HUNT THE BANKER

HUNT THE BANKER

Alexander Lebedev

Translated by Arch Tait

Quiller

Contents

Copyright © 2019 Alexander Lebedev

First published in the UK in 2019
by Quiller, an imprint of
Quiller Publishing Ltd

British Library Cataloguing-in-Publication Data
A catalogue record for this book is available
from the British Library

ISBN 978-1-84689-303-2

The right of Alexander Lebedev to be identified
as the author of this work has been asserted
in accordance with the Copyright, Design and
Patent Act 1988

Design by Guy Callaby

Photographs and other archive materials
are the copyright/property of the author
unless otherwise stated and credited

Printed in the Czech Republic

Quiller
An imprint of Quiller Publishing Ltd

Wykey House, Wykey,
Shrewsbury SY4 1JA
Tel: 01939 261616
Email: info@quillerbooks.com
Website: www.quillerpublishing.com

PART II

The New Hunting Season: Ten Years On

'The audience has not, to my knowledge, demanded anything of the sort. However, in view of your distinguished position, Arkadiy Apollonich, I will – since you insist – reveal something of our technique. To do so, will you allow me time for another short number?'

'Of course,' replied Arkadiy Apollonich patronisingly. 'But you must show how it's done.'

Mikhail Bulgakov, *The Master and Margarita*[1]

Mikhail Bulgakov, *The Master and Margarita*, tr. Michael Glenny, London: Vintage Books, 2004, p. 151.

What is the Third Colonialism?

Money can't buy you happiness

All my life I have been fascinated by how people react to wealth, serious money and what it can buy. There was a time when I lived with my parents and brother in a thirty-square-metre apartment. For years I darned my one and only pair of jeans. As a boy it took me three weeks to save the seven kopeks needed for an ice cream, and as a student I thriftily collected the deposit on bottles of the cheap alcohol I and my friends drank (which cost at most a ruble twenty, or a ruble fifty for an 800 ml 'fire extinguisher').

I was far happier then than I was in the noughties. Even making it on to the *Forbes* rich list was no big deal. It seems to me that if you have a few thousand dollars a month to cover the everyday necessities (what it is now fashionable to call an 'unconditional basic income'), then anything above that will not make life appreciably better, and may well make it worse. I find that the only people with a fortune who deserve respect are indifferent to it or, better still, despise it.

We spend a third of our lives sleeping, and asleep everyone is equal in the property stakes. What difference is there between us in the shower, washing our faces, brushing our teeth, combing our hair? We all pay the same for water. Okay, there is social differentiation in the toiletries we buy, but no evidence to suggest that costly creams or lipsticks do anything for us. In fact, we see plenty of examples around which suggest the opposite. Expensive operations to alter lips, noses, breasts or backsides often leave their victims looking not more but less attractive. You can buy sports clothing, but not the shape, the fitness of your body. How well you work out on the treadmill, horizontal bar or weight machine depends not on how much you pay, but on how much graft, sweat and time you put in.

We spend several hours every day eating, and the truth is that the simpler and cheaper the food, the more wholesome it is. The ideal menu consists of buckwheat (40 rubles, 60 US cents, a kilo), extra virgin flaxseed oil, vegetables, and a modest amount of fish. For this bounty you will pay 60–70 rubles, about a dollar a day. Everybody earns at least a dollar a day, except perhaps for some Papuans or pygmies living on the verge of starvation, and the average standard of living of the world's population is equivalent to an income of at least several hundred dollars a month.

There are differences in how we dress. Someone's well-off mistress will be able to array herself in jewellery and finery costing tens of thousands of rubles, and still not look a patch on a girl with the willpower needed to make a hobby of pole dancing, practise yoga, to keep fit and run for two hours a day. You cannot, alas, learn a foreign language by paying money: you need a flair for it, or at least motivation and perseverance. Buying a university degree is no longer encouraged even in Russia, and if someone pays to put you on the stage, they will succeed only in making a laughing stock of you.

Sex, of course, you can buy, although only unlovable addicts manage to spend big money on it. I know quite a few who do, but even so their budgets add up to no more than a few hundred thousand dollars a year. Well, maybe that is a lot, but don't be jealous: try to get it for free.

Nothing in life is achieved without effort, and wealth makes it no less strenuous. You can write a good book or create a successful business only through ability and hard work, and neither is contingent on finance. Quite the reverse: easy money often leads only to losses and failure.

The person with billions frequently has a physical sense of alienation from their capital. Money warms only a shallow soul. It shrivels the heart, gives no peace, and problems proliferate. You are at risk of acquiring bad habits, not least the habit of paying girls for their services, a sin I too have been guilty of.

Fortunate are those who compensate by spending millions of dollars on charity in all its forms. My urge to invest in the least easily realisable projects – agriculture, wholesome food, hotels in Crimea (rather than the Maldives), air transportation, affordable housing and so on was evidently prompted by a subconscious longing to free myself from the burdens of wealth. In the middle of the second decade of the twenty-first century, I had the good fortune to be relieved of a considerable portion of my business interests: my share of Aeroflot, my banking, my Red Wings budget airline and the Ilyushin Finance Company. Paradoxically enough, this has all been to the good. I have gone back to trying to achieve things in life for myself, rather than in order to make money.

Is the life of a billionaire all that different from the life of averagely well-off people who are in harmony with themselves and the world around them? We can discount the virtual money in bank accounts which, as we have discovered, contributes nothing in terms of personal development. There is one clear difference, of course, and that is how much *stuff* they have. I have noticed that the average person on the *Forbes* rich list has at least one business jet, five or six mansions and apartments, and a yacht (sometimes two). The rest of their money, however, is tied up in their businesses.

On close inspection, you find there is an inverse correlation between the impression they make as human beings and the amount they have invested in real estate. It rarely exceeds some hundreds of millions of dollars, but the more they have invested, the less personable they are. They have lacklustre eyes, look abysmal, have a toxic personality and an off-putting physical appearance. This is the result of trying to buy something that can only be obtained through your own efforts, willpower and hard work. People are so much more pleasant who have not been spoilt by wealth, people like Warren Buffett, who gets around by taxi where he lives in Omaha.

Do people really feel at home if they live in a house with 5–7,000 square metres of floor space and the odd twenty-five bedrooms? Well, maybe. The passion for accumulating expensive properties is rooted in vanity. They aim to show off their needy superiority to the rest of the world and have no other way of doing it. Many of the super-rich hardly use the things that belong to them and would be glad to be rid of them, but that is not easy. The human race is developing a kind of consensus on the level of personal consumption expected of billionaires. I hope the social networks will soon ridicule those who emulate Philip Green rather than Warren Buffett, and instead respect people who put money into hospitals, libraries, museums and other public amenities.

I would also like to see closer public scrutiny of how money raised for charity is actually spent, because of the half a trillion dollars donated annually, at least half ends up in the pockets of fundraisers and 'managers'. Perhaps I should write another book about that. In Russia and abroad it is very much in evidence. Recently a diva prominent in the lush pastures of charity fundraising invited her sponsors to her town. They knew that over the past twelve years she had raised over $100 million, yet all she had now to show them was a couple of children's playgrounds and a facility for sick kids that extended to all of a hundred square metres. Not much, you might think.

With this digression, which is important for understanding my motivation, let our story begin. I hope that some day I and the venerable Professor Vladislav Inozemtsev, one of Russia's most eminent economists, will jointly be awarded the Nobel Prize for our discovery of the Law of the Third Colonialism (unless by then it is being awarded to whoever gives the biggest bribe). The prestige of the Nobel Prize, alas, has been severely dented after it was so inexplicably awarded to Barack Obama, and to a European Union which is falling apart before our eyes.

Black holes of the global economy

Just as Adam Smith discovered, and Karl Marx elaborated, the theory of surplus value featuring money, goods and labour, so Inozemtsev and I have discovered and described a system of black holes in the global economy into which money disappears simultaneously throughout the world and then, after laundering, reappears in a certain secret pool. Hard work, knowledge and experience have no bearing on the contents of this pool, and we feel fully justified in claiming for ourselves the status of a Stephen Hawking, only in economics.

Let us picture the economic system as an organism in which money is the blood supplying vital energy to the various organs. Banks are the circulatory system and serve a purely technical function: the heart pumps blood and the arteries deliver it to where it is needed. Adam Smith wrote in *An Inquiry into the Nature and Causes of the Wealth of Nations* of the importance of trust in the 'fortune, probity and prudence' of those seeking credit.[2] In the case of a banker, a country's population needs to be confident that he will be able to redeem on demand such of his promissory notes as may be presented to him. Where that is the case, his notes are accepted as readily as cash.

In the modern world, however, everything is different. Let us suppose you have a legal income. Part of it is immediately taken off you by the state in taxation. Another part you spend on your personal needs. If there is anything left over, you deposit it in a bank. But whereas you can keep a close

---

2 Adam Smith, *An Inquiry into the Nature and Causes of the Wealth of Nations*, The Glasgow Edition of the Works and Correspondence of Adam Smith, vol. II, ed. R.H. Campbell and A.S. Skinner, Oxford University Press, 1976, p. 122.

eye on the money in your wallet, once it is with the bank it is out of sight. Keeping an eye on it is now, in theory, the responsibility of the Central Bank, but it can only too easily fall under the influence of dishonest bankers and their patrons, who give little thought to the welfare of society or, indeed, even to ensuring that the money you deposited is at least secure.

Shortly afterwards, having been transformed from rubles, rupees, pesos, dinars and yuan into US dollars, the money ends up in an immense, fetid reservoir, that very same pool of the world's leading banks and investment funds in thirty-three unassailable offshore tax havens protected by lawyers, lawcourts and politicians. You will be told (if you presume to ask) that there has been a crisis, a bankruptcy, force majeure or whatever. The outcome is invariably that the money has gone from your wallet and is now in someone else's pocket. Every day the money of millions of people pours into the pockets of an elect circle of people, and nobody does anything about it.

The international organisations whose job it is to monitor this, estimate that the reservoir of dirty money contains in excess of 60 trillion dollars, which is close to the annual gross domestic product of Planet Earth. Every year another trillion is added to it. This is many times more than the revenues from drug trafficking, prostitution and the trade in human organs, against which a relentless battle is waged. Why do we hear nothing about that trillion dollars derived from white-collar crime? Is that odd or is it odd?

The reason is that this vast slush fund is managed by an international financial oligarchy, and the slush fund's VIP clients are corrupt officials and bankers, businessmen and, not to put too fine a point on it, fraudsters, with the corrupt officials usually providing protection, the criminal *krysha* or 'roof', for the latter. For pumping the money on its way, a whole empire of offshore jurisdictions has been created where these parasites can call on the services of top-notch lawyers, nominee directors, and tens of thousands of companies dedicated to the laundering and storing of dirty money.

As a result, entire continents – Africa, for example, – are bled dry. The parasites, having laid their larvae in these bespoke gardens of Eden, then scuttle off to a 'promised land' where they can rely on the local courts to defend them vigorously from criminal prosecutions brought against them in their homeland. Even when there are investigations, their victims soon have it explained to them that the reason their savings have evaporated is something to do with the workings of the latest economic crisis, or simple mismanagement.

The public face of the international financial oligarchy is such multinational banking groups and investment trusts as Goldman Sachs, JP Morgan Chase, Credit Suisse, Franklin Templeton, Blackstone, BlackRock, Lone Star, HSBC, Bank von Ernst & Cie, Coutts, and their ilk. Along, of course, with lawyers, auditors, rating agencies and other service personnel.

One typical example is Franklin Templeton. This is a 'fund of funds', an American finance and investment group that manages assets of almost a trillion dollars. Of these, just under eight billion are Ukrainian government bonds, amounting to almost half the country's sovereign debt. These securities ended up with Franklin Templeton in 2013 after an 'unofficial' visit to the company's headquarters in San Mateo, California, by the then first deputy prime minister of Ukraine, Sergey Arbuzov, finance minister Yury Kolobov, and the director of the tax service, Alexander Klimenko.

What were they discussing there? It is not impossible that it was the placing of money, embezzled in Ukraine and laundered in the United Arab Emirates, Hong Kong, Uruguay and Cyprus, to purchase Ukrainian Eurobonds through 200 low-profile funds at a fifty-per-cent discount. (A number of warnings by Ukrainian government officials about the possibility of a default had caused the quoted price of these securities to nosedive.)

The Ukrainian president, Viktor Yanukovych, could not then in his worst nightmares have foreseen what would happen in six months' time. He was probably confident that he would soon be able to buy the securities back at close to their nominal value, using the money of his taxpayers or Russian loans. (The Russian Federation had by then issued loans amounting only to $3 billion out of an anticipated $16 billion.)

The popular view in America is that in 2013 the Ukrainian people took to Maidan Square to rebel against the corrupt regime of Yanukovych who, being a Kremlin agent, did not want his country integrated with the US and Europe. Maybe so. But if Yanukovych was controlling the lion's share of Ukraine's debts through an American financial company? Are we really to believe the ex-president of Ukraine and those in his circle, who had from every ministry been miraculously extracting $10–15 billion in cash every year, wanted to work in Russia's interests and would have shifted the money to the United States?

The Kremlin Ukrainologist who wrote that Yanukovych was 'a son of a bitch, but our son of a bitch', was naïve. If my understanding of the Franklin Templeton story is correct, Yanukovych was using the company for money laundering and he was America's son of a bitch. The only reason he fled to

Russia was because the situation on Maidan had got completely out of control.

It seems to me that Natalia Yaresko, a US citizen and Ukrainian minister of finance who in 2015 was working on restructuring Ukraine's national debt, effectively confirmed this was the case. 'All this could be possible, because these bonds can be freely bought and sold,' she said in reply to a question on the Ukrainian TSN television programme in connection with my publications. 'They are sold on the Irish stock exchange. I have no way of knowing who is the beneficial owner.'

The 'restructuring' which the creative Ms Yaresko had lobbied for proved beneficial primarily to one side in the negotiations: Franklin Templeton. Despite setting back repayment of the debt capital to 2019, in the course of the restructuring, government derivatives were issued with the return to creditors tied to the percentage by which Ukraine's GDP increased. A complete innovation in the history of restructuring sovereign debt! In other words, the more the Ukrainian economy earned, the more it would have to pay. Having accomplished her valiant labours to the benefit of the creditors, Yaresko retired.

Given the catastrophically low baseline of Ukraine's GDP in recent years, this triumph, for which Yaresko was awarded a 'valuable gift' in the form of a decorated shell case by interior minister Arsen Avakov at a meeting of the Ukrainian government, may leave the Ukrainian nation in hock to Yanukovych and Franklin Templeton (if it is the case that both are in on the deal). It is true that a portion of Ukrainian bonds held in accounts of Yanukovych's team in Oschadbank, the state savings bank of Ukraine, was recently confiscated by the present authorities, but this seems to have been only a small proportion, an easy way of not repaying $1.5 billion of debt. The current Ukrainian authorities may yet show Yanukovych's people a thing or two.

The evolution of robbery

Advocates of conspiracy theories claim there exists a shadowy, oligarchic, behind-the-scenes government that actually manages the global economy, and they recall the Rothschilds and the Rockefellers. Our discovery puts this previously unconfirmed hypothesis on a solid scientific basis. Is there a single gang capable of managing such colossal resources, as it sees fit and to its own advantage? Is it making use of vast sums of money to inflate financial bubbles in the global market, which lead to such cataclysms as the 2008 collapse? The bankruptcy of Lehman Brothers bank was only the trigger: the force behind the crisis was a massive 'subprime debt' mortgage scam of bonds underwritten by substandard security. The trillions of dollars involved in the operation came out of the infamous reservoir, and Goldman Sachs and Deutsche Bank relieved their customers of billions of dollars.

At the G20 summit, it was officially acknowledged that the biggest crisis facing humanity is corruption and unjust redistribution of wealth. China, almost the greatest economy in the world, is making enormous efforts to stop the diversion of the wealth of developing countries, which is being exported by corrupt elites and finding a home in bank accounts in London, Paris and Geneva. The leaders of the Western world acknowledge the need for cooperation in these efforts, but in practice their support amounts to no more than a little speechifying. Why?

I have discussed this problem with many of them, not least with three British prime ministers: Tony Blair, Gordon Brown and David Cameron. I detected no interest in the issue. Not one of the people I talked to had a vested interest in suppressing discussion, so is it somehow outside their remit? Do they consider it unimportant? Their attitude seems to be that there is nothing anyone can do about it. They seem to think mankind has more urgent problems to deal with: terrorism, nuclear weapons, wars, climate change, ecological crises. These are the issues politicians are taking seriously, and this small matter of the embezzlement of a trillion dollars a year is something they never quite seem to get round to. Is that not odd?

It is completely obvious that corruption in Third World countries, a result of the way their societies are structured, is one of the causes of this enormous problem. If there was no plundering of resources by corrupt plutocrats in Africa, Asia, Latin America and the Middle East, people there would be better off, would not feel they were being denied their human rights and, probably, would be less susceptible to the influence of extremists. It is, however, Europe and the United States which, by creating a whole industry for sucking out and laundering money from Third World countries, have introduced an insidious new form of colonialism, whose existence is studiously ignored by political leaders. The United States is exploiting the situation to its own advantage.

For six centuries, European countries have dominated less economically developed regions of the earth. This period of history is admirably described by evolutionary biologist Jared Diamond in his Pulitzer Prize-winning book *Guns, Germs and Steel*.[3] Europe has excelled the rest of the world in technology, especially military technology. Thanks to this superiority, the 'superior' white race ruled over the natives in their colonies. Spanish, English and Dutch conquerors were the first to build fleets that could reach lands rich in gold and silver, minerals, silk and spices. And slaves.

But the age of the First Colonialism, with its reliance on brute force, which often endangered the lives of the colonisers themselves, came to an end in the twentieth century, when the political, military and financial costs of reigning over vast territories in Africa or Indochina began to outweigh the value for Europe of the plunder.

Decolonisation became mainstream, and by the mid-1970s the political atlas of the world was multicoloured. The problem was that Europe remained dependent on the commodities of its former colonial possessions, especially in respect of natural resources. Accordingly, after an orderly retreat that lasted into the 1960s, the Western world found a new form of colonialism. In future it would rest on two main pillars. The first was penetration of the economy of the Third World by transnational corporations. They brought with them much-needed investment and technology, but at the same time occupied a dominant position in the economy and infrastructure of Third World countries, expropriating the financial gains of development.

The second pillar of this expansion was private banks, which began making loans to developing countries in the 1970s. Field Marshal Kwame Nkrumah, sociologist, philosopher and the first president of Ghana, in the late 1960s labelled this 'neocolonialism'. For simplicity's sake Professor Inozemtsev and I call it the Second Colonialism.

Less bloody than the First Colonialism, it became more brazen and no less cruel. Both the First and Second Colonialisms focused on material resources and slaves. In the nineteenth century, up to forty per cent of Europe's imports and exports were between the great powers and their colonies. This so-called free trade brought misery to the peoples of the colonies, but great wealth to the 'mother' countries. In 1999, the African World Reparations and Repatriation Truth Commission estimated the loss to the Black Continent as $777 trillion.

---

3 Jared Diamond, *Guns, Germs, and Steel: The Fates of Human Societies*, New York: Norton, 1997.

This is certainly an exaggeration, but looking back at how Madrid and Lisbon, London and Paris, Brussels and Amsterdam expanded in those years, it is clear that this form of colonialism too was highly profitable. Even after the writing off of debt of the poorest countries under the aegis of the Paris and London Clubs at the turn of the millennium, the financial burden of the Third World was around $2 trillion, and net interest on these loans brought the West over $200 billion per year.

It is indisputable that this could not have come about without the connivance of corrupt or incompetent local potentates, but it is no less obvious that the Second Colonialism, like its predecessor, was developed and operated by European and Trans-Atlantic civilisation under the patronage of the world's new superpower. There is nothing surprising about the fact that it was US banks that faced default in the early 1980s, when Mexico, Argentina, Venezuela, Peru and other countries proved unable to continue to service their debts.

Colonialism was a hot topic in the 1980s and engendered a host of human rights movements. Hollywood celebrities demanded debt forgiveness and a new, fair world order. Despite huge sovereign debt and the trade restrictions they faced, many Third World countries were, nevertheless, beginning to clamber out of extreme poverty. The technologies which had been transferred to them were having an effect, and their goods were being granted preferential export terms to the markets of the 'metropolitan' countries.

It was at this point that a new phenomenon emerged, which we have called the Third Colonialism. This form of exploitation operates in a subtler and more insidious manner, which explains why until now it has hardly been described anywhere other than in a few inarticulate protest broadsides and, to some extent, in commercials released by Donald Trump in the course of his campaign for the US presidency. We see the Third Colonialism as more effective than its predecessors.

If the First Colonialism was grounded in military force, and the Second in the financial power of loans, the Third Colonialism is based on the subversion of elites, teaching them how to manipulate finance and siphon money into offshore centres that are part and parcel of the Western economies. To make matters worse, the countries being exploited in this manner often rack up debt. It is not within their power to raise the quality of life of their populations to anything like the standards of the Golden Billion, but their elites are desperately keen to enjoy the benefits of Western-style civilisation. Because most of these states still lack democratic institutions and dependable rule of law, the riches of their elites have been gained through corruption and could be called into question by the current or future regimes.

Very few people at the highest levels of power feel secure enough to keep their wealth in their homeland. Increasingly, the wealthy elites of Africa and Asia buy property in London, set up offshore companies and open secret bank accounts. This state of affairs is warmly welcomed by the financial services industry of the West, and that too is hardly surprising, because it is the cornerstone of the Third Colonialism.

Through the efforts of Western banks, lawyers and accountants, corruption, which for centuries was largely a national problem, has become an international phenomenon. It has been globalised. It is based on links between the corrupt elites of poor nations and the international financial centres of the West. No longer is there any need to establish East India Companies and send in the troops, as in past centuries, to conquer far-off lands: the natives themselves fly in, bringing their riches with them.

This is happening on an impressive scale. Today, by even the most conservative estimates, the net outflow of financial resources from Third World countries is about $1 trillion a year: at the beginning of the millennium it was estimated at less than $200 billion. To put it another way, corrupt government officials and fake entrepreneurs are stealing from their poor countries some five times more money than their nations are paying on loans from international banks. For sheer brazenness, the Third Colonialism has left the Second far behind.

In spite of that, even such highly respected international organisations as the Financial Action Task Force and Transparency International prefer not to notice the phenomenon and undertake practically no measures to counteract it. Instead, they periodically deliver speeches on the need to ensure financial transparency. The international network of corruption is the most wretched byproduct of globalisation. The key to combating global corruption is to be found, not in the corrupt countries themselves, but in the United Kingdom and in Europe as a whole, which are the birthplace of this and the earlier forms of colonialism.

It was Europe that created the new financial architecture through which the flows of dirty money from poor and badly ruled countries stream. The West allows corrupt national elites to enrich themselves in criminal ways, and reaps the benefits. In these circumstances there is no possibility of the poor nations defeating corruption on their own. What is needed is for the rich nations of the West to stop promoting it.

As we have noted, the international system of corruption did not just happen: it was deliberately established in order to perpetuate the West's dominance over the rest of the world. In maintaining this global status quo, however, in redistributing the world's resources to its own benefit, Europe is placing itself at risk. By promoting corruption in the Third World, the First World is destroying itself. The populace of plundered countries become an easy prey for extremists and religious fanatics and the ensuing wars generate torrents of refugees. These have flooded the Old World and caused a migration crisis.

Ultimately, international networks of corrupt officials have sprung up that would have been unimaginable in the past, a close-knit alliance of venal elites residing in both the First and Third Worlds. The huge amounts of dirty money at the disposal of a small circle of individuals increases the risk of it ending up in the hands of terrorists.

The Third Colonialism will lead, sooner or later, to a global economic collapse and the end of civilisation in its present form. It is not unreasonable to liken the international financial oligarchy to a cancerous tumour that is feeding on mankind and, as we know, a tumour dies only with the death of the entire organism. Money does, however, act in accordance with the first law of thermodynamics: it never just disappears. Every stolen dollar or ruble can be found: all that is needed is the will to do so and to undertake global chemotherapy. It will hurt, it will be unpleasant, but without it we will not survive.

As I am writing these lines, new sanctions are being imposed on Russia. The Russian Foreign Ministry has announced it is working on retaliatory measures. It could not be simpler! Russia needs officially to propose (or better still, to demand) that the West return the more than $100 billion stolen from Russian citizens by criminal bankers and salted away abroad. We should formulate a national policy for getting this money back, involving all the appropriate institutions and levels of government, from the Ministry of Foreign Affairs, the Ministry of Finance and Parliament to the Prosecutor General's Office, the Interior Ministry and the state-run media.

The way I reached these conclusions, and the impact my investigations have had on my life, is the topic of the book you are reading.

PART I

'A Person Resembling the Prosecutor General', and a Bunch of Gangsters

CHAPTER 1

Allow Me to Introduce Myself ...

We have all learned step by step

I was born on 16 December 1959 in Moscow, in the maternity hospital on Proletarskaya Street. We lived in a communal apartment on Avtozavodskaya (Automotive Factory Street) and a little later, when I was three, the family's fortunes improved to the extent that we moved to a small 36-square-metre apartment of our own.

At that time my parents could hardly have imagined how their younger son's career would develop. My father, Yevgeny Nikolaevich, had a doctorate in engineering and was a professor in the education department of the Bauman Higher Technical College in Moscow (now the Moscow State Technical University). There he forged elite engineers for the land of triumphant socialism. My mother, Maria Sergeyevna, taught history to the next generation of Soviet people and, later, the language of the 'probable adversary', namely, English. They had no idea what the First Directorate of the KGB of the USSR might be, and for them millions of dollars were to be found only in the novels of John Galsworthy and Theodore Dreiser.

I owe my secondary (and very middling) education to School No. 17, which offered 'intensive study of the English language'. It was what was known in those days as a 'specialised school'. I had the privilege of attending a representative specialised school at the height of the Soviet Era of Stagnation. We had some fine teachers of, for example, English and literature: reading and studying Shakespeare and Robert Burns in the original was seen as nothing out of the ordinary. Many years later, already in adult life, I was able on a couple of occasions to surprise British friends by reciting Hamlet's monologue.

I studied well enough, but consistently got bad marks for conduct, which meant my parents were regularly called in to the school to hear expressions of concern. These were not infrequently about tricks I got up to with Sasha Mamut, with whom I had been friends since first grade. He was eventually moved to a different class: from B to C.

In arts subjects my marks were excellent, but in physics, chemistry and mathematics, less so. I blame the teachers. I did not warm to them, and they left me with a life-long aversion to their subjects, even though the shelves in our apartment housed dozens of books my father had written and which contained wall-to-wall maths as applicable to optical engineering (and not without military applications). For me, though, that was terra incognita. The situation was quite different with my mother: English, history, literature ...To this day I enjoy nothing more than reading Gibbon on the Roman Empire or Sebag-Montefiore on the Romanovs. I think my father was a little envious.

As was typically the lot of a professional family in the USSR, we lived modestly but were reasonably well provided for by the standards of the time. I was taken aback years later by a photo posted on Instagram by my already adult son, Evgeny. It showed the refrigerator in his home in London with at least sixty bottles of different kinds of vodka. He boasts an excellent wine cellar of over 100,000 bottles! Such a thing was beyond imagining in the two-room apartment I shared with my parents and brother.

Even had I come into the possession of such a quantity of alcohol, two dozen friends would have helped me despatch it in a couple of days. ('Head on over, lads, my folks are away. The *flet* is ours!') And afterwards Mamut and I would have taken the bottles to the collection point and wrangled with the fat women there over every supposedly disqualifying chip on the necks of the bottles.

I emerged from secondary school with a commendable certificate. There was no *blat* (parental string-pulling) involved, even though my mother taught at the prestigious Institute of International Relations and was a member of its Communist Party committee. Before applying for a place I had a year's tutoring, and even gave up water polo, which I had been playing since a child. I was beginning to have trouble with my eyesight. I couldn't see well and there were no contact lenses.

In those days *blat* was fairly common, especially at IIR. My cohort included many progeny of members of the Politburo: Andrey Brezhnev, for instance, grandson of the general secretary of the Party, or Ilkham Aliev, whose father was a member of the Politburo and future president of Azerbaijan. Nowadays Ilkham is president of the republic himself. Vladimir

Potanin, today the CEO of Norilsk Nickel, was in the year below mine. I remember a great fuss when my mother, who was very honest, failed Brezhnev in English. The other lecturers began avoiding her, giving her a wide berth when they passed her. About a month later she was walking along the corridor when she met Andrey. 'Maria Sergeyevna!' he exclaimed. 'Guess what? I've already managed a "very good"!'

The institute's principal was also called Lebedev. He was no relation of my mother but pretended he was. Brezhnev's wife had phoned to request that Andrey not be expelled but moved from Maria Sergeyevna's group to a different one. The end result was that the principal ended up on good terms with the general secretary's family. There was serious jiggery-pokery in the USSR, at the highest level.

Twice a week I went to the food shop to stand in five or six queues. There were separate ones for making a purchase and paying for it. At times the shop would run out of eggs or milk, cheese or sausage, and at best there were only a couple of varieties. You could choose between Soviet cheese or Russian cheese. Eggs were always called 'Extra', sausage was always 'Gourmet'. Often at home I would take a mouldy 13-kopek loaf from the cooking pot in which the bread was kept, cut off the crust, pour water over it and put it in the oven. I would retrieve half a month-old pack of *pelmeni* dumplings from the freezer and douse them with mayonnaise. Spongey, sprouting potatoes, eggs, frozen pollock or cod – such was pretty much my diet for twenty years or so.

How I came to be recruited by Yasenevo into the foreign intelligence agency remains something of a mystery. I had been planning to write a thesis at the Academy of Sciences' Institute of Economics of the World Socialist System and go into academic research. I had even chosen my dissertation topic: *Problems of Debt and the Challenges of Globalisation*. In my final years at IIR, however, headhunters from the KGB's First Directorate began taking an interest in me.

This was despite the fact that, in the first place, I shunned all work for the Young Communist League, the Party, and any other social commitments. Secondly, I was sceptical about Marxism-Leninism, read Solzhenitsyn and Shalamov (discreetly), and told political jokes. In short, I showed every sign of developing into a dissident. As a result of these proclivities, I blotted my copybook at the very beginning of my career as a spy.

Nevertheless, ideological shortcomings apart, my professional qualifications fitted the role rather well. I had English, I had quite respectable

Spanish, I was married and had a child. Was the world of intelligence in those years secretly some anti-Soviet 'Union of the Sword and Ploughshare'? After all, the people who worked in it were well educated and knew the reality of how foreigners lived. They could not be taken in by Soviet propaganda, because they were the ones who concocted it.

My fourth year was a year abroad in Libya. Translators were needed from the higher education institutions that were considered most trustworthy. The contract was for six months and the pay was what you might have expected if you were a 'grown-up' working for a foreign trade organisation. It was everything a Soviet citizen could hope for!

The USSR had signed a contract with the Libyan Jamahiriya to build a nuclear research facility with a 10-megawatt light water reactor in Tajura, a forty-minute drive from Tripoli. Its purpose was to train future specialists to work at a nuclear power plant Gaddafi was proposing to build on the Gulf of Sidra (Great Sirte). The would-be local specialists turned out, however, to be a bunch of ne'er-do-wells from wealthy families who had no desire to study and only wanted to move to America or the United Kingdom at the first opportunity.

In June 1981, shortly before we arrived, Israel carried out Operation Babylon in Iraq, bombing an Osirak class nuclear reactor near Baghdad, which the French had sold to Saddam Hussein. The Israeli Prime Minister, Menachem Begin, had publicly threatened to bomb Tajura as well, so the situation was tense. There were a lot of Libyan soldiers posted at the facility, very young men (at times they seemed to be just boys with enormous boots and assault rifles). We had anti-aircraft defences. In the event of an air raid, we were to hide in a shelter that had survived since the Second World War, a legacy of General-Field Marshal Erwin Rommel, commander of the Third Reich's Afrika Korps.

Drinking alcohol was prohibited in Tajura and the law was quite severely enforced: for a booze-up you could find yourself in a *zindan* punishment pit. We broke the law regardless, and distilled moonshine. One time everyone got poisoned and some people ended up in hospital, but our superiors turned a blind eye. Political unreliability was a different matter. On one occasion I told a joke at a party:

> Okay, there's this big gala event in the Kremlin Palace of Congresses to celebrate the anniversary of the October Revolution. Everybody's there, the Party and government leaders, the Heroes of Labour, the

Young Pioneers, the astronauts. It's being compèred by none other than People's Artist of the RSFSR, Joseph Kobzon. He announces, 'And now we invite to the stage the legendary Sidor Kuzmich, who saw Lenin. Twice.'

The hall goes silent. A decrepit old man clambers up on to the stage. Kobzon asks him, 'Tell us, Sidor Kuzmich, how did you come to meet the leader of the world proletariat?'

'Er, let me think,' Sidor Kuzmich wheezes. '1917 it was, in Razliv (that's near Petrograd). So, I'm in our village bathhouse. I've got one foot in this basin full of hot water and the other in a basin full of cold water. Really good birch-twig switch, and all the people around are just so nice! Only thing missing is the vodka: ban on drinking alcohol there was. Suddenly in comes this nasty little bare chap, really small, bald too. In he comes to the bathhouse, doesn't even close the door behind him. Walks straight over to me. "Look here, geezer," he says, "how about you let me have one of those basins?" So I says to him, "How about you get stuffed!" That's how I saw Lenin for the first time.'

Everyone in the hall is shocked. Murmuring. Kobzon does his best to smooth over the embarrassment. 'Comrades! Let us not misunderstand. Sidor Kuzmich is getting on in years. His memory is no longer what it was. Sidor Kuzmich! Tell us about how you met Lenin the second time.'

'Ah, yes!' the old man replies. 'The second time it was at the Mikhelson factory. I'm standing there, grinding some widget on the lathe. Suddenly the door to the shop floor opens and in comes a whole crowd of people, must've been twenty of them, all in those leather coats, with revolvers and pistols, and there with them is that bald chap I saw in the bathhouse. I'm standing there, shaking like a leaf. Anyway, he walks straight over to me. He comes over and I've got all these people surrounding me. The little bald chap is looking out from behind this tall fellow, had a goatee beard – Dzerzhinsky that was, I think – anyway, he looks out and says, "Look here, aren't you that geezer who wouldn't let me have a basin in Razliv in 1917?" I'm thinking, "If I admit it, they'll shoot me on the spot. If I say it wasn't me, they'll shoot me anyway." So I says to him, "How about you get stuffed!" Yes, that's how I saw Lenin the second time.'

Everyone laughed. My friend Alexey told the joke to his dad, who worked in the Second Directorate of Counter-intelligence and was in charge of the section controlling entry to and exit from the USSR. His dad told the story to another person and they laughed too, but someone said, 'What kind of people are you recruiting there to work in intelligence?' To make matters worse, my mother had been on a couple of delegations to the United States and was corresponding with Americans. The upshot was that after IIR I didn't get the attestation I was expecting and was packed off as an ordinary Joe to the translation bureau.

I drudged there for three years or so. My colleagues – and about fifteen from our course went into intelligence – were getting paid four times my salary, and in the evenings on the bus driving us back from First Directorate headquarters in Yasenevo, they would pat me condescendingly on the shoulder and say, 'Never mind, old man, it'll work out in the end!'

Oddly enough, translation matters too, even if it is uncreative. I put in the hours, took on extra work, burned the midnight oil, and the fruit of my labours was a certificate of commendation from the director of the KGB, Vladimir Kryuchkov. Also a knowledge of Portuguese and Italian.

No cloak, no dagger

At just this time 'an opinion' was forming at the highest political level in the USSR – in the mind of Yury Andropov, I believe – that there was something we were not getting right about the decay of Western capitalism. It had been decaying for many decades now, but showed no sign of collapsing. In fact, things appeared to be moving in the opposite direction: the USSR's problems as it competed with the West seemed to be piling up. The authorities' response was to engage in resolute positive thinking with the aim of persuading themselves nothing could be wrong, because theoretically nothing should be.

Andropov, the general secretary of the Central Committee, started asking questions. He summoned the most trusted advisers with responsibility for the struggle against capitalism and said, 'You keep repeating that capitalism is in the third stage of its general crisis, when it is certain to collapse, but I have the impression things may not be quite so straightforward. Can you explain to me why the USSR's foreign debt is increasing and we know nothing about it? And why grain prices are so high and oil prices so low? Why are we having to buy grain from the States and Canada? Why are foreign exchange rates so unfavourable to us? Why are we lagging behind so drastically in technology? And why are our financial arrangements with the countries of the socialist camp so much to our disadvantage?' The comrades either did not know the answers, or thought it better not to give them.

The questions were readdressed to the Academy of Sciences, where the academicians put their tails between their legs, well aware that they would get no thanks for telling the truth and that, in any case, these were classified matters they were not supposed to think about. Andropov turned to the intelligence community, which also proved clueless. In the end someone had the idea of setting up a small department in the information analysis directorate of the KGB, which had been processing economic data.

This was why I had been headhunted from the Academy of Sciences, then sent into exile as a translator, but was now being set to work. At some point this junior employee had come to the attention of Nikolai Leonov, the head of the directorate. My translations of financial topics landed on his desk and he was impressed by my understanding of them. 'So, you are an economist? We need economists for the department.' With a time lag of three years, I got my attestation.

The task of an analyst in the directorate was to sort through tons of information discovered and supplied by agents in the field, to throw out the rubbish and compose short notes from what was of value. This was sent on up to the chiefs of the intelligence community and from them, if they felt something specific needed to be reported, to the country's leaders. As they liked to tell us, 'You need to write so that even an idiot can understand it.' The length of this report for idiots could be as little as half a page, although it was usually permissible for it to extend to two or three pages. Without neglecting my work at the coalface, I graduated from the Red Banner Institute of the KGB and was awarded my captain's epaulettes.

Leonid Shebarshin, the head of the First Directorate, approved my candidacy to work in a residency. As was traditional, I was found a job in the Ministry of Foreign Affairs, where I worked with genuine commitment for almost a year. The people at Smolensky Square did not at first sniff out who I was: a sociable chap who enjoyed a chinwag with the rest of the staff? But then, after three months or so, someone put it around that I was from the 'deep-drilling section'. One fine day I arrived at work to find everyone stony-faced and searching their memories: 'God Almighty, have I blabbed to him about anything?' They did not know whether I was working for intelligence or counter-intelligence. I had clearly been overenthusiastic in my penetration of the MFA, but with time everything settled down.

After my stint at the Ministry of Foreign Affairs I was sent, by now a diplomat, as an attache to the London embassy. The days of the Soviet Empire were coming to a close and perestroika was in full spate. The country was changing before our eyes. My family lived where I had been posted, but each year we flew back to Moscow for a month's leave (our tickets were paid for). In the evenings we watched the programme *Vzglyad* ('Look') on television, and read newspapers that had begun telling the truth.

My specialisation was financial and economic information, but I made useful unofficial contacts in the City, meeting many senior managers of banks and companies. In the Soviet Union a new class of entrepreneurs was being born. Comrades making the first easy money felt an urge to visit the financial capital of the world and, as the member of the embassy responsible for economic matters, I looked after them. Some turned up at our address in Kensington Palace Gardens, some I met at Heathrow, others I drove around in my little Ford, and some even stayed at my house.

I met Mikhail Prokhorov, who was flaunting a wad of fifty-pound banknotes beyond the imagining of a humble Soviet official; Vladimir Potanin; the late Vladimir Vinogradov, proprietor of Inkombank; Sergey Rodionov and Vitaliy Malkin, the owners of Imperial and Russian Credit, the first commercial banks; Oleg Boyko, who traded in computers and engaged in currency operations. My school friend Alexander Mamut was there in the commercial whirlpool and, as a lawyer, was servicing almost everyone: he flew in to open accounts in London for Mikhail Khodorkovsky. With my salary of a few hundred pounds a month it was an eye-opener to see how the 'New Russians' partied at night in the clubs and restaurants.

In April 1989, while Margaret Thatcher was still prime minister, Mikhail Gorbachev, the general secretary of the Central Committee, came to London on a second official visit (the first had been in 1984 when he was still only a member of the Politburo). According to my calculations, the USSR was heading for a default on its foreign debt and the situation had become critical. The embassy had its own internal politics, and I was allowed to meet Gorbachev only at two o'clock in the morning. Leonid Zamyatin,

Ambassador Extraordinary and Plenipotentiary, had no wish to report my very own scientific discovery, although he believed it was entirely correct. 'You go. You tell him,' Zamyatin said.

The general secretary was sitting at the ambassador's desk, in a secure space where there were jammers to frustrate attempts at bugging. Some twenty people were in the room and the air was so thick with cigarette smoke you could see nothing. The ambassador introduced me: 'This, Mikhail Sergeyevich, is one of our near neighbours [an ominous silence ...], but he has something to report.' Zamyatin thus prepared himself a path for a hasty retreat, making it clear that if my report did not go down well, it was nothing to do with him.

I told Gorbachev it would soon be impossible to service our national debt, explaining how and why. Someone raised objections and I was, as it were, booed off the stage. Nobody could believe such a thing was possible. The Soviet colossus seemed to be standing firmly on its feet. Just a year and a half later, however, Gorbachev was to send the following telegram to John Major, the newly elected prime minister of the United Kingdom:

> *Dear John,*
>
> *I am writing to you as coordinator of the 'Big Seven' with an urgent request for financial assistance.*
>
> *Despite all the measures we have taken, the currency situation is in danger of collapsing. By the middle of November, the deficit of liquid currency resources needed to fulfil the USSR's foreign debt liabilities will be about $320 million, and by the end of the present year may reach 3.6 billion. All the underlying calculations were submitted to experts of the 'Group of Seven' in Moscow on 27–28 October.*
>
> *In order to avoid matters taking an undesirable turn, John, I am asking you to make available liquid resources in any form acceptable to you in the amount of $1.5 billion, including $320 million before the middle of November.*
>
> *Mikhail Gorbachev, 2 November 1991*

The default of the USSR, about which I had warned, followed shortly after that. It occurred on 28 November 1991, when Vneshekonombank (the Bank for Foreign Economic Affairs) ceased operations and declared itself de facto bankrupt. A week later, in Belovezhskaya Pushcha, the leaders of Russia,

Ukraine and Byelorussia announced the dissolution of the Soviet Union, and on 25 December Gorbachev appeared on national television to make a farewell address as president of the USSR to his fellow citizens.

How to make a billion while retaining your integrity

In early 1992, by which time I was a lieutenant colonel, I returned from my 'extended foreign business trip'. More precisely, I did not return: I was recalled. A high-ranking 'open' diplomat, who had close links with our service, harboured unfounded suspicions about my relations with his wife and reported that I had lost some ridiculous unclassified document. I was referred for investigation. He had given me the document himself, together with permission to mention it at an open conference, where I had read it out.

Before my departure, I spent two days composing a lengthy telegram of some fifteen pages about how our economic intelligence system should be structured, which areas it should focus on, how it should be subdivided, what questions it should address, how its staff should be trained, and so forth. This was in response to a request. As I later learned, my note found its way to the desk of the newly appointed director of the Foreign Intelligence Agency, Yevgeny Primakov. Not involved in the internal politics of the service, he asked for me to be found and, just three days after my return, I was in his office.

Primakov knew me a little from the past. I had been friends with his daughter and visited them at home. 'Hello, Sasha! As you see I am reading your telegram.' And indeed, there was my telegram in front of him, covered in scribbles, pasted with stickers, and annotated with different coloured marker pens. 'We discussed this telegram yesterday for two hours. But why are you looking so miserable?' I explained I was suspected of something totally absurd.

Primakov discussed my suggestions for an hour, at the end of which he phoned the head of my directorate. 'Have you got some misunderstanding there about Lebedev? Kindly trust him. He is an intelligent and disciplined officer.' He gave me the option of either being promoted to the rank of general to run the foreign economic intelligence service, or return to London.

'You know, Yevgeny Maximovich,' I said. 'Your intervention will put me in a very awkward situation. If some lieutenant colonel gets made a general and placed in charge of a new directorate, he will be cold-shouldered and you will not be able to protect me. I will put in another three months or so, then leave the service and go into business.'

Primakov responded, 'As you will.'

I got my things together and left the service. At that moment in time I possessed a hard-earned £500 and a 1977 Volvo with left-hand drive. The capital city of my native land had turned into one big flea market and presented a dismal aspect, but I viewed life through rose-tinted spectacles. I had no experience of living and surviving under capitalism with a Soviet face and believed anyone could succeed in business. The reality was to fall short of that.

The firm I set up with Andrey Kostin, the counsellor at the London embassy, was called the Russian Investment Finance Company. We took on everything that came our way, piling, as was considered normal at the dawn of capitalism in Russia, into one thing after another: property, consultancy, trade ... on the whole, unsuccessfully.

For example, we bought a wagonload of women's shoes from South Korea, only to find they were all size 34 and for the same foot. Another time we bought a batch of televisions that did not work. We planned to supply barbed wire from Russian detention facilities to UN troops in Mogadishu, but it turned out that Soviet barbed wire was not up to modern standards. We did nevertheless turn a modest annual profit, a five-figure dollar sum.

The Russian Investment Finance Company then rented an office from the Interior Ministry's medical section in the basement of a half-ruined mansion at No. 23, Petrovka, which had been designed in the late eighteenth century by Matvey Kazakov. It was just across the street from the capital's police headquarters. We sank all our meagre profits of around $40,000 into refurbishing the mansion.

While the renovation was going on, we were stuck in the basement with no toilet and no heating. During the winter we heated the place with a heat gun. When the fashionable renovation was finally complete and we moved into a wing, tattooed gangsters turned up and said, 'The cops have sent us round to get you out.' They were followed by the deputy interior minister, an individual with the eloquent surname of Strashko, Mr Fierce, who personally supervised the eviction. Needless to say, they paid us not a kopek.

That dark period lasted several years. Eventually I felt I could take no more, and even Freud's doctrine about spiritual anguish paving the way to happiness did not help. I sat on the sofa and stared fixedly at one point, acutely aware of my own uselessness, not wanting to do anything, unless perhaps to disappear. 'You don't want to do anything? Not even to smoke?' Until that moment I had been unable to give up smoking, and got through a couple of packs of cigarettes a day. That state of not wanting to do anything was enough to enable me to kick the evil habit, and to this day I try to use my lapses into depression (which still recur) to mobilise hidden reserves and engage in self-improvement.

Finally, in 1995 Lady Luck smiled on me. We were acting as consultants for Sergey Rodionov at Imperial Bank. I had advised many people to buy up sovereign debt in foreign markets, but no one knew what kind of beast that was, and no one believed it was possible to make good money from it. Rodionov, however, became interested in a deal I proposed to buy 'Brady bonds', named after the US Treasury secretary, Nicholas Brady. These were the national debts of Mexico, Venezuela, Nigeria and Poland, and were highly volatile.

On my advice, Imperial bought $7 million worth of these securities and in six months made $3 million on them. (Subsequently they tried to play the game without me and got in a right pickle.) We received a highly acceptable commission of about half a million bucks. What were we to do with what seemed to us an unbelievable fee? We spent some of it on a yacht trip in Greece, and knocked together a couple of offshore companies. Bankers were making the best money at that time, and I decided to spend $300,000 on one of Oleg Boyko's numerous dwarf 'banklets'. It had the imposing name of National Reserve Bank, although in reality it was no more than a licence with no actual assets or liabilities.

How this shell was transformed in the course of two years into one of the leading banks of the Russian Federation remains a mystery to many people. They keep looking for 'Communist Party gold' and 'KGB money', where in fact there is no mystery. Everything is completely transparent. At that time the person with most influence in the Russian economy was not the first President of the Russian Federation, Boris Yeltsin, or even Prime Minister Chernomyrdin, but a modest 34-year-old deputy minister of finance called Andrey Vavilov, who carried drafts of the budget to the State Duma in a string shopping bag. He was the person managing the state's finances, controlling the nation's entire banking system, pulling the strings and allocating the deposits of the Ministry of Finance to private banks.

Vavilov kept these balances in Khodorkovsky's Menatep bank, Boyko's National Credit, Smolensky's Stolichny [Metropolitan] Savings Bank and a dozen other major banks. That was where all the money circulated. Today's all-powerful state-owned banks, Sberbank (Savings Bank) and VTB (Vneshtorgbank, Bank for Foreign Trade) were not yet playing any role, and the Central Bank just sat very quietly and did not interfere.

A secret commission, chaired by Vavilov, reported to the Ministry of Foreign Trade, and all the intelligence agencies with an interest in foreign debt issues were represented on it. This was the moment when a Russian secondary market for foreign exchange bonds was being formed. These were, in the first place, the government's domestic foreign exchange bonds, issued by the Ministry of Finance in late 1993 against the liabilities of the bankrupt Vneshekonombank (Bank for Foreign Economic Affairs) of the USSR. They were also known as Taiga bonds or *Vebovki* – VeeBees). These bonds were on the balance sheets of foreign trade associations, and they did not know what to do with them. In the second place there were credit claims by Russia and its foreign trade associations against other countries and companies.

I proposed a scheme. Suppose a thousand Western companies owed us debts totalling billions of dollars. They might simply find someone to bribe and have them written off in return for a kickback. My proposal was to set up a consortium of banks that would buy up these debts at a fifty-per-cent discount. I persuaded Imperial Bank, National Credit, Capital Savings Bank and Menatep that this was a good idea, and thereby brought to my own bank some very solid clients among the state-owned foreign trade associations. I had money from the Ministry of Finance on the books of National Reserve Bank.

Our next success was with Gazprom, around which the greater part of business at that time was literally 'circling'. Many future oligarchs spent days and nights in the reception room of Rem Vyakhirev, chairman of the board of the monopoly. However, unlike those who wanted to embezzle the nation's assets, or at least grab themselves as large a slice of the national cake as possible, I saw a real problem Gazprom was facing and came up with a solution.

Ukraine owed Russia a huge debt for gas. The now independent republic was diverting 'blue gold' from the Soviet export pipeline for its own consumption, and settling the bill not with cash, which it did not have, but with promissory notes, so-called *gazpromovki*. In 1995, ten series of a total of 280,000 bonds were issued with a nominal value of \$1.4 billion. I suggested the Ukrainians should convert these notes into sovereign debt. That is, Ukraine should issue bonds, place them on the stock exchange in Brussels where they would be bought in the stock market, and Gazprom would get its money.

The Ukrainians did not issue them in electronic form, though, but printed them as bits of paper, which they deposited in the basement of the National Credit Bank branch in Kiev. What good, you might well ask, were they going to do there? It was something out of the nineteenth century! 'Well, pal,' someone told me, 'that's a lot of paper you got issued …'

I promised to think of something, and a day later was back in Vyakhirev's office, to find him and his deputy Vyacheslav Sheremet waiting. I made them an offer. 'We're going to give you a benchmark price. National Reserve Bank buys these bonds for seventy-five per cent of the nominal value in a bilateral arrangement, and you invest that amount in me as capital. No cash has to be exchanged: all that is needed is the recording of a transaction between banks.' The upshot was that the omnipotent gas monopoly became a shareholder of National Reserve Bank without having to pay a kopek.

Someone who is today an oligarch, and whom I often met at that time in the venerable reception room on Nametkin Street, commented as I was leaving, 'Our financial Mozart!'

CHAPTER 2

The Xerox Paper Box

'Choose or Lose!'

At the beginning of 1996, 'democratic' Russia was experiencing its latest lurch down the rusty spiral of dialectical materialism. The state was seriously ill: getting drunk, thieving, and the people were in financial difficulties. There were vain attempts to seek salvation by calling in the Varangians (American spin doctors), by pleas to the International Monetary Fund and the likes of George Soros.

All the traditional idiocies were repeated, with no one recalling the earlier stages of Russian history or learning its lessons. Soviet citizens, who had been promised the capitalist paradise and a life 'like they have' in Europe and America, had had their full share of revolutions, counter-revolutions, hyperinflation, voucherisation, the MMM pyramid scam, elections and referendums, a little civil war in the centre of Moscow and a much more serious war in the Caucasus.

The population, penniless and half-crazed, was listening to official reports about military operations 'to restore constitutional order in the Chechen Republic', which had been going on for two years, was getting used to subsistence living, and wondering what else it had left to sell, from an inherited parental fur coat to the infamous (and mythical) 'red mercury' for making pocket-sized atom bombs. Such was the cultural and historical background as Russia braced itself for another presidential election.

There was a serious power struggle. The Communists had won a crushing victory in the December 1995 State Duma elections and were preparing to besiege the Kremlin. In February, Gennadiy Zyuganov displayed himself at the World Economic Forum in Davos, where the international business elite hold their annual gathering. While Anatoly Sobchak, still mayor of St Petersburg, was sitting at a table giving an interview to twelve French models Petya Listerman had rounded up, the general secretary of the Communist Party of the Russian Federation was hard at work.

His declaration that his party was no longer the old Communist Party of the Soviet Union, that he was all in favour of a mixed economy, and that foreign investors would find the climate under his regime hospitable, enabled the leader of the CPRF and the 'patriotic popular forces' to make a favourable impression on the event's participants. After all, by this time they had been doing business successfully for over ten years years with the predictable Chinese comrades, investing billions of dollars in the economy of the Celestial Empire.

Things were not going well for President Boris Yeltsin. First Deputy Prime Minister Oleg Soskovets had been appointed head of his election campaign. The former director of the Karaganda Metallurgical Group and former minister in the government of the USSR had not a clue about popular politics. In line with Soviet tradition, he put his trust in 'administrative resources', supposing that all that was needed was to give the order and another 'election' would proceed according to plan.

In a country being torn apart by contradictions, where there was no 'vertical of power', and where officials in the provinces kept their CPSU membership cards under the pillow and openly admitted their support for Zyuganov, that was fundamentally impossible. Faltering half-measures and colourless speeches turned Yeltsin into a laughing stock. The president's approval rating fluctuated around the margin of statistical error, and a number of officials in the government began putting out feelers to Zyuganov, offering to deliver him the head of Tsar Boris in return for future employment.

Soon, however, there was a drastic change in the incumbent president's election campaign. His rating shot up so sharply it ultimately brought Yeltsin a second term. This miraculous transformation of the outsider into the winner gave rise to the myth of the all-powerful 'Seven Bankers' (by analogy with the Seven Boyars who ruled Russia at the end of the Time of Troubles in the early seventeenth century). This meme, as people say nowadays, was unleashed by Boris Berezovsky, who always had a tendency to self-demonisation and exaggeration of his personal role in the history of mankind.

After the election, in an interview with the *Financial Times* in November 1996, he gave the names of seven individuals who, he claimed, controlled over fifty per cent of the Russian economy and jointly influenced the taking of the major domestic political decisions in Russia. They were: Vladimir Potanin (Onexim Bank), Vladimir Gusinsky (Most-Bank), Mikhail Khodorkovsky (Menatep), Mikhail Fridman and Pyotr Aven (Alfa-Bank),

Alexander Smolensky (Stolichny Savings Bank, renamed from 1997 SBS-Agro), and himself, Boris Berezovsky (United Bank, 'Obedinenny Bank', which in Russian lent itself to an unfortunate obscene abbreviation). To this canonical list were subsequently added Vladimir Vinogradov (Inkombank, Innovative Commercial Bank), as well as Vitaliy Malkin and Bidzina Ivanishvili (Rossiysky Kredit Bank).

The legend was officially set out in an article 'The Seven Bankers as a New Russian Take on the Seven Boyars', shortly after Berezovsky gave an interview to journalist Andrey Fadin of *Obshchaya Gazeta*. It suggested that oligarch bankers, fearing the Communists might come back to power and take away all their hard-earned loot, had laid aside their commercial rivalries and joined together to protect their covert power and influence. They had had a whip-round, set up a slush fund and hired sorcerers (some possibly even from America). These wizards had addled the brains of the Russian public and had their puppet, the half-dead Yeltsin, resurrected and re-elected.

This elegant conspiracy theory bore not the slightest relation to harsh Russian reality. The truth is that the influence of the guild of merchants on those in government, under Yeltsin and all the more so after him, has been minimal. Their dependence on bureaucrats, and especially those in the security ministries, has, on the contrary, been absolute. The private sector today, twenty years later, does not represent even a third of the Russian economy, and back then it was just displaying the first shoots of a potential 'people's economy' culture.

In Russia, the state has always been the principal entrepreneur, and many high-ranking officials, ministers, governors and heads of national corporations could see off any businessman featured in the *Forbes* rich list. An unofficial ranking does exist, but is never made public. These bureaucrats were the real driving force behind the bourgeois revolution that put an end to the socialist distribution system.

The distinguishing feature of the Soviet *nomenklatura* system of privileged officialdom, despite all its shortcomings and bureaucratic overregulation, was that it was impossible for officials to enrich themselves. Even if they succeeded in embezzling funds, there was nowhere for them to spend the money. Inside the Soviet Union there was the watchful Department to Combat Embezzlement of Socialist Property, and neither could they get up to anything in the world outside, because of the KGB and the Iron Curtain.

After 1991, incomes increased out of all proportion. You could safely 'earn' tens of millions, hundreds of millions, even billions of dollars, depending on your place in the hierarchy. We call such officials '*dolbins*', businesscrats, officials with business interests. In them the state and private capital coalesce into a single entity or family. For example, a governor issues building permits to his own construction firm; a federal minister, purchasing medicines from the budget for people exempt from paying for them, orders them from his own pharmaceutical company. There was nothing actually illegal in such arrangements.

'What do you mean, corruption?' the businesscrat would retort indignantly to any suggestion there might be anything improper in such behaviour. 'That's an outrageous slander! It just so happens that my brother (brother-in-law/other relative) is a successful businessman. He won the tender! What? My sister chaired the tendering committee? Well, she has two postgraduate degrees and experience in this area going back to the Byzantine Empire. Anyway, show me the law against it or I'll see you in court!'

A typical example is the former mayor of Moscow, Yury Luzhkov, who back in 1996 was one of the most powerful people in Russia and had his eye on the presidency. I once witnessed a curious scene at a dinner party given by the renowned practitioner of monumentalism, Zurab Tsereteli. When someone asked Luzhkov's wife, Yelena Baturina, whether family ties might in any way have contributed to her place in the rich list, she elbowed her husband, who was seated next to her, and said, 'What?! If he did not keep getting in the way, I would have made not five but thirty-five billion dollars by now!' Her husband nodded, ruefully rubbing his ribs.

Most of those called oligarchs became rich thanks to the state, and were perfectly aware that it could, whenever it chose, reduce them to penury. That was the fate of Vladimir Vinogradov, who died a poor man. The entire Menatep coterie ended up in jail or emigration, and Berezovsky came to a bad end. Oleg Deripaska, the owner of Rusal aluminium, very succinctly articulated the Russian oligarch's credo in a 2007 interview with the *Financial Times*. 'If the state says we must renounce (the company), we shall do so. I do not see myself as separate from the state. I have no other interest.'

This is why the oligarchs, with the exception of Berezovsky, have either steered clear of politics completely, or preferred not to keep all their very valuable eggs in one basket. The renowned Seven Bankers went out of their way to find opportunities, if not to do a deal with the Communists, then at least to square the circle. In April 1996, *Nezavisimaya Gazeta* (Russia's *Independent Newspaper*) published a letter, 'Let's End This Deadlock'.

It was signed by all seven of the bankers, as well as by Sergey Muravlenko and Victor Gorodilov, the CEOs of the Yukos and Sibneft oil companies (which were not at that time owned by Khodorkovsky and Abramovich); by Alexander Dondukov, president of the Yakovlev Experimental Design Bureau; Nikolai Mikhailov, president of Vympel International Corporation; and Dmitry Orlov who owned the Vozrozhdenie Bank. In their letter, crafted by Sergey Kurginyan, who was close to the Communists, they upbraided both Democrats and Communists and called upon them to 'make a concerted effort to find a political compromise and avert dangerous conflict.'

Yeltsin, however, was not a man of straw, but a charismatic politician with a startling appetite for power and a nose for anything that threatened it. When he saw plainly that Soskovets and his team were heading for defeat, a new campaign team under Anatoly Chubais suddenly appeared. The key players in it were Yeltsin's daughter, Tatiana Diachenko, and Viktor Ilyushin, who had been Yeltsin's assistant since he was first secretary of the Moscow City Communist Party Committee. Unlike the bureaucrats and security ministry people, they recognised that relying solely on administrative resources would get them nowhere, and that popular support now needed to be worked for using capitalist methods.

They launched an ambitious public relations offensive, 'Choose or Lose!' To this, advised by the top experts in the newly emerging art of spin-doctoring and by talented directors of Russian show business, they attracted to their banner the famished creative intelligentsia, the celebrities of art and culture. All this, of course, came at a considerable price but, also of course, the money was not paid through this presidential candidate's election fund.

The bankers really did shell out for Yeltsin's election campaign, but less from fear of the Communists or from any great love for the ruling regime than because, as would have been the case in Soviet times, the incumbent told them it was their duty. He also provided them with tools for the job that enabled them, even as they financed his campaign, to make a little money for themselves.

A pyramid for Yeltsin

A neat fundraising mechanism was devised. Selected banks invested money the Ministry of Finance had on deposit with them in government short-term bonds, a financial pyramid created by the ministry itself. Everyone participating in the market at that time bought the bonds, because the return was ridiculously high: over 100 per cent per annum and, one might assume, with no risk attached because they were, after all, state bonds. Deputy Finance Minister Andrey Vavilov sent round a memorandum to banks who were using the ministry's money in this play, stipulating that half the income was to go to the Yeltsin campaign fund, in cash. That was the source of Yeltsin's election slush fund, of which more below.

It had a very specific address: No. 2, Krasnopresnenskaya Embankment, which happened to be the head office of the Government of the Russian Federation, known as the White House. It was a perfect location for dispensing cash – a hypersecure facility with all amenities, including an almost free canteen and a ready supply of alcoholic beverages.

Cars bringing money drove in directly from the embankment. There were two teams at work in adjacent rooms. One, under Alexander Korzhakov, who headed the president's personal security service, received and counted the cash and put it into wads. The other, delegated from Chubais's headquarters in the President Hotel on Yakimanka, collected it for current expenditure and removed it from the building. In between performing these important patriotic duties, the lads drank brandy, smoked, played computer games (the Internet was not yet available, so they played Solitaire or Minesweeper) and hung around the young White House secretaries and waitresses.

Throughout the campaign, this mechanism worked like clockwork. Crafty Berezovsky and Gusinsky avoided having to pay the cash by persuading campaign headquarters they would make their contribution by exploiting their television channels, ORT (now Channel One) and NTV. Ordinary bankers from the coalface were rather miffed they were having to shell out their honestly acquired cash on propaganda, rather than just issuing orders to the menials who managed TV channels for them, but could not make specific complaints for lack of evidence.

National Reserve Bank, like other donors, dutifully paid over the prescribed amounts to campaign headquarters. The money was used to send pop stars all over the country to urge their fellow citizens attending gigs to 'vote with your heart'. Ten million copies of a free colour newspaper, *God Forbid!*, were printed and explained that Zyuganov was worse than Hitler. The Communists were regularly lambasted on the airwaves.

As a result, in the first round of the election, held on 16 June, Yeltsin overtook his main rival, gaining 35 per cent of the vote against Zyuganov's 32 per cent. They went through to the second, decisive round, held on 3 July. Yeltsin managed to strike a deal with General Alexander Lebed, who unexpectedly came third with an honourable 14.5 per cent. On 18 June Lebed was appointed secretary of the Security Council 'with special powers', and publicly endorsed the incumbent president. Chubais's headquarters were all ready to open the champagne, but the very next day something unexpected happened.

That Wednesday our staff, as usual, brought another instalment of 'sponsorship donations' to the White House in our bank packaging. Actually, it was two instalments. Yeltsin's headquarters were preparing a final mega-concert in Red Square and needed a whole bunch of money. Sergey Lisovsky, one of the pioneers of Russian show business, whose remit at Yeltsin HQ was the 'Choose or Lose!' campaign; Chubais's assistant, Arkadiy Yevstafiev; and seconded from our bank, staffer Boris Lavrov, appropriated $538,000 of the money they had been brought for preparations for the event, put it in the first box to hand (which happened to be for photocopier paper) and walked serenely towards the exit.

Right by the entrance, all three were detained, sent for questioning, and the money was confiscated. There was a great scandal. Chubais, speaking on television, all but accused Korzhakov, FSB Director Mikhail Barsukov and their 'father confessor' Soskovets, of attempting a coup aimed at disrupting the election. All three were fired the following morning.

The motive behind the security officials' action would probably be comprehensible only to a very heavy drinker. Conceivably, the minions of Korzhakov and Barsukov were jealous because the minions of Chubais were walking away with the lion's share of the cash. Years later, Korzhakov described the incident as a move against embezzlement at Yeltsin's campaign headquarters. Militating against this is the fact that his own people were sitting in the next room, knew perfectly well how much money the couriers were taking and why, and had actually allocated them the disputed $538,000.

The only rational explanation for the whole episode seems to me to be that a person or persons were drunk out of their mind. The Presidential

Security Service officers, who were working as the campaign's cashiers, were indeed seriously imbibing while on duty and may simply have forgotten what they were supposed to be there for. To cap it all, according to people involved in the event, a vehicle bearing $5 million was on its way to the White House but, after the incident, vanished without trace.

At Yeltsin's headquarters it occurred to someone to pass the buck to … me. Well, who else but the 'ex-KGB agent' must have set the whole thing up in cahoots with Korzhakov? I suspect the source of the rumour was Gusinsky, in order later to demand an interbank loan to prop up his TV-Most, which was becoming seriously wobbly. Until Chubais was able to run to Yeltsin and turn the situation to his own advantage, he was very cross.

In the evening, I was summoned by Vavilov, the campaign treasurer, to his dacha. He was in a foul mood. His young new wife, with whom Andrey was head-over-heels in love, had a flaming row with him in front of me. He went straight on to blame me for the disaster with the ill-starred Xerox box. I had landed everybody in it. I tried to reason with him. 'Just a minute, guys! Someone tells me a car is on its way, I fill up a box, the car goes off with it. This is not the first month that's been going on. What am I being blamed for?'

At that Vavilov suddenly demanded I should immediately transfer $50 million to Gusinsky's Most-Bank, because he was supposedly not able to settle up with Gazprom. I was so tired myself I could barely stand and just told him what he could do with his 'peace initiatives'. Andrey hinted darkly I would be sorry I'd said that.

I attached no special significance to his words. That day everyone was overwrought. Anything can happen. In any case, two weeks later Yeltsin was re-elected president by 'the democratic will of the Russian people'. Meanwhile problems were snowballing. There was no money to pay state employees' salaries, no money to service foreign and domestic debt. We would have liked to support the ruble in the foreign exchange markets, but the Central Bank had no reserves. A triple whammy: papering over cracks, airhead solutions, and we ran out of time.

CHAPTER 3

Nothing Personal,
Just Business

More banks. Some good, some less good

The Soviet banking system was as straightforward as a glass of soda water from a slot machine on Gorky Street and rested on the four pillars of Gosbank (the State Bank), Stroybank (the Bank for Construction Projects), Vneshekonombank (the Bank for Foreign Economic Affairs), and Gostrudsberkassy (the State Labour Savings Banks). The State Bank of the USSR was analogous to today's Central Bank. That is, it acted as a regulator, but was also a universal finance and credit institution. Stroybank serviced industry.

Vneshekonombank operated in the import-export sector. In the Gostrudsberkassy the Soviet people, following the advice of Georges Miloslavsky in the movie *Ivan Vasilievich Changes Profession*, deposited all they had acquired by straining every sinew at their workplace. During Perestroika, the State Bank was stripped of its retail banking and credit-deposit functions, which were transferred to specialised institutions: the Industrial and Construction Bank, the Agricultural Industry Bank, and the Housing and Communal Services Bank.

In 1990, the Supreme Soviet of the RSFSR adopted a directive transforming the regional headquarters of these specialised banks into commercial banks and the state-run monsters rapidly collapsed. Numerous new 'banklets' sprang up and by 1994 there were 2,439 banks in Russia, the greatest number in the post-Soviet period. In this we were becoming comparable with America, where there are more than 7,000 banks.

Unlike the United States, however, where this anomaly has historical roots, in Russia 'bankers' sculpted their finance and credit institutions while sitting on a stool in the kitchen of a slummy apartment from the Khrushchev era, or a shabby cubbyhole in some plant-breeding research institute, whose director, needless to say, figured on the bank's 'board of directors'. The requirements for authorised capital were minuscule and could be bulked up with all manner of waste paper. Is it to be wondered that the criminal world found this nutrient medium so much to its liking?

The first murder of a bank chairman in Russian history occurred in Moscow on 29 December 1992, with the shooting of Vladimir Rovensky, chairman of the board of a certain Tekhkobank.

Kommersant reported, 'Rovensky was the executor of a major financial fraud which resulted in $140 million disappearing into foreign bank accounts. The scam was extremely simple: Tekhkobank made loans to fictitious firms against fake collateral. These loans were never repaid, but were instead converted into foreign currency and transferred abroad. Credit resources from other banks, underwritten by Tekhkobank, were also discovered in foreign bank accounts. The only person who knew all the beneficiaries of the embezzled funds was the head of Tekhkobank. According to the Ministry of Security of Russia, he was killed just ten hours after the last payment was completed.'

The resources of any state, even one as rich as ours, do sooner or later run out. Finding itself in a tricky situation, the government was compelled to look for sources of money in addition to government short-term bonds within Russia. However, nobody abroad was still lending. The executive branch was unable to think of anything original, so resorted to a method used several times previously: new issues of VeeBees: government domestic foreign exchange bonds. This supplementary issue was for over $5 billion. It is one thing to print bonds, though, and quite another to place them for actual money. Thus, bonds of the 6th and 7th tranches had 10- and 15-year maturities, but even the coupon yield could not make them attractive.

At that moment National Reserve Bank was one of the top ten banks in Russia and, apart from us, a similar decision to support the issue was taken only by Sberbank (the Savings Bank) and Stolichny (Metropolitan) Savings Bank. The rest preferred to look the other way. At the government's request, we granted it a loan secured by a holding of bonds for over $100 million. It soon became clear that the state would be unable to redeem the bonds in the near future, and we began looking for possible buyers. Andrey Kostin was in charge of National Reserve Bank's day-to-day activities. He was good at reaching agreements with people and finding ways out of the most intractable situations.

I remember a curious episode we had involving Yulia Tymoshenko, when she was head of Unified Energy Systems of Ukraine. Early one evening I had a phone call from Rem Vyakhirev, the head of Gazprom, who was a shareholder of NRB. He asked me to see Yulia from Ukraine. Shortly afterwards, an energetic young woman in high-heels and a skirt of purely symbolic length came into my office, sat down opposite me and crossed her legs. She crossed and uncrossed them periodically as gracefully as Sharon Stone in a celebrated scene in *Basic Instinct*, and suggested we should sell her *Gazpromovki* (the Ukrainian currency bonds issued in 1995 on account of money Ukraine owed Gazprom for gas supplies).

My guest was talking of nothing less than a package of securities with a nominal value of $200 million, which she hoped to acquire for next to nothing. She was offering no more than ten per cent of the face value, on top of which she wanted to pay not with money, but with 'horilka vodka and bacon fat'. I did my best to explain politely that this would not be happening.

Time passed. I could hardly just kick out a protégé of the chairman of Gazprom. At 11.00 p.m. our polite conversation showed no sign of coming to an end and I was desperately wondering what to do next when Kostin came to the rescue. I left him in the office with Tymoshenko and departed by the back door. I do not know how he sweet-talked her, but in the morning the future princess of the Orange Revolution and prime minister of Ukraine left empty-handed, a little tipsy, and in a good mood.

Soon afterwards an opportunity presented itself to sell at least a proportion of the bonds. The bank did not take long to make its mind up, because there was simply no market at all at that moment for the long-term bonds of the 6th and 7th tranches. The offer came from Mosbiznesbank, which was owned by a certain Victor Bukato. On behalf of a 'round-table of businessmen', he had signed statements supporting the re-election of Yeltsin, was a member of government commissions on the financial market, and was at the helm of the Control and Inspection Commission of the Russian Union of Industrialists and Entrepreneurs.

Bukato's biography did not arouse suspicion, or even vague doubts. He was a native of Pinsk in Belarus and had worked from a tender age in the local branch of Gosbank, then as director of the republic's headquarters of Stroybank, and finally became head of Zhilsotsbank (the Bank for Financing of Communal and Residential Construction of the USSR) which, after the collapse of the Soviet Union and with the support of the Mayor of Moscow, Yury Luzhkov, was reincorporated as a joint-stock company and changed its name to Mosbiznesbank. The agents dealing with the purchase of the bonds were others – one a company and the other a private individual. We knew little about him then, but had no time to worry about that.

The private individual was Igor Fyodorov, born in 1952, a graduate of the naval school in Peterhof and former submariner. Bukato liked telling us the tale of how he too had almost become a submariner. In 1958 he was summoned to the enlistment commissariat and asked to write in detail about himself and, more importantly, about his parents and all his relatives. He discovered that a crew was being chosen for the first atomic submarine. Twelve places had been allocated to his province but, when Victor arrived at the assembly point, there was already a full complement.

After his time in the submarine fleet, Igor Fyodorov taught at the Naval Academy in Leningrad, and then emigrated. To the United States. So he emigrated: what of it? There had been no USSR for five years; a lot of people emigrated. And anyway, Fyodorov and Mosbiznesbank appeared to be our only customers.

These were the circumstances in which National Reserve Bank and Edge Investment Group Inc., an American company that Fyodorov represented in Russia, concluded a swap agreement. The bank undertook to transfer to the firm bonds of the 6th and 7th tranches with a nominal value of $90 million, and in return Edge Investment Group would exchange bonds of the 5th tranche with a nominal value of $50 million, which were traded on the stock market and cost more.

This absolutely legal transaction was of interest to us for two reasons. Firstly, it enabled us to unload the problematical bonds of the 6th and 7th tranches that did not have an established price, and to receive in return foreign exchange bonds of the 5th tranche, which had long been in circulation on the financial market and were quoted on it. Secondly, the bonds of the 6th and 7th tranches were being transferred to a foreign company at the same price as our bank had purchased them from the state so that, from a financial point of view, the bank was incurring no losses on its balance sheet.

Sleight of hand and just plain fraud

Shortly after signing the contract, we obtained some further details regarding the personality of Igor Fyodorov. In 1988, having retired from military service, he had applied to emigrate permanently to Israel at the invitation of relatives of his wife. Permission was denied on the grounds of his having had access to state secrets of the USSR. The US State Department applied for a review of the decision, and in October 1989 Fyodorov and his wife were permitted to emigrate to reside permanently in Israel.

Some time after that, the couple were in the United States, where Fyodorov obtained a consultancy job on a classified anti-submarine defence programme with a company working for the Pentagon. In 1992 he began exporting consumer goods to Russia, and in 1994 started engaging in financial operations with some degree of success. He established a relationship of trust with the management of Mosbiznesbank, and registered a number of offshore companies abroad.

If we had known these nuances ahead of time, we would have thought twice about whether this deal was such a good idea. But we did not. National Reserve Bank transferred a portion of its bonds to Edge Investment Group, and the company in turn transferred its bonds to our account. Subsequent transactions went through smoothly. By the time only the last batch of bonds for Edge Investment Group was to be transferred, our bank's management was seriously considering continuing cooperation with Fyodorov and placing a batch of bonds through him.

We transferred the last bonds of the 6th and 7th tranches to Edge Investment Group's account at the beginning of June 1996, but the grand culminating chord in a major key was unexpectedly replaced by a jarring chord in which minor notes increasingly predominated. In return for this final transfer, our bank was due to receive bonds of the 5th tranche from Fyodorov to a value of $25 million. We did not.

Fyodorov disappeared. He did not return to his room in the Intourist Hotel and made no further contact with our bank staff. We were on the verge of notifying the matter to the law enforcement agencies when Fyodorov suddenly phoned, told us all was well with him and, in the same breath, added that he considered that neither he nor his companies now had any outstanding obligations to National Reserve Bank.

We made inquiries. It transpired that on 14 May 1996 Fyodorov had indeed concluded a brokerage contract with Mosbiznesbank, but not on behalf of Edge Investment Group, which would have been logical, but on behalf of Jacobson & Associates, a company registered in the US, but which for some reason had its account with a bank in the Cayman Islands. (A quick chronological digression: later, during an internal investigation by the bank, we established that Fyodorov had earned a healthy commission on the swap of the bonds of the 6th and 7th tranches with National Reserve Bank: some $100,000.) At that moment, however, we were more concerned about the fate of the final batch of bonds our bank had transferred to Fyodorov's account.

We found that this batch, like the first two, had indeed been sold by Fyodorov to Mosbiznesbank, and the money for the deal, amounting to $7,228,750, was, on the seller's instructions, transferred to the account of Delta Associates with a bank in the Cayman Islands. In breach of the swap agreement, however, Fyodorov gave no instructions to buy bonds of the 5th tranche at their face value of $25 million for National Reserve Bank.

Our worst fears were confirmed: a swindler had gained the trust of our bank's top management, concluded and partly executed a deal, but had failed to honour the last part of it. He had, as it was fashionable to say at the time, suckered us. Our calculations and conclusions suggested he had misappropriated over $7 million before scooting back to his new homeland. A complication was that the swap agreement between National Reserve Bank and Edge Investment Group expired only in 1997, so we could not go to court or bring in the forces of law and order immediately.

It was obvious we had made many mistakes. Well, we were not the first and will not have been the last: the only people who never make mistakes are those who never do anything. Some American banks – and major ones at that – now rest in peace while we are still here. Of course, we did notify the 'competent authorities'. Fyodorov was already sticking his tongue out at us from the other side of the Atlantic, knowing full well we would not embark on a dispute that could only end in tears.

We needed to get back, and soon, the money that had effectively been stolen from us. Procrastination would play into the hands of the villain. I first approached the New York agency Kroll Inc., but soon wearied of the saga of the search, instigated by Yegor Gaidar, for the 'CPSU'S gold', of multi-million-dollar fee rates, temple-like office complexes and hyped-up search reports. Within a month, the Interfor investigation agency of Juval Aviv, a former Mossad officer, tracked our money down to Switzerland and the Banque von Ernst & Cie.

Aviv did everything legally, which surprised me not a little, given my impression at that time of banking confidentiality in Switzerland. Swiss lawyers took the matter to court, the agency provided its evidence, and the court agreed to freeze the money he had discovered. However, the consent of Mosbiznesbank, which we had at that time (the money had after all gone out of their account), was withdrawn under puzzling circumstances, and Aviv (probably not without inducement) later switched to Fyodorov's side. Another investigative agency was regularly sending us a load of professional-looking garbage, a standard method of stringing customers along.

Juval Aviv had informed us that the money stolen from our bank was in Fyodorov's personal account No. 12178 in Banque von Ernst & Cie. Aviv had evidently presented his investigation as a search for the property of Holocaust victims, and the Swiss judiciary had unquestioningly believed the results he achieved to be publicly available information, as if he had found it on a rubbish dump. Before delivering a final verdict, the Swiss court agreed in the interim, at the request of our lawyers, to block Fyodorov's accounts.

This meant we would only have to wait until 1997 for the court to rule that the money he had misappropriated should be returned to us. At this point, though, events started to unfold in a manner that would have made the twists and turns of an ingeniously constructed thriller seem like a banal soap opera.

CHAPTER 4

Operation Boar on the Run

Money, especially tainted money, prefers stillness

In real life, unlike in geometry, parallel lines frequently do intersect, and sometimes rather elaborately. This is exploited in films, where two or more stories develop separately, only to meet in a final, culminating moment. A classic example is *11:14*, with Hilary Swank and Patrick Swayze, where the fates of multiple characters suddenly converge. In the present instance, the course of my life intersected with that of a classic swindler, gangster and fixer for the Russian authorities, Ashot Yeghiazaryan.

Ashot was born on 24 July 1965 into the cultured family of Gevorg Yeghiazaryan, head of the Industry Department of the Economics Faculty of Moscow State University. After graduating from daddy's faculty, Yeghiazaryan worked briefly as an engineer in the Expocentre exhibition group on Krasnopresnenskaya embankment, then at the Sverdlov Silk Factory in Moscow. At the age of twenty-five, the young financial star became chairman of the Fund for Socio-Economic Development of the Moscow Region, which was founded by, among others, Tokobank, Avtobank, the Moscow Banking Union, the Academy of the National Economy of the USSR and, of course, Moscow State University.

In 1993, Yeghiazaryan and his brother Suren founded the Moscow National Bank. Mosnatsbank rapidly made its way into the top 100 banks in terms of assets, becoming also the fourth largest in terms of loans underwritten by the Ministry of Finance. Its borrowers were understood to include the Interior Ministry of the Russian Federation, the Federal Border Agency, the Ministry of the Defence Industry, and the Ministry of Communications.

In the summer of 1996, Ashot Yeghiazaryan was installed in Unikombank, which had been established in 1990 on the basis of the Moscow regional division of Zhilsotsbank. It positioned itself as a regional bank.

It is perhaps overly diplomatic to say he was installed. As *Novaya Gazeta* reported, its investigative department received the recording of a telephone conversation between a certain great chief of Oneximbank (let's call him X) and an inquisitive lady acquaintance, who was also involved in the world of big business (let's call her Y):

Y: I wanted to know a bit more about Yeghiazaryan. Who is he? What kind of person? What does he do?
X: He is a very bright young man. I don't know him personally. For one thing, he got in with us with no greasing.
Y: Who is 'us'? The system, do you mean?
X: Yes. And as a result he got Unikombank.
Y: And who was he in Unikom? [...]
X: He sits there. Has an office. Actually he has nothing to do with Unikombank. Never had, to be precise. That's as much as I can say.

Although formally Yeghiazaryan was only the deputy chairman of the board of directors of Unikombank, and the majority shareholder was the Administration of the Moscow region (the chairman of the board was officially, as is considered only proper in the world of businesscrats, Victor Vlasov, first deputy of the governor), the real boss was Ashot, who had brought his pocket-sized Russky Dom (Russian House) Bank on to the register of shareholders, as well as several other commercial institutions.

In June 1996, the Administration of Moscow region received a loan from the Ministry of Finance in the form of government domestic foreign exchange bonds totalling $656 million. The socially concerned Moscow authorities intended to pay off the salary arrears of state employees from transactions involving these securities. Officials immediately transferred the bonds to Unikombank for trust management at 3.5–4 per cent per annum. (The average rate of Russian banks that could be taken seriously was 12–16 per cent.)

Unikombank promptly passed the bonds on under a repurchase agreement[4] and agency agreements to Mosnatsbank and another of Yeghiazaryan's companies, International Financial Club (MFK) Bank, which distributed them among other associated entities. When the time came for

---

4 A repurchase agreement, or repo, is an agreement to buy (or sell) securities, with an obligation to sell (or buy) them back after a particular term and at a price specified in the agreement.

the Moscow Region authorities to repay their loan to the Ministry of Finance, Unikombank, by way of repayment, bought a batch of Ukrainian state bonds from the Ministry of Finance. Their value was only $40 million. As a result, the Ministry of Finance was paid back just $40 million instead of $315 million, which was the actual market price at that time of the Russian government bonds.

Yeghiazaryan conducted the same operation with OVVZ bonds for $237 million allocated to that flagship of the Russian military-industrial complex, the MiG Moscow Aviation Production Corporation, for a fictitious contract to supply MiG-29 fighters to India. According to documents signed by Maxim Tkachev, financial director of MiG, all the money again went to Unikombank and International Financial Club Bank. By coincidence, at just that time a little money-laundering banklet was opened in Bridgetown, the capital of the sunny island state of Barbados in the Caribbean. It was called Louis d'Or Investment and was managed by Andrey Gloriosov, first deputy chairman of Unikombank.

The saying 'Money prefers stillness' is attributed to Mayer Amschel Rothschild, the founder of the Rothschilds' financial empire. In fact, the proprietor of the Frankfurt exchange office at the end of the eighteenth century taught his sons four principles: not to allow women into business; to live in love and harmony; to concern themselves with the public good; and not to display their wealth.

In Russia his maxim is treated as meaning that money is best made away from the light and the bustle of publicity. Of course, if you are a swindler and your money is tainted, then behaving like a cockroach is perfectly natural. Accordingly, Ashot Yeghiazaryan, despite the vast scale of his business dealings, tried to stay beneath the radar.

Because of the nature of my early career, I have retained more curiosity than is deemed appropriate about banking operations other than my own. I have long been aware that a substantial number of representatives of the financial world see no difference between their own and their clients' money. Yeghiazaryan was a typical example of this. Curiosity killed the cat, however, and it was not long before my life took a new turn and came to resemble a cross between a crime novel and a western.

National Reserve Bank under bombardment

During the night of 23 August 1996, a hand grenade was hurled through the window of our office at the bank and exploded, seriously injuring one of the security guards. The others called the police. The duty squad arrived, inspected the premises and departed. A couple of hours later other people, in plain clothes this time, appeared. They scrutinised the scene of the crime, took measurements in a very professional manner, wrote things down on special forms and then … arrested two of the guards on duty that ill-starred night. The policeman in charge bore an uncanny resemblance to Conan Doyle's Inspector Lestrade.

The hapless guards were released from the cells only after other buildings of our bank were fired at from a grenade launcher. They told us the police had suspected them of having brought the hand grenade to the bank themselves and that the explosion had come about because of careless handling of munitions. This far-fetched theory was soon disproved when plastic explosive was laid by the corner of one of our bank buildings. Finally, one day when I arrived at my office, I trod on a bullet. Another was lying directly under a bullet mark in the wall at the level of my head. Both had penetrated the bullet-proof protective membrane on the window panes.

There appeared to be no rational explanation for these attacks. National Reserve Bank worked like clockwork and had no conflicts with anyone. The only unresolved issue in our work was the unfinished business with Edge Investment Group. At no time in the bank's history had there been any similar threat to our personal security. Was this the work of Fyodorov? It hardly seemed likely. By now it was too late for him to influence anything, because the Swiss court had already ruled that our money should be returned to us and we were just waiting for that to happen. Could he be trying to intimidate us? It was doubtful. He was a fraudster, not a gangster. Swindlers do not usually mutate like that.

The law enforcement agencies failed, as usual, to find any suspects. After two months of preliminary investigation, the proceedings in both cases were suspended 'in view of non-detection of the individuals who committed the criminal acts'. A cold case, in professional parlance.

At the end of 1996, a fax had been sent from the United States to Yury I. Skuratov, prosecutor general of the Russian Federation. We only learned of its existence a year or so later (*see opposite*).

енеральному Прокурору
Российской Федерации
Г-ну Скуратову Ю.А.

От г-на Федорова И.И.
почтовый адрес:
322 E.Broadway
Hopewell, VA, 23860
fax: (804)4582349

19 ноября 1996 г.

Уважаемый Господин Генеральный Прокурор.

Весьма неприятные обстоятельства вынуждают меня обратиться к Вам с настоящим письмом.

Весной текущего года руководители так называемого "Национального Резервного Банка" (НРБ) в Москве, господа Лебедев и Костин (последний не так давно назначен на высокий пост управляющего Внешэкономбанком), ответственный сотрудник Мосбизнесбанка (МББ) г-н Чистилин, а также известный в банковских кругах финансист г-н Швецкий пригласили меня для участия в международной финансовой транзакции, механизм которой сводился к следующему.

Используя тесные личные связи с некоторыми руководителями Минфина и ЦБ России, в частности, с руководителем ЦБ г-ном Дубининым (жена последнего работает на ответственной должности в НРБ), указанные лица получили для НРБ от соответствующих правительственных учреждений исключительное право осуществлять на рынке ценных бумаг, российском и международном, операции с тогда новыми, 6-м и 7-м траншами валютных облигаций Минфина России (ВЭБовки). Суть сделки состояла в обмене 6-го и 7-го траншей на 5-й. Вполне легальная операция, часто практикуемая финансовыми организациями.

Получив в свое управление ВЭБовки 6-го и 7-го траншей номинальной стоимостью 300 миллионов долларов, НРБ при моем посредничестве и при

To Mr Yu. I. Skuratov, Prosecutor General of the Russian Federation
From Mr I.I. Fyodorov
322 E. Broadway, Hopewell, VA, 23860
Fax: (804) 4582349
19 November 1996.

Dear Mr Prosecutor General,
    Highly disagreeable circumstances oblige me to send you this letter.
    In spring of the present year, the directors of the so-called National

Reserve Bank (NRB) in Moscow, Messrs Lebedev and Kostin (the latter has recently been appointed to the important position of CEO of Vneshekonombank), Mr Chistilin as the authorised representative of Mosbiznesbank (MBB), and the financier Shvetsky, who is well known in banking circles, invited me to participate in an international financial transaction the mechanism of which was as follows.

Exploiting their close personal ties with certain senior figures at the Ministry of Finance and the Central Bank of Russia, in particular the director of the Central Bank, Mr. Dubinin (the wife of the latter works in a senior position at NRB), the aforementioned individuals obtained from the relevant government institutions the exclusive right for NRB to conduct operations in the securities markets, Russian and international, in respect of the then new 6th and 7th tranches of foreign exchange bonds of the Ministry of Finance of Russia (VeeBees). The essence of the transaction was to swap bonds of the 6th and 7th tranches for bonds of the 5th. This is a perfectly legal operation, commonly practised by financial institutions.

Having acquired VeeBees of the 6th and 7th tranches with a face value of $300 million, the NRB, through my mediation and with the participation of Mosbiznesbank as broker, began selling these bonds on the international market, after which they supposedly intended to buy bonds of the 5th tranche and transfer them to the RF Ministry of Finance. In accordance with the agreement concluded, the commercial companies under my direction were assigned the legitimate role of intermediary in the above-mentioned transaction.

However, in the course of executing this financial transaction, it became apparent that the above-named gentlemen had no intention of buying VeeBees of the 5th issue, and they began simply transferring the proceeds from the sale of the 6th and 7th tranches (approximately $300 million) to the accounts, mainly in Swiss banks, of front companies specially registered in various countries. I received instructions on the transfers as supplements to my mediation contract.

When the criminal nature of the activities of Messrs Kostin, Lebedev, Chistilin and Shvetsky became apparent to me, and in particular after the disappearance of most of the documentation from my temporary office, I announced that I was withdrawing from this business. At this, the gentlemen listed attempted to dissuade me from this step, citing *as their principal argument the fact that the deal on the fictitious exchange of VeeBees was being carried out with the knowledge and consent of Mr Chernomyrdin, and it was accordingly risk-free. When, however, I learned some time later that other businessmen who were, like me, intermediaries in transactions involving foreign exchange bonds of the 4th and 5th tranches were being murdered, I immediately withdrew from this business and flew to the United States.*

The aforementioned gentlemen did not leave me in peace even in the United States. I began receiving insistent demands that I should return to the VeeBees business, which then developed into outright threats of physical violence against me and my family. Moreover, in every threat it was emphasised that the gentlemen threatening me had secured support in high-level Russian circles, including also from Mr Chernomyrdin (which I do not believe).

About a month ago, the gentlemen from Mosbiznesbank and National Reserve Bank, having forged a number of legal and financial documents, succeeded in misleading the courts of the Swiss Republic, as a result of which a portion of my funds was frozen, which had a very negative impact on the functioning of my business.

In addressing this letter to you, Mr Prosecutor General, it is my sincere hope that you will afford assistance in protecting my family, my property and my resources from the criminal encroachments of the dishonest gentlemen whom I have mentioned above.

Otherwise, I shall be obliged in a few weeks' time to inform the media, including the Russian media, and the US legal authorities of the information I have about the criminal activities of representatives of the Russian financial community, including details of the bank accounts in which dishonestly obtained multi-million dollar sums are deposited.

With sincere respect,

I. Fyodorov

You do not have to be an expert on the subject to imagine that hundreds, if not thousands, of such appeals arrive in the Prosecutor General's Office every day. Crooks and their mistresses complain about investigators who, they claim, beat and torture people with household irons and electric shocks; neighbours in communal apartments complain about each other; professional stool pigeons denounce honest people; psychos write about their private obsessions, and so on.

Most of these communications go straight in the bin. Some, no doubt, do the rounds of various offices until they end up with luckless officials who have no one else to forward it to and so are obliged to check it out themselves. Perhaps they would have dealt with the complaint conscientiously, but how can anyone be expected to verify all the details when there are only a few tens of thousands of people working in the Prosecutor's Office to cover the whole of Russia?

By a 'fortunate coincidence', Fyodorov's appeal proved an exception to the usual practice of the prosecutor's office. But what so caught the attention of the clerk there? Perhaps, indeed, of Skuratov himself? Could it have been the names of Chernomyrdin, Dubinin, Lebedev or of other less well-known persons? Or the sincerity of the applicant with his imaginary fears for his life in the United States? Or the frozen money (stolen from our bank)?

This ludicrous epistle landed on Skuratov's desk, not thanks to the vigilance of the upholders of law and order, but because someone was waiting for it. Everything had been agreed in advance and all that was needed was an excuse to start the ball rolling. The letter carried a marker, a signal addressed to the 'right person'. I think that Skuratov, shortly to become famous as 'someone resembling the prosecutor general of Russia', knew the names of the congenial skeletons in his cupboard backwards, because puppet-masters as yet unknown were tirelessly making sure he did, and had a film projector at the ready for the evening bulletin of the *Vesti* television news programme. 'We wouldn't want any trouble,' they doubtless told him, 'only ...' and so on.

What is the most crucial part of this letter? Fyodorov's motivation was, of course, purely mercenary. Predictably, the Prosecutor General's Office picked up on evidence in his appeal of 'treason and murder most foul' committed by Lebedev and his accomplices. It immediately set to work on Fyodorov's communication as a top priority. Over the Prosecutor General's signature, top secret orders and requests were instantly despatched to the FSB and the tax police. The texts of these documents already imply that a fiscal crime has been discovered, of which it only remains to clarify certain details and formalise everything in the appropriate official manner.

The staff in the Prosecutor's Office who received Fyodorov's appeal were undeterred by the fact that their informant lived on the other side of the Atlantic. He would, of course, need to be cross-questioned, available papers obtained, and documentation requested. All this would need to be analysed and compared and further questioning conducted if inconsistencies came to light. Not only that, but when there was 'himself' sitting on the other side of the wall, directly supervising the course of the investigation and, indeed, playing the central role in it, then clearly the person in charge of the investigation was in an unenviable position.

In the end, however, it all blew over. The deadlines stipulated in the legislation expired, no evidence of a crime was discovered (because no crime had been committed). No decision to proceed was taken and nobody got hurt, glory be to Themis. It had, however, all been worth the effort, because Fyodorov's letter that had led nowhere was, without any legal justification, quietly attached to the materials of a new criminal case, filed as early as 15 July in the following year of 1997. Indeed, it featured as the principal charge.

On the eve of the New Year, there was another explosion outside our building, and again the police failed to find the culprits, as we had no doubt they wouldn't. It did occur to us, though, that Skuratov's office might be able to shed light on what was going on. A remarkable reply was received from the Prosecutor's Office of the Central Administrative District of Moscow to the effect that firstly, after examining all three criminal cases relating to the armed attacks, those with the task of supervising the progress of the investigation had discovered that no work was actually being done on them. Secondly, substantive progress could be made on the cases if the investigation focused on the theory that those responsible for the crimes were members of the bank's staff who were employed to guard it.

The scenario being suggested was that, in the opinion of the police and the Prosecutor's Office, the guards had, under the noses of the bank's senior management, organised a criminal gang, obtained arms and ammunition, and used the security office as a training ground. Sometimes, obviously, not very successfully. On other occasions, however, they worked at night, meticulously, invisibly and – brainlessly, evidently forgetting that at night the bank was closed.

Bearing in mind that during the day the guards performed their duties very professionally, the logic of the Prosecutor's Office was going to need bolstering with convincing insights from research in parapsychology and experiments conducted while the moon was full. This had the makings of the script for a film starring Louis de Funès.

Enter the Tormentors

Until February 1997 (and not yet knowing anything about Fyodorov's appeal to the Prosecutor's Office), we could not imagine what was behind all that was happening to our bank. As winter drew to a close, however, we gained a new insight into the causes and consequences. Officers from the tax inspectorate arrived at the bank for an unannounced audit of our compliance with tax legislation. We would probably not have seen any great significance in this, but for the fact that less than a year had passed since our last comprehensive inspection. In the course of 1996, officers of the local tax inspectorate visited the bank on several occasions. In May 1996 a comprehensive audit, with involvement of the Central Bank, was conducted and did not turn up any serious irregularities.

Something that put us on the alert this time was the presence in this composite team of officers of the tax police. We were given no explanations, not even of the reason for this unscheduled inspection. Some time after it started, we discovered that the bank was obliged for such unexpected scrutiny due to a letter from Deputy Prosecutor General Katyshev to the National Tax Service. A touching correspondence was taking place at this time between Fyodorov and the prosecutors.

I doubt whether any fraudster had ever previously enjoyed such sensitive and solicitous treatment from the prosecution service staff. None of the law enforcement officers I have spoken to since then could believe a letter of this sort could have been written, let alone from the Prosecutor General's Office on Bolshaya Dmitrovka. Some were sure it must be a forgery, but alas this letter was indeed sent to Fyodorov.

It is startling to find the Prosecutor General's Office providing a thief with details of the legal measures being taken by a bank to defend its property, and urging him to agree to a personal meeting.

Dear Mr Fyodorov,

As a result of checks carried out in respect of your statement to the Prosecutor General's Office of the Russian Federation, we have received partial confirmation of the information you provided. This indirectly indicates possible negative consequences that may befall you and your family. Representatives of National Reserve Bank are enquiring whether you have sent a statement to the Prosecutor's Office, what your whereabouts (address) might be, and are making counterclaims of a financial nature.

We have also learned that they have sought the services of a foreign detective agency to freeze your accounts through the courts, submitting false documents with material claims against you.

The situation urgently requires maintenance of direct contacts, both for obtaining additional information and for a joint discussion of practical measures to protect your interests.

Issues regarding the provision of security can be discussed only in person, taking account of the relevant circumstances. This can be arranged at your discretion either in the US (where you are resident) or in a third country (for example, Cyprus or the Czech Republic), to which our representatives are ready to travel without delay upon receipt of your reply.

Kindly confirm receipt of this fax.

S.A. Aristov

Later, former investigator Kirsanov related that in September 1997 he had been instructed to investigate the factual claims in Fyodorov's statement. At that time, all the case materials amounted to were the account Fyodorov himself had given the FBI and a large quantity of bank and other documentation yet to be translated into Russian. From the available evidence, it was impossible to draw even preliminary conclusions. Everything needed to be done from scratch, from the buying of the bonds by National Reserve Bank to Fyodorov's transfers of money.

It took Kirsanov to almost the end of 1997 to complete the job, by which time he had drawn up a diagram. The tax audit report was completed only on 27 June 1997, although Aristov's letter to Fyodorov had been sent in April. It was promptly put to good use. Upon receiving the fax Fyodorov took it to the Swiss court and succeeded in getting his personal account unfrozen. He thereupon withdrew the money and concealed it somewhere less detectable.

Pioneers of black PR

We wrote several letters to the Prosecutor General's Office, but received no response. At around this time our bank, and I as its director, were on the receiving end of a campaign of vilification unleashed in the media. Not a week passed without an article appearing somewhere, 'exposing' me and demanding that I should be called to account. Yury Ryazhsky and Leonid Krutakov were particularly active in the capital's most widely read newspaper, *Moskovsky Komsomolets*, as was Yulia Pelekhova in the most influential business periodical, *Kommersant*.

Pelekhova's subsequent fate aptly illustrates the saying, 'God, unlike Antoshka, does not see all'. In 2004, she was sentenced to seven and a half years' imprisonment for attempting to extort $100,000 from a female entrepreneur by threatening to publish compromising material.

For the most part, the article headlines made laboured play of the fact that *Lebed* means a swan in Russian. So we had 'Swan Lake', 'A Swan in the Bush ...', and so on. Some were more original. Here is a fairly typical article by a certain Pavel Nekrasov (a pseudonym, needless to say), published on 13 August 1997 in *Moskovsky Komsomolets*:

A Wild Boar on the Run
Is Chairman Lebedev of National Reserve the hunter or the game?

In the banking world, the man in the spotlight in the first half of August is rightly considered to be Alexander Lebedev, chairman of the board of National Reserve Bank. Let us remind readers that it was Lebedev that former Deputy Finance Minister Andrey Vavilov pointed out to the Prosecutor General's Office, accusing him of attempting to misappropriate a batch of government debt bonds worth $460 million.

Lebedev it is who figures in a statement written by former Russian citizen Igor Fyodorov, accusing him of spiriting several million dollars out to the West during Boris Yeltsin's election campaign last year. The authorities reacted to that by searching Lebedev's premises two weeks ago. Having absorbed all these unpleasant experiences, the banker seems to have got his second wind and thrown himself into a counterattack.

Today Lebedev is proclaiming throughout the land that neither he personally nor NRB have been involved in anything criminal, although you will agree it would be surprising if he were to admit his guilt openly. The friends and patrons of Lebedev are, however, a different matter.

The most powerful of these is rightly considered to be Sergey Dubinin, chairman of the Bank of Russia, who, it would appear, combines in his person the functions of Russia's most senior banker and of Lebedev's defence lawyer. Thus, according to information received by this newspaper, Dubinin has several times personally telephoned the Prosecutor General's Office, trying to influence the investigation and even to tell its staff how to do their jobs.

Significantly, it is not only Dubinin who has been phoning the Prosecutor's Office. Lebedev's fate is causing concern to top officials in the Presidential Administration and bureaucrats in the Russian government close to Victor Chernomyrdin's clique. Whether the chairman of NRB is guilty or not is for the competent authorities to decide.

What we would like to point out is something different. All those who have been phoning the Prosecutor General's Office, including Dubinin, the chairman of the Central Bank of the Russian Federation, are allowing themselves liberties unheard of for officials at their level and which, let us remark, are hardly compatible with what is expected of the highest servants of the state.

Dubinin, indeed, actually went so far as to issue a public statement in support of National Reserve Bank and reprimanded the law enforcement agencies for their (in his opinion) unduly close scrutiny of Lebedev and lack (in his opinion) of professionalism. Perhaps the most comical voice, however, in this chorus of Alexander Lebedev's defenders has been that of Lapshin, the leader of the Agrarian Party who, in some extraordinary way, contrived to link the 'attack' on NRB with possible disruption of the harvest in Russia.

We should probably expect analogous interventions in the near future from Zhirinovsky (who will readily find a link between this banker's problems and negro domination in America), Zyuganov and other such like characters. But now we need to talk more seriously. We will try to understand why Dubinin, Russia's leading banker, is so doggedly speaking out in the interests of one of the very people he should, in theory, be scrutinising more closely than anyone else.

Some will say, well that is his job as head of the Central Bank, speaking out in the interests of his cronies, the smaller bankers. He certainly does that, but we seem to remember Sergey Dubinin had nothing to say when Angelevich, the president of Montazhspetsbank, was arrested; that he assiduously pretended nothing was happening when Tveruniversalbank went to the wall, or when Inkom lurched into an extremely serious crisis. We could list dozens of similar examples.

Perhaps the reason for Dubinin's present fervour is that it is not so long ago that he and Lebedev were working shoulder to shoulder at Imperial Bank and have stayed on extremely cordial terms ever since. How did that old schoolchildren's song go?

Friends, I tell you I'm not scared
If a bear should run
At me when I've got a friend
And the bear has none.

Or perhaps Mr Dubinin is making such efforts also because he very much loves his wife who, by one of those coincidences which happen only in life, works for Mr Lebedev's bank. The logic could not be simpler: if someone is being horrid to NRB, he is being horrid to my wife, and that I will never allow ... Actually, I would like to suggest the government puts out to tender the right to employ Sergey Dubinin's wife in a commercial bank.

If the winner is being guaranteed protection by a *krysha* in the person of the governor of the Bank of Russia, he will be only too glad to pay for the privilege – and the state's revenue from the tendering process will be little less than it got from floating Svyazinvest or Tyumen Oil.

However, joking apart, the two bankers are doubtless bound not only by the bonds of friendship and almost family relations but also by purely commercial shared interests. We have not forgotten how only a year ago, by courtesy of Dubinin, Lebedev successfully acquired shares of Unified Energy Networks of Russia (we have already written about the $300 million which the governor of the Central Bank ordered should be allocated to NRB to complete this transaction).

It only remains to add that, having received these state funds, a commercial bank immediately made a profit of $700 million owing to the rise of Unified Energy Networks' share price on the stock market. The notorious 'global speculator' George Soros is said to be looking to his laurels. Incidentally, according to some sources, the company Energomenedzhment complained to the Prosecutor General's Office about this purchase, accusing NRB and Lebedev personally of fraud and violation of current legislation.

These are the muddy waters in which Sergey Dubinin is currently operating. At one moment he is trying to do the Prosecutor General's job, the next he is trying to become the handler of all the law enforcement agencies, and then, far from the capital, he is furiously reforming the currency. In the opinion of most experts, this latter operation by the governor of the Central Bank – shearing 'superfluous' zeros off the currency – (about which not even people in the Ministry of the Economy knew) was an admirable smokescreen behind which Dubinin could hide from all the scandals of recent months.

Flying off to see the president and successfully persuading him to immediately announce revaluation of the ruble, Sergey Dubinin undoubtedly strengthened his position, which had been in jeopardy after the failed attack on Onexim and Unikom banks. Even so, people in the Russian business world are unlikely to forget his blunders against those targets. One can only wonder what will happen if Dubinin carries on missing the mark like this. He knows well enough how it could all end for him, and yet goes full speed ahead. His comrades-in-arms ...

If we look closely at this, it is manifest claptrap, but its author is adroitly manipulating the prejudices of the man in the street. What is important is not facts, but the continual innuendo. At that time this genre was just beginning to emerge, and it was Russian 'journalists' who were leading the way. In the years ahead, I was frequently to be the object of similar campaigns, and have adopted the attitude Mark Twain counselled, that any mention in the press, even the most negative, as long as it is not an obituary, is an advertisement. Alas, the mass reader does not take that view.

The article was published shortly after Dubinin, as governor of the Central Bank of Russia, had written to Prime Minister Viktor Chernomyrdin demanding a criminal investigation into the theft by Ashot Yeghiazaryan, through Unikombank, of domestic foreign exchange bonds issued by the

Ministry of Finance of the Moscow Region Administration. The article's title is wholly unrelated to the text, in which there is not a word about hunting. The mention of a wild boar might appear entirely beside the point but in fact, as later became evident, it was yours truly who was the game being hunted.

The systematic terrorist attacks on our offices, raids by the tax police, criminal court cases, searches and confiscations, and mud-slinging in the media, were all links in a single chain. That title in *Moskovsky Komsomolets* was a coded message that the hunt was on. It was a gesture analogous to the custom of the Italian Cosa Nostra or 'Ndrangheta, who send their prospective victims a rotten herring in newspaper.

Among themselves, the organisers of the hunt called their victim 'the piglet', perhaps mindful of a humorous story by Anatoly Trushkin, 'Characteristics of the National Hunt':

A. Was that your lot whacked the banker yesterday?

B. Hell, no. What do you take us for? We do deputies, restaurant owners, shopkeepers. Bankers? Never. Well, unless a wounded one came running in our direction. Not likely.

A. Do you feed officials?

B. 'Course we do. They used to be timid, but now they take food out of our hands.

A. What, really?

B. Swear to God! There can be people around, nothing frightens them. Help themselves, don't even blink.

A. Out of your hands?

B. Right out of our hands. Offer them anything, they'll take it. You mean, you don't feed officials?

A. Nah, we're more politicians. How they breed, though! It's terrible. Last year they ruined the harvest.

B. No, really?

A. Swear to God. We catch them with applause. Just clap your hands and there they are, jumping out of nowhere. And they sing. No, beautifully though! You should hear them trilling away! Tweet-tweet-tweet … tra-la-la … tweet-tweet-tweet!

B. Just like that? Tra-la-la and all?

A. Tra-la-la and all. No sweat. They might sing about their salary, their housing, or their pension. You just stand there thinking, 'Time for me to bump you off, pal,' but you're transfixed.

B. What, don't they scent danger, then?

A. They're a bit short of something, politicians are. Thick skin, maybe. When one opens its mouth, its ears close.

B. Is that right? Well, mother nature, eh? What she comes up with! Too bad they've screwed up the environment: all the crime bosses have flown off to warmer climes to hatch their eggs there. The New Russians in the past though, eh? Now you take one or two of them to a prostitute, zilch!

A. Yeah, it's our own fault. Mutants everywhere. Look at them from the front, they're a politician. Look at them sideways, they're a hitman!

B. Lord, protect and have mercy on us!

Who was behind all these events? What did these people want? They were hardly likely to be interested in me personally, unless for my money. It was also clear that the person behind the incidents was not Fyodorov the Fugitive: he was at best a pawn in someone else's game. A massive onslaught in the press would hardly come cheap, and that's before all the bribes to the law enforcement agencies.

CHAPTER 5

In the Crosshairs

Shortly afterwards, the head of the FSB's Economic Counterintelligence Directorate, Lieutenant General Alexey Pushkarenko, came to my office on Novokuznetskaya, told me a vague story about an attempt on my life they had thwarted, and invited me to meet the director of the FSB, Nikolai Kovalyov. In his gloomy office on Lubyanka, Mr Kovalyov received me dryly. They were not in a position to disclose details of the operation; the person who commissioned the crime had not been identified; the FSB could not guarantee my safety, and accordingly he recommended I should leave Russia. Temporarily, of course.

I tried to find out if there were at least any lines of enquiry. 'We can tell you nothing. Decide for yourself who might have benefited,' Kovalyov replied. In all sincerity, I spread my arms wide – and did not believe a word of the story. The FSB was, if without enthusiasm, assisting the Prosecutor General's Office in the Fyodorov saga and working against my National Reserve Bank. I asked about this, plainly irritating the director of the FSB, and we parted no closer to a meeting of minds.

Years later, a former officer of the criminal police, completely unknown to me, gave me a letter with a detailed account of that story from the now distant past. What it primarily shows is that Kovalyov was telling the truth, and that I had reacted unwisely. Here it is:

In spring 1997, as a senior officer of the Economic Crimes Department of the Criminal Police of the Interior Affairs Directorate of the Northeast Administrative District of Moscow, I received a call on my home telephone from my over-eager subordinate, Agent Kubik, who said he needed to see me urgently about a very important matter. I was about to go to bed, so went out to meet him in not the best of moods. For this chancer every case was extremely urgent, and invariably ended up with my delivering him a homily on how idiotic, wicked or illegal his latest wheeze was.

'Hello, there.' 'Good evening, Volodya!' [*The former Economic Crimes Department officer's name is Vladimir Vasilevsky – AL.*] 'I've got this guy with me. Tell you all about it later. In front of him you need to call me Vladimir. I'm a major in the CID.' 'You are?!' 'It sounds daft, but it adds up. No time to explain. Follow my lead.'

Sensing this was not going to end well, I nevertheless agreed to play along. It would have been good to know what my own role was, but there was no time for that. This was going to call for improvisation.

The warm May rain was rustling the leaves. Kubik called to some character lurking in wet bushes away from the light of the street lamps. He was heavily built, about six foot six, had the face of a grunt in the army, and could best be described as a bruiser.

Our newly promoted major took the initiative and I, nodding affirmatively and feeling a complete prat, gathered that a joint operation between the CID and Economic Crimes Department was approaching its logical conclusion. Having been hired, paid an advance and given a mission, a hitman had been detected, exposed and, facing impending criminal prosecution, declared himself ready to cooperate with the security agencies. I gathered the guy had come to turn himself in, but I had no idea why he thought he needed to. Kubik to the rescue. He very convincingly and professionally allowed our guest to explain everything himself.

Oleg (the bruiser) said he had been trapped. He did not want to go through with the hit, because he could see he would be a dead man within a month of doing the job. It would be cheaper and safer for the gang to get rid of him than pay him for the hit. He could not publicly turn himself in, because then he would be dead within a week. He could only give up and trust us to treat him fairly. 'If you don't,' he said, 'I'll deny everything, and anyway I'm not giving you my full details, I'm not ratting on my pal, and I'm not signing anything.'

So he did not trust us. Well, that was understandable, only to be expected. Our 'major' said that, man to man, he had come to feel sorry for Oleg, and they had become buddies while he was being processed by our units, He wanted me, as an old friend and colleague, to support his initiative on the collegium. 'What an idiot!' was my reaction. Would that be the collegium of the Interior

Ministry he had in mind? Just the place for majors and, all the more so, senior lieutenants to get a respectful hearing!

I had learned to expect the unexpected in my job but was, to put it mildly, perplexed by what I heard. I played my role to the very limit of my acting ability and said I had not expected such creativity from the CID, that I could not tell how his superiors would react, but that I would lend him my support, not, of course, at the collegium but at the level of my own superiors, who usually went along with my opinion.

We agreed to proceed in the light of how the situation developed, and shook on that. Oleg departed back into the bushes and I, after allowing enough time to be sure he had gone, told Kubik in language traditional within our service exactly what I thought of him. [*Some text excised here from considerations of ethical censorship – AL.*]

His excuse was that, trying yet again to evade his creditors / criminals with a grudge / enemy agents he had outwitted, Kubik had rented an apartment on the outskirts of Balashikha. He had two dependants: a young and beautiful mistress and a sturdy dog, a Staffordshire bull terrier I think, which provided the fugitive with at least some modicum of security. While taking the terrier for a walk on the local embankment, Kubik had met Oleg, walking his own faithful mongrel. They discovered they lived on the same staircase, became friends, and had recently joined forces to celebrate a national holiday.

Some time later Oleg, clearly tormented by doubt, let the cat out of the bag.

'Volodya, I don't know what to do. I'm in real trouble. This old friend of mine, Zhenya, he works for the Medvedkov gang. Well dressed, solvent, helps the guys get round problems of some sort. It seems not to be dangerous. I pestered him a couple of times to have a word and see if they might find a job for me. I fought in Afghanistan, and not as a rookie. I know how to handle a rifle, shoot, at people too. I can do all that if need be. Zhenya tries putting me off. "You don't need this." But I stick to him like a leaf in the bathhouse. "Take me to meet the guys, just do it."

'In the end, he does. They have a talk with me, a month later tell me they've got the brothers and cops to agree and I'm in. Didn't give me any work, but paid me on the nail. Not a lot, probably, but more than I'd ever dreamed of. This goes on for half a year or so. I'm already taking it easy. But two weeks ago, they tell me there's this job: whack a merchant. Well, what would you have done in my place?'

'First of all, I am not in your place. Secondly, you're not a little kid. You signed up, you sort it out. What's wrong with you? Can't take the heat?'

'You know, it's not that I'm chicken, but I'm up shit creek, Volodya. Think about it: the job's worth six thousand bucks, and they've given me eight hundred up front. Said I've got two weeks. When it's done, I get the rest. I'm to whack some guy called Lebedev. Instead of a photo, they show me a magazine cover, it's called *Profile*, and there he is on the cover. I'm thinking, if he's on the cover he's got to be famous, and they reckon he's worth a full six thousand bucks. That means they're going to owe me another five thousand two hundred. Big money! Offer three rubles for taking me out and they'd have a queue!

'I don't know what to do. I tried talking to Zhenya, but he didn't want to know. "It was your idea. Don't say I didn't warn you." I thought of going to the cops, but no one would take me seriously. They'd want a written confession, and then what? I've got no proof, nothing. They'd start hauling the guys in to the cop shop, they'd play dumb and get back out while I'd be off for pre-trial investigation and they'd get at me there. Either the guys or the cops, and all for those three rubles.'

'Okay, kid. Here's a second chance. You'll owe me, though. In short, listen up. I'm a major in the CID. My name wouldn't mean anything to you, because I'm undercover and my real name is so secret, I've forgotten it. My wife isn't my wife, she's another staffer, and what her mother called her I don't know myself. We've been keeping tabs on your brigade for a long time, but for other stuff, wet jobs too, old ones. Do you think I moved out here and take my dog for a walk because I've got nothing better to do? Why are you looking so down? Pull yourself together. You should have thought about all this before. As your lot say, live up to your big talk.'

Oleg was totally downcast. 'Now what? Do I get an hour with my family, to say goodbye?' The 'major', as an excellent psychologist, decided to kick a man when he was down.

'You're a good lad, Oleg, I saw that right away, and it would be a shame to ruin your life just because you've been a fool. I'm sorry for your wife too, and your little girl. You don't have a cat in hell's chance without me. I can promise they'll do you in, not so much for the money. What matters is you're a witness, a thread that can be followed if push comes to shove. With you out of the way, the thread disappears. You have a problem, man! I could have dealt with it, but this is a joint operation. The Economic Crimes boys have been brought in on it.

'There's some questions about fraud for the Medvedkov gang to answer. Seems they've been providing protection for con artists. That's what I hear. They have a good cop there, though, and I've known him for a long time, a big wheel the men at the top trust. We need to speak to him. Go home for now. Talk to someone if you want to, but it's better if you don't or you could land me in it. Don't try to make a break for it. Without my say-so, they won't let you. I'll try to phone through to my colleague. Come back in ten minutes. If I don't get through, we'll go there unannounced.'

Oleg was so moved by Kubik's big-heartedness, he was almost in tears and gratefully shook the would-be detective's hand. Kubik did get through to me, though, and so we met. 'Look,' I said when he finished, 'did it not occur to you he might just take your head in one big hand and tear it off your shoulders? Did you see the size of his mitts?' 'But I had the dog with me!' 'Playing on his emotions. He had a dog too! Or he might have just pulled a gun and rubbed out both of you there and then.' 'I never thought of that.' 'Why did you ever get into this?' 'I don't know. Wouldn't you have done the same with information like that?' The look of crazed opportunism reappeared in Kubik's eyes.

'I don't know either. Probably not. This is totally insane!' I told Kubik he was an idiot, a half-wit, an opportunist, but could not help admiring his panache. We started thinking what to do. I told him my superiors would never wear it. It was not our line of work. Ours was the kind of thing Soviet teams investigating 'theft of socialist property and speculation' used to deal with, shop assistants making money out of sausage leftovers. Well, okay, they had wised up over the last three years, but they would want nothing to do with a contract killing.

We couldn't rely on the Regional Directorate on Organised Crime, and in any case doubted their reliability. (They were forever asking us for 'solved' crimes.) Empty poseurs with maroon jackets and medallions. Criminal Investigation? There were some bright sparks there, but they would elbow us out and take over everything themselves, turn Oleg inside out, maybe even follow the latest government decree and jail him for thirty days, and that would not save Lebedev's skin if a hit had been commissioned.

To meet Oleg's conditions, we needed someone with special authority. The FSB! But we had no contacts there. Or rather, we had, but only at our regional level and that too would be pointless: by the time they had checked everything out, written up their reports and their superiors had had time to react, Oleg would long have disappeared. He would have done a runner, Lebedev would have been dispatched and his body would be on our conscience. 'On yours too, Comrade Major!' I added.

'Wait a minute – I do have contacts in the FSB!' Kubik said. 'I know a couple of guys in the Moscow divison! Do the names Antakov and Petukhov ring a bell?' 'No. How come you know them? Who are they? Although ... what does it matter?' I replied. 'Give them a call. We have no option.' 'Right. I'll phone them tomorrow. So long.'

The next day I was feeling distinctly uneasy. I could picture the scale of the forthcoming operation and had not the faintest idea of where to start or how to finish it. There seemed to be no solution: if there was an order for a hit, it was going to happen. I reported everything to my boss, but that did not help. Barannikov [*Sergey Barannikov, Vasilevsky's immediate superior – AL*] supported me, but himself had only questions. Puchkov [*Andrey Puchkov, at that time acting head of the Economic Crimes team for Northeast Moscow – AL*] was unavailable and one of his deputies just twisted his fingers at the side of his head and advised me to calm down and stop giving myself a hard time over a lot of nonsense. I really just wanted to wash my hands of the whole affair. I wanted the situation somehow to resolve itself. I wanted Oleg to disappear and the FSB not to respond.

It was not to be. On the contrary, Oleg turned up to our meeting on the dot. So did the FSB, in plain clothes. One (Petukhov, or Antakov – I don't remember which) was probably, to judge by his age, a lieutenant colonel. The other was younger, almost as massive as Oleg, and asked us to call him Said, despite bearing not the slightest resemblance to a Said.

We met on Lubyanka, walked down a side street and went in the front entrance of a mansion with no name plate and old-fashioned, half-height, Soviet-style net curtains on the windows and a duty officer in the entrance hall. The panelling and furniture were light oak, there was a dark brown leather sofa, a black telephone – all very Soviet. In fact, Khrushchev-era.

There were no introductions. The FSB officers immediately went to work on Oleg. I was flattered that they prefaced some of their questions with 'if our colleague from the Interior Ministry has no objection.' There was immediate hard bargaining, no holds barred. Oleg needed guarantees, the FSB needed serious information ('What the fuck have you come running to us for, pretty boy? We don't waste our time on minor stuff.'). The Interior Ministry also needed information that would provide a reinforced concrete lead, and it had to relate to economic crime.

Oleg's expression changed constantly. At times he squared up like a boy in a fight, then wilted under the pitiless pressure of the negotiators. In the end he gave in. The discussion moved on to economic crime, our ground. We decided to act immediately. (That is, of course, the FSB officers decided and I nodded assent.) They made Oleg call his clients and tell him he was practically ready and wanted the tool for the job. The brothers in the gang already had mobile phones which identified the caller, but Oleg's fears were abruptly dismissed. 'The Office' was in charge, stop worrying and do as you're told.

A lot of calls followed. The idiots on the other end of the line effectively appointed Oleg coordinator of the operation, constantly giving our new friend more and more contacts, and even phoning Tallinn. The Office rubbed its hands gleefully.

The end result of many phone calls was that, firstly, the hired hand told the subcontractor the 'tool' he was being given was completely unfit for the job. Oleg checked out the location. It proved unsatisfactory, because there were no safe getaway routes. He needed a more distant firing position and a suitable tool – a good rifle, for instance.

Secondly, it was arranged that on a certain date the Tallinn–Moscow train would arrive at Leningradsky station and in carriage number so-and-so the conductress, Nina, would be waiting. Oleg would meet her, collect a bag containing the requisite tool, and Zhenya would cover his colleague's back.

Before we left the FSB that day, I was asked to go out to the street and wait there, so what was subsequently discussed with Oleg I neither knew nor cared. It was evidently something it was best for me not to know.

I reported back to Puchkov. He listened carefully, asking detailed questions, then said, 'Go for it!' That, by tradition, meant, 'This is your top priority. Drop everything else (but only for now: nobody has abolished the Plan, let alone our departmental meetings). And any other member of the department who can assist you is at your command.'

A couple of days later, I had a call from the FSB inviting me to check out the prospective scene of the crime. Our usual team met at Bolshaya Nikitskaya: me and Kubik, Oleg, the lieutenant colonel and Said. Our 'elder brothers', as we called the FSB officers, were understanding about Kubik's original legend and throughout the operation he retained his rank of a major in the CID and was addressed as 'Vladimir Vladimirovich'.

We came to Romanov Street. Block 3, Building 1, if I remember correctly. This was evidently a fixed point on the target's route. As we were walking, the elder brothers told me who that was: Alexander Yevgenievich Lebedev, formerly of the Foreign Intelligence Agency and now one of the directors of the rapidly and inexplicably expanding National Reserve Bank.

He had supposedly come to see the director of the FSB, asked to be provided with protection, but received the reply, 'Of course, most certainly. Could you just put in writing from what and from whom exactly you want to be protected?' Lebedev hesitated, and a few days later sounded the retreat and decided to make his own arrangements.

I arrived with my colleagues Sasha (Alexander Anikin), Sergey (Shuverov) and Denis (*Toropov, all at that time senior agents of the Economic Crimes Directorate – AL*) at Komsomolskaya Square. We needed to select a convenient spot for observing the meeting with

Left: *Legendary football player Lev Yashin, a friend of our family (right), congratulates my father on his fiftieth birthday. On the left – my mother, Maria Sergeyevna.*

Right: *We practised fencing with my older brother Alexey sometimes*

Below: *Happy student years*

Left: *With my son Evgeny in London, 1990*

Below: *Christening of our youngest son, Yegor*

Left: *A photo with a view of the entrance to the office of the National Reserve Bank, made from the neighbouring house – the place where the killer was hiding who tried to blow me up with a grenade launcher*

Above: *Potato fields of the National Land Company, Tula region*

Above: *Now I am a master of the potato harvester*

Below: *With the head of the Ukrainian Orthodox Church, Metropolitan Vladimir, and Metropolitan of Simferopol Lazarus, at the opening of the lighthouse church in Malorechenskoye, Crimea.*

Left: *The lighthouse church in Malorechenskoye is one of the new sights of Crimea*

Below: *Chekhov's theatre in Yalta, Crimea, after reconstruction*

Below: *Press conference with Kevin Spacey and John Malkovich in Chekhov's theatre, Yalta*

Right: *Spa-hotel More in Alushta, Crimea*

Below: *The Presidents of Russia and Ukraine Vladimir Putin and Leonid Kuchma in Hotel More. Crimea, 2004*

Left: *Meeting with the President of Russia on the civil aviation development. Moscow, 2001*

Above: *In the conference hall of the Ukrainian parliament – the Verkhovnaya Rada. Kiev, 2006*

Right: *In the assembly shop of the aircraft plant in Voronezh*

Above: *With USSR ex-president Mikhail Gorbachev in Italy*

Left: *With Ugandan President Yoweri Museveni. We discuss the problem of saving the elephants from poachers. Kampala, 2015*

Below: *Meeting with UK ex-Prime Minister Margaret Thatcher*

Left: *Meeting with Boris Johnson (at that time – Mayor of London) at a Charity Gala, 2009*

Right: *With ice hockey Olympic champion Vyacheslav 'Slava' Fetisov*

Below: *With theatre and film director Kirill Serebrennikov*

Nina of Tallinn. On the opposite side of the square from Leningradsky station, we found a suitable building next to the Moskovsky department store and agreed with the management that we could get upstairs without hindrance at any time. We took some trial photos of the area and some more close-up, developed them and found they were fine.

When Nina arrived, we had everything ready for her rendezvous. We used up the whole film but got clear portrait photos of Nina and Zhenya, who had come to the station with Oleg. Lena [*Yelena Barchenkova, at that time another ECD operative – AL*], who had been introduced to Oleg, followed him and signalled to my pager from a public telephone that he had met Nina. Oleg helped Nina carry her bags and conducted her across the square to a spot beneath our windows, where Zhenya met them at the car. They put the luggage in the boot and drove off.

The tool had been delivered. It later proved to be a rifle adapted from a hunter's single-barrel gun. It had a threaded insert for a 7.62 x 39 cartridge, a handmade orthopaedic butt, handmade multi-chamber silencer, and a standard issue but very ancient telescopic sight. A single-loader but with a cartridge extractor, which would aid speedy reloading.

The next few days were very tense. The FSB was demanding that implementation must be delayed under any pretext, while the intermediary for those commissioning the murder was insisting it should be done as soon as possible. I was playing the role of a faulty telephone between Oleg and the FSB, trying to moderate the attacks from both sides, and being pestered several times a day. I had to exercise great self-restraint in order not to tell them all to go to hell. Oleg was adamant he needed to meet Said's boss and I had to insist on a face-to-face meeting so both sides could reach some sort of consensus.

We met again, and Oleg spent half an hour trying to persuade the others he had put every conceivable explanation for his dilatoriness to the contact and had now run out of excuses. It transpired that the villains were intending to monitor the implementation of their hit and all but make a movie of it. Voices were raised. The outcome was that The Office came up with a solution of almost embarrassing simplicity. Apparently, there were no cartridges for the rifle, and in any case it would need to be sighted in. It could turn out that it was completely unusable for getting an accurate shot. The villains would be able to see that for themselves and the time pressure would be relaxed for a while.

Nevertheless, our elder brothers declined to help us find ammunition and accordingly it fell to the ECD to solve the problem. Not the gangsters, not the CID, not the army or the FSB, but the Economic Crimes Department, the 'sausage and mattresses' specialists. It was enough to make you weep! With little expectation of a positive outcome, I reported the situation to Andrey Puchkov, and the issue was instantly resolved.

Puchkov explained the situation to Alexander Ivanov [*then chief of the criminal police department for Northeast Moscow – AL*], and within half an hour, by oral order of General Kharchenko, head of the Moscow Interior Affairs Directorate, I was issued thirty assault rifle cartridges without any questions or filling in a single form.

The next day, in an abandoned quarry in the Medvezhiye Lakes district, Oleg and I sighted the rifle in. Finding a large sheet of cardboard and a dozen tin cans in the mountain of litter was no problem.

The rifle turned out to be ideal for a single shot. In the first place, the firing accuracy was, in more senses than one, striking. This was doubtless due to the long barrel (the initial velocity of the bullet was probably 1,000 m/s or more) and the precision of the fitting of the junction between the barrel and the breechblock. Secondly, the handmade silencer proved highly effective. I had never fired a firearm with a silencer before and had nothing to compare it with, but the feel was unbeatable: a recoil to the shoulder, a click, and a short hiss of emitted propellant fume, as if you had disconnected the hose of a pump from the valve after inflating a tyre. 'Pss!' Nothing more.

The sights were more of a problem. We used up half a pack of cartridges on the sighting in. We fixed the sight to the swallow tail rail as tightly as we could and it was clear there could be no question of dismantling it subsequently. We unfastened the foregrip, removed the barrel, reassembled and fired again. No change. It was ready. There were about ten rounds left.

I phoned The Office, told them all about it, and we agreed to meet that evening. I was asked not to bring the 'comrade major' with me.

Only Said turned up, and he quickly explained the plan. First, Oleg needed to inform the contact that the rifle was not self-loading and had shown terrible firing accuracy. At the same time, he was to report that he had found another way of carrying out the hit: by chance he had spotted an ideal position for firing a grenade launcher: the roof of a house near Lebedev's office. He would suggest to the contact that he should be supplied with a grenade launcher, either an RPG-7 or a single-shot RPG-18.

At this point Said enquired which grenade launchers Oleg was familiar with. It did not matter which, but an RPG-18 (*Mukha* – the Fly) would be preferable. It was less bulky and easier to get hold of. That was a legacy of the Chechen war, evidently.

Second: the grenade launcher he was given was to be 'upgraded' by specialists to misfire. As he was leaving, Oleg would be stopped by police but manage to escape. All this was there to be observed by the enemy's spies. If everything went smoothly, the outcome would be a news sensation, which would not protect Lebedev, but would at least force his enemies to lie low for a while. Oleg for his part would get 100 bonus points from the gang and be able to demand compensation from the contact responsible for delivering a substandard tool. At best he would finally get clear of the whole business.

Oleg was delighted with the plan. Now he had been saved he was a different person, confident and relaxed. I, needless to say, had no objection to it. I was just a little alarmed when, after Oleg had left, Said asked me not to mention this new version to his superiors, to prepare suggestions on where my officers should be positioned and, after agreeing the finer points of the performance with Said, instruct said actors to ensure the premiere was a brilliant success.

I do not know who the genius was who devised this plan – and make no claim to authorship – but to this day it strikes me as beyond criticism. It really was the only right solution.

The Office's crafty scenario had just one flaw: it did not deal with the problem of the rifle. 'Once in a year even a stick will fire,' goes the saying. Well, this 'stick' would be guaranteed to fire again, and not into thin air but into a person. What was to be done about the rifle? Returning it to the gangsters could not even be considered. Doing that would contravene the law. At the very least it would demonstrate extreme negligence, perhaps even complicity in the trafficking of firearms. As for how it would sit on anyone's conscience ...

Oleg talked to his contact exactly as planned. He liked the idea of the grenade launcher and got to work on the new approach, but it was clear he would not forget to ask for the rifle back. We decided to seize the initiative. Oleg got in touch with the contact himself and told him he had taken a shine to the rifle. Although unfit for purpose as it was, given a bit of effort it should be possible to get it back into usable condition. He asked whether he could buy it with the fee he would be due for completing the job. No, was the answer. The tool either had to be bought straight away (and the price was $3,000), or returned to Nina on her next trip, which meant practically by the time the train would be leaving the following day.

Oleg gave me a full account of his conversation with the contact and relaxed, supposing he had done everything he could. 'Give me the rifle, Vladimir Anatolievich,' he said. I could not do that! I tried appealing to his conscience, explaining how wrong it would be to return a firearm to gangsters. He wasn't listening. I said, 'Right. Let's give it a day. I'll ask the FSB to allocate the money, and my superiors too.'

My superiors reacted with lightning speed. 'Don't even think about it. We haven't enough money to pay our staff their salaries. And there's no heading in the budget we could possibly put it under. If you try to get it authorised it will take a good six months, and even then it's unlikely.'

'But they will kill someone! It's a certainty. If not today, then tomorrow, or the day after tomorrow, or in a year's time. A year from now at most we'll see it again on the television, abandoned by a gunman at the crime scene.'

'People get killed every day. We are not all-powerful, we can't save everyone. Anyway, is the rifle in your possession? Hand it in. Say it's been seized, or found somewhere. And then forget all this if it upsets you. Why, doesn't your gunman still want it?'

'No, they've called it off for now. We've got a week. After that we'll see how it goes.'

The FSB also said no, without offering any explanation. 'We don't do that sort of thing,' was all I got out of them. They had been reluctant from the outset to take on all the hassle connected with this case although, to give them their due, anything they did agree to they carried out with filigree precision. The issue of the rifle remained unresolved.

I put the question bluntly to my team. They found my arguments noble and deserving of respect, but as to subscribing personally? No, it was just too expensive.

'Right,' I said. 'You can all get lost. I'll buy it on my own.'

'Where are you going to find three thousand bucks?' they wondered.

Three thousand dollars I really did not have. I had earned $400 standing guard while goods were unloaded for a businesswoman I knew. My mother-in-law had given us six hundred bucks from the sale of an aunt's house. I had another nineteen I had squirrelled away in the box with her dollars while moonlighting as a taxi driver in the city at night when customers sometimes paid with dollars.

I spent rubles and saved dollars. The total came to $1,019. Sasha, with whom I shared an office, agreed to lend me another nine hundred. I called Oleg to come that evening, gave him what I had raised, revealed the sources of the finance and said, 'That's all there is. Half of it is not mine. I have to pay it back later myself. Do as you please. Subtract expenses from Nina or your contact, say the cartridges you bought were special, just spin them any line you like, but I am not going to give you that rifle back. If it's not enough, you'll have to put in some of your own money. That's my last word.'

Oleg left without protesting unduly, and in the morning phoned to say everything was sorted. The contact had taken the money and would settle up with Nina.

Then everything went like clockwork. Oleg got his RPG-18 (the *Mukha*), I collected it from him and drove straight to the Moscow FSB building. I was met by people I did not know, who reassured me (I was evidently looking stressed), took a double plastic bag from the boot, and briefly and very succinctly gave me my instructions. A few hours later, in early morning, I drove back there and directly up to the main entrance. I switched on my flashing light, got out of the car and saw an officer in the uniform of a traffic policeman already approaching.

I thought he would start questioning me, but no. He asked me to wait a couple of minutes. Two more immediately came over. I did not notice that while one was saying hello to me and and asking how things were (doubtless a topic of great interest to him), the second had already put the package back in the boot. I heard the lid slam, turned, and he indicated that was all and I could be on my way. In a word, neatly done.

At the end of Lubyanka, a white Mercedes with a flashing light caught up with me and ordered me to stop. There was only the driver, also in traffic police uniform. He got out and introduced himself. I showed my ID. As he was about to leave, he asked what was in the boot. I answered, with what I hoped was a relaxed smile, 'A dead body'. He smiled back, got in his car and immediately drove off. After briefly pondering what the significance of that episode might have been, I too left. For Balashikha.

Oleg reported to his contact that he was ready. I explained the details of the plan to my colleagues, took them to see the location, and we discussed and talked through their roles. We had then to wait for zero hour on the day appointed by the contact, who was evidently well informed about Lebedev's schedule. Meanwhile, through me Said summoned Oleg to Vishnyakovsky Street, where they inspected the site for the shot and the place where Lebedev's car would drive in.

The day dawned. 11 June 1997. I drafted in almost all the officers of the department for the operation, including my brother (*Alexander Vasilevsky, at the time a senior operative for particularly important cases of the ECD - AL*) and Sergey Nikolaevich, the head of the department. The key roles were distributed as follows: 'Policeman on the Beat', Kostya [*Konstantin Svishchev, then an ECD operative*]; 'Militia Volunteer', me; and 'Random Taxi Driver', Sergey. The others provided counter-surveillance, transport, cover and backup.

The first half of the day was lovely, sunny weather. Vishnyakovsky Street. Oleg arrives with Zhenya and the getaway driver. The car is placed under FSB field surveillance. Oleg, bearing a large package from which several centimetres of the casing of a grenade launcher protrude, goes up to the roof of No. 23. Zhenya settles down below, sitting on the steel railing round an area of lawn. 'PC' Kostya in a police uniform and I in plain clothes are chatting at ease, outside Zhenya's field of vision but able to keep the entrance door of the staircase under observation.

As Oleg told us afterwards, he climbed up the attic ladder to the roof, looked around and readied his weapon for firing. He was about to light up a cigarette, but at that moment a car, and behind it a jeep with a security detail, drove into the courtyard of the house which was the zone for the hit. He aimed, closed his eyes with fright and pressed the trigger. There was a click and ... nothing more. He quickly stuffed the extended casing into the polythene bag and went downstairs.

Kostya and I did not have long to wait. From the outside everything looked like this: a door opens and a suspicious-looking character with a no less suspicious-looking bundle emerges. (This is Oleg with a package from which there protrudes half a metre of grenade launcher in full battle readiness with its cover hanging open.) A militiaman and a volunteer approach this person and look pointedly at the package. The character looks at the policeman in consternation and, when he salutes and introduces himself as Lieutenant Pupkin, punches him in the face and takes to his heels along the pre-arranged route.

Kostya is the largest of us, which is why he got the role of policeman. He knew the script contained a stage direction, 'violently repulses the militiaman', but clearly was not expecting the punch to his jaw. As a consequence, he furiously pursued his attacker ... and was clearly catching up with him! (Nobody had thought to ask Oleg how fast he could run.)

The situation was saved by a puddle. Kostya was almost level with the fugitive when Oleg slipped at the edge of a puddle and landed right in it, sending spray all over the place. This provided Kostya with some stage business and he started brushing off the mud, enabling Oleg to get up and make it to the nearby 'taxi'. Sergey's heart sank as he watched a massive, mud-spattered ballbreaker pile into his own personal car.

Our counter-surveillance colleagues told us everything

happened in full view of Zhenya. He twisted like a snake in a skillet and headed like an athlete in a walking race towards his own getaway car. He departed, driven this time by professional spies.

Everything went quiet, but quiet was not part of our plan. We had yet to make a commotion in Lebedev's office so there would be a reaction, a natural intensification of personal security, changes to planned activities, and other logical consequences. We were not well received. While our elder brothers were talking to someone behind closed doors in the office, the clerks and guards were scowling at us as if it was all our fault. Needless to say, no one offered us coffee: the atmosphere was not right for that. They saw us off the premises promptly, unambiguously, emphatically. We could rest assured, however, that there would be plenty of fuss.

Oleg had also saved his own skin. He played his part in our admirable plan to the full, and during a heartfelt conversation in a secure environment conveyed to the gang's intermediary the trauma he had had to endure. His words were directly confirmed by one witness, and indirectly by another. The members of his labour collective, as well as representatives of the Medvedkov branch of the trade union of robbers and racketeers, were on Oleg's side. The verdict was that there had been a cock-up, but he should be paid anyway. The amount of the advance was considered fair recompense and nobody owed anybody anything.

When the hour of reckoning came, Oleg yielded up Nina to us, although we would in any case not have neglected such a lead. We were given a nod when Nina was coming back with more goods. There was, after all, no certainty she was gun-running every time her train came to Moscow.

The more combat-ready half of our department went to meet her and detained her in much the same place where she and Oleg had transferred the rifle into the car boot. We deliberately did not search it: if the boot was empty, we would apologise; if not, we would be on our territory and nobody condemns a winner.

In the presence of witnesses of the female sex the luggage of detainee Nina Mironova, citizen of Estonia, was searched and a Parabellum pistol and Sudaev machine pistol discovered. The weapon was in a pretty poor state and had probably been supplied by 'grave robbers'.

Our investigation section was reluctant to bring a criminal case. It was clear from Mironova's statement that she had been arrested in the vicinity of the station, so the line department of the Transport Police Directorate should have brought and investigated the case. Our regional superiors were not, however, going to relinquish anything as rare as an Article 188 (Smuggling), Part 4, and the investigators had to give in. The more so since the crime was discovered and registered on the territory of the Northeast Administrative District in my office, where the search had been conducted. Masha Tumanova took on the case and very competently brought it to court.

The next day our FSB colleagues told us that, two hours before the train was due to leave, they had raided the siding where the carriages were waiting to be assembled for its return journey and found dozens of icons, pieces of church plate and other valuables. To this day I'm not sure how I feel about that. I only know that Mironova was tried for smuggling firearms and there was no mention of the icons. Perhaps they figured in a different hearing.

We had no more meetings with our elder brothers. Only once, within the framework of the same overall case, did they ask us to act as extras, to conceal some operational hi-jinks. We had little difficulty coping with this in the line of duty. We had to eat, to down some beer, to steam ourselves in a bathhouse, and were even thanked personally by those in charge.

After reading this tale, I recalled policemen coming and showing my security people the malfunctioning grenade launcher, which only convinced me there had been something staged about the assassination attempt. I drove to the crime scene at the bank's old office and found the building and the roof where the sniper had supposedly lurked. From there the courtyard my car drove into every day was fully exposed to view. A perfect position for an assassination attempt.

The gang that had undertaken the job, the Orekhovo-Borisovo organised crime group, carried out numerous such murders entirely 'successfully'. In my case, fate had decreed otherwise.

CHAPTER 6

Werewolves in White Uniforms

A leviathan against the Bank

While one of the FSB's units was working to avert an assassination, the officers in a different unit were discussing the target's security with I. Fyodorov. In June 1997 agents were sent from FSB headquarters to see him. I know of no other case where officers of Russia's foremost intelligence agency have travelled to the United States for a meeting with a run-of-the-mill fraudster.

Here is the transcript of a curious telephone conversation prior to Fyodorov's interrogation in June 1998:

Fyodorov: He was carpeted today …
S: [*an FSB officer – AL*]: Who?
Fyodorov: Filin [*head of the investigation team at the Prosecutor General's Office dealing with the National Reserve Bank case – AL*]. […]
S: Right … Well, tomorrow we'll know what they pulled him in over. […] You know what? Don't forget, make really sure you mention that they forged the documents. That's so that if they suddenly start disputing it in court, we'll already have everything documented in the Prosecutor's Office. You got that?
Fyodorov: Er … Yeah, sure. Okay. I'll pass that on to Yulia [*Pelekhova – AL*].
S: And then, you also need to talk about the forging of documents in London and Switzerland. And about the rescinding of the court ruling against you. Get those ideas out there, and exhibit the documents. You know what I'm saying?
Fyodorov: Er … Well, yes. Yes! I'll pass it on to Yulia.

S: Yes, but she already knows all that. And you talk about it in your vlogs too. Because if those get shown later in court it will all resonate. Get it?

Fyodorov: Yes, yes, I get it. Certainly I'll do all that.

S: There's one thing that could be sticky, which not everyone is absolutely clear about [*meaning Investigator Kirsanov in the Prosecutor General's investigative team – AL*].

Fyodorov: What thing is that?

S: How you came by this money [*the money Fyodorov stole from NRB – AL*]. [...] And something else ... Do you think we can put out information about the credit cards you have? My colleague Yury is taking an interest in them too.

Fyodorov: What credit cards?

S: You know ... You gave us the statements. Where they were issued, by which companies, who uses them.

Fyodorov: Ah, yes. I see! Of course, do whatever you want with that information.

I presume these phone calls were recorded by the Americans. It would be odd if the FBI failed to take an interest in an émigré who had formerly captained a nuclear submarine and was, moreover, playing an important role in a case brought by the Prosecutor General's Office and the FSB against a former intelligence officer. When I received transcripts of these discussions between FSB agents and Fyodorov from a certain journalist, I sent them to Kovalyov with a request to 'Take whatever measures you deem necessary.' However, the case became even more complex and tangled than might have been expected.

While these recently recruited knights of the cloak and dagger were playing games in the streets with no less recently conscripted malefactors, Ashot Yeghiazaryan was hard at work in a parallel world. For example, he was conducting shady financial operations involving a state television centre, the famous Shukhov Tower on Shabolovka. This institution was transformed into a joint stock company called RTR-Signal, and 74.5 per cent of the company's shares were promptly acquired by Unikominvest-Centre, a company owned by Yeghiazaryan, which paid for them with a loan from Unikombank.

Having acquired control of RTR-Signal, Yeghiazaryan (watch his hands closely) deftly withdrew all his 'investments', along with a $28 million grant from the government for 'modernising broadcasting networks,' and exchanged them for Unikominvest-Centre promissory notes.

Another high-profile case of those years was the Angolan debt to Russia, which was carved up between Yeghiazaryan and Arkadiy Gaidamak, a former cleaner of the Moscow Circus and French-Israeli businessman, who had recently been released from prison in France. Gaidamak had been on amicable terms with the corrupt government of Angola since 1980, to whom he had been supplying arms on a questionable basis for their war against insurgents. (For this he subsequently ended up in the dock alongside Jean-Christophe, the son of the French President, François Mitterrand.)

The regime of José Eduardo dos Santos owed the Soviet Union over $6 billion for fraternal assistance which Russia, now in the unenviable financial position of legal successor state to the USSR, would have found very helpful indeed. For Angola, repaying that amount was completely out of the question. It was almost two-thirds of the country's GDP. Gaidamak volunteered to resolve the problem.

On the recommendation of Mikhail Kasianov, the government decided to write off seventy per cent of the debt, and the remaining 1.5 billion dollars were converted into promissory notes, which were to be paid off between 2001 and 2016. However, Abalone Investment, a company owned by Gaidamak and registered on the Isle of Man, unexpectedly offered to buy up these promissory notes at a discount of fifty per cent. Needless to say, our incorruptible officials agreed. The end result was that, of the $773 million paid by Angola to an intermediary company, only $161 million finally arrived at the Russian Ministry of Finance, and even that money vanished into Mosnatsbank, which Yeghiazaryan 'sank'.

Those entrusted with enforcing the law in Russia could hardly be expected to waste their time on so a trivial a matter, so I had to do it for them. In tandem with the investigation into embezzlement at Unikombank and Mosnatsbank, I began asking too many questions in closed circles and giving interviews. The campaign against NRB intensified accordingly. The Tax Service, following a letter from the Prosecutor General's Office, conducted a comprehensive audit. Nobody had any intention of considering objections.

On 15 July 1997, Deputy Prosecutor General Katyshev initiated Criminal Case No. 18/171845-97 on suspicion that a crime had been committed under Article 199, Part 2 of the Criminal Code of the Russian Federation. Searches ensued, and very odd searches they were. Investigators are usually looking for materials relevant to a case, and they remove specifically those. In our case, the brigade of people bearing authorisations who descended upon the NRB office could have been replaced by removal men: they simply gathered up all the bank's documents, dumped them in a van and departed.

Some new areas of 'investigation' were added to the existing accusations of 'non-payment of taxes' and 'fraud'. For my birthday, friends gave me a gun, having obtained the necessary permit. This should have been accompanied by a medical certificate and notes from various clinics. I could have gone the rounds of the doctors myself, but my friends replaced this vexatious procedure with something more straightforward, and unfortunately nobody warned me. The result was an attempt to charge me with 'illegal possession of a firearm'.

Hot on the heels of the criminal charge came a refusal to consider National Reserve Bank's objections to the report of the tax audit. We disputed its conclusions in court and the verdict went in our favour, but the juggernaut of the criminal case proceeded unabated. There was no reaction from the Prosecutor General's Office to the evidence provided by the bank proving no crime had been committed.

Therefore, in early 1998 I wrote to Anatoly Kulikov, the minister of the interior, asking him to open a criminal investigation into the fraudulent acts to which we had been subjected. The top people at the Interior Ministry instructed officials at the National Directorate for Combating Economic Crime to look into the matter.

Their examination was nearing completion, their agents preparing materials to pass to their investigations unit for a procedural decision when I was telephoned by one of the top officials at the directorate and told that the Prosecutor General's Office was requisitioning all the materials relating to the examination, with the result that the Interior Ministry was now unable to resolve our application. Such was the law. The upshot was, once again, a refusal to bring a criminal charge of fraud against Fyodorov.

Cui prodest? (Who benefits?)

For two years now, I had been in the dark as to who was commissioning this onslaught against us and what their aim was. We had no business conflicts with anyone. NRB had not participated in the privatisation and 'loans-for-shares auctions', had not prised any titbits of the Soviet economy off anyone, had not seized any oil wells or steelworks. Those were the kind of grounds that occasioned shoot-outs in those days. We were playing in a different court, making money in financial markets, mostly foreign, devising complex but legal schemes and instruments. Neither could the motive be political: if I participated in elections and other political games at all, then it was only on the correct side.

There came a glimmer of light after a meeting I had with the administrator of the Prosecutor General's Office, Nazir (Krym-Geri) Khapsirokov. This former second secretary of a district committee of the Young Communist League and director of a bathhouse and laundry complex in Karachai-Cherkessia was personally in control of the state's prosecution 'business' and the entire staffing aspect of the 'Eye of the Tsar'.

The manager of the guardians of the law was to all intents and purposes analogous to the keeper of a slush fund for a gang of thieves. He decided who got apartments, dachas in the country, cars, holiday trips to sanatoria, special passes, and flashing lights for their car. His proximity to Prosecutor General Yury Skuratov made Khapsirokov an éminence grise. As he informed me at his first meeting, 'I ain't, of course, the first in importance in this building, but probably I ain't just the second neither.'

Chain-smoking, inserting one cigarette after another in a long, diamond-studded Cartier cigarette holder, Khapsirokov told me that the person behind all my vicissitudes in the past year and a half was his boss, Prosecutor General Yury Skuratov. Why would this intellectual-looking gentleman with a decent reputation and who, before this appointment, had been engaged in teaching and research (first as dean of the legal prosecution faculty of Sverdlovsk Law Institute, then as director of the Institute for Research into Consolidation of Legality and Law Enforcement of the Prosecutor General's Office) decide to organise a campaign of harassment against a businessman remote from the oligarchic Seven Bankers?

Khapsirokov's answer was straightforward: we were queering the pitch for Ashot Yeghiazaryan's business interests; we were upsetting respected people, so we were being invited to get out of the way, cease working with foreign debt, forget the path to the Ministry of Finance, and pay condign compensation. Khapsirokov accompanied his speech with folksy sayings like, 'We jail who we please, and release who we please', 'We sort fings by phone', and also by issuing coupons guaranteeing immunity from audit to certain people entering the office.

I looked at the dazzlingly white jacket of this general of the justice system and at the office portrait of his boss in equally ceremonial dress. (I had come to Khapsirokov from Skuratov, who had afforded me just five minutes of his time. Skuratov was much less frank and had difficulty uttering even a few meaningless sentences.) What a mockery of the expression 'the honour of the uniform'. Well, at least the situation could not be any clearer. There being no reason for me to stay longer in that office, I left without troubling to say goodbye.

Some time later I was told that, at a reception in the Kremlin to celebrate State Security Officer's Day, Skuratov had promised in the presence of several top security officials to 'jail this Lebedev'. He had every confidence he was going to win the game of Hunt the Banker. Everything fell into place.

Deputy Prosecutor General Katyshev wrote a report that was submitted to Skuratov just one month after my letter to the Interior Ministry. To Katyshev's credit, he made no secret to Skuratov of the fact that Fyodorov had transferred $7,228,750 to his personal bank account and that Lebedev, chairman of the board of National Reserve Bank, had stated this. Katyshev effectively invalidated the criminal case.

As we see from the report, the case was based 'on the offence of repeated large-scale evasion of payment of taxes by the directors of National Reserve Bank'. The investigation, however, had come to a different conclusion (*see opposite*).

'As a result of further checks, specialists of the National Tax Inspectorate of Moscow have come to the conclusion that there has been no violation of tax legislation by officials of the NRB commercial bank.'

The only legal decision for the Prosecutor General's Office to take under these circumstances was to halt a criminal case initiated on suspicion of repeated tax evasion, on the grounds that no offence had been committed. Now, however, it at least became clear why Katyshev, who had initiated the case, could not close it.

A document appeared in the file of the case that confirmed the lack of any procedural possibility of continuing investigative actions. If there were any legitimate reasons left for pursuing other lines of enquiry, these needed to be separated out into new cases and investigated without further reference to tax offences now seen to have been fictitious.

Skuratov who, in his own words, was personally in charge of the investigation, did not give a damn about that. The investigation into the alleged tax evasion simply continued and no decision was taken on National Reserve Bank's complaint of fraudulent activity by Fyodorov.

Генеральному прокурору
Российской Федерации
Скуратову Ю. И.

Докладная записка по уголовному делу N 18/171845-97.

Настоящее уголовное дело возбуждено 15 июля 1997 г. по фактам неоднократного уклонения от уплаты налогов в крупном размере руководителями Национального резервного банка (НРБ).

Расследование проводится по следующим направлениям:
Первое направление:
----

1) Уклонение от уплаты налогов руководителями НРБ.

Второе направление (основное):

а) Перевод Лебедевым, Костиным и Швецким денежных средств на заграничные счета.

б) Перевод Федоровым на свой личный счет 7,228,750 долларов США. Заявление председателя правления НРБ Лебедева о присвоении Федоровым указанной суммы.

Третье направление:

Учреждение руководством НРБ фирм с целью использования их для необоснованного увеличения уставного капитала банка и для получения учредителями этих фирм незаконной личной выгоды.

Четвертое направление:

Незаконное получение Лебедевым, Кудимовым и Костиным удостоверения личности частного охранника, разрешения на право ношения служебного оружия при исполнении служебных обязанностей, лицензии на частную охранную деятельность.

ПЕРВОЕ НАПРАВЛЕНИЕ
По данному направлению расследование завершено.
В результате дополнительной проверки специалисты ГНИ по г. Москве пришли к выводу, что нарушений налогового законодательства

The Prosecutor General's Office continued to correspond with Fyodorov, updating him on the situation:

Your appeals to the Prosecutor General's Office of the Russian Federation have been considered.

I wish to inform you that the investigation is examining

publications in the mass media relating to the investigation of the criminal case known to you.

The investigation agrees with your viewpoint that A. Lebedev is intentionally misleading journalists, giving them information that does not correspond to reality.

By acting in this manner, Lebedev is attempting to draw the investigation into a polemic on the pages of newspapers and thereby obtain information of interest to him.

In this connection, it is not at present expedient to refute in the press the articles you have mentioned in your appeals.

I would like you to be aware of the position of the investigation, which does not share the point of view expressed by Lebedev in the media.

Senior Investigator of Especially Important Cases
Prosecutor General's Office of the Russian Federation
State Counsellor of Justice 3rd Class

A.D. Filin

On the eve of a visit to the United States by an investigator from the Prosecutor General's Office, FSB officers continued their telephone conversations with Fyodorov:

Right, then ... our Madonna [*Yulia Pelekhova – AL*], a stallion with balls, is coming to see you. What have you got for her? Think what you can give her to move things on. Make it sound like you are just defending yourself. Understand? Keep it fairly mild, but confident, so that for reasonable people it will hit home or compromise you-know-who ... Okay, you get the message, eh?

'You-know-who' is, of course, me. By the spring of 1998, the investigation had practically worked its way through all the episodes, but the materials they had collected were not enough to press charges. Only the Fyodorov episode remained incomplete. Fyodorov flatly refused to leave the US, and the Swiss prosecutor's office had demanded additional data. As a result, Fyodorov announced during one of his phone calls that he was not willing to give any testimony at all, and only changed his mind after much persuasion. A detailed list of questions, with documentation attached, was prepared, but the head of the investigation team refused to fly to the United States. In the end, Fyodorov's questioning was conducted in June 1998 at the Russian embassy in Washington, D.C.

The Prosecutor General's Office never did take any interest in Fyodorov's personal account at Banque von Ernst & Cie in Switzerland, which we had discovered and had frozen. Perhaps when Skuratov was studying at university he skipped the course on Electoral Law, and when he later noticed the heading in his academic record book, assumed it meant you could elect to apply the law or not as you saw fit. He turned Russia's system of law enforcement into a service for gangster businessmen who coveted other people's businesses.

CHAPTER 7

Nothing Secret That Shall Not Be Made Manifest

The aberration of the default

From the internal memoranda circulating in the Prosecutor's Office, it appeared that the prey was completely entangled in their web and on his way to jail. During the Stalin period, Mikhail Zoshchenko, who found he was a candidate for incarceration, would cross to the other side of the street when he saw an acquaintance approaching in the distance, in order not to come face to face with him and thus avoid the necessity of exchanging greetings.

I followed his example, and began noticing an expression of relief on the face of many of yesterday's friends. The omnipotence of the Prosecutor General's Office was obvious: it initiated criminal cases, investigated them, and was itself in charge of supervising observance of the law.

In August 1998, the modern history of Russia succumbed to its latest aberration. The government and Central Bank declared a default on the main types of government securities, which by then had become the principal vehicle for speculation on the stock market. The Short-Term Government Bond pyramid scheme collapsed, followed by a collapse of the ruble, which lost over two-thirds of its value against the dollar. A middle class that had not yet properly formed was ruined. In Moscow you could see yesterday's New Russians in their crimson jackets moonlighting as taxi drivers in their Mercedes.

The financial collapse led to resignation of the government of 'young technocrats' under the premiership of Sergey Kirienko. With the connivance of Yavlinsky and the support of the Communist majority in the State Duma, Yevgeny Primakov's team came to power. Yeltsin finally turned into a lame duck, the next presidential election was not that far off, and the usual catfight for the Kremlin broke out.

A weird kind of unofficial triumvirate emerged. It consisted of Prime Minister Yevgeny Primakov, Moscow Mayor Yury Luzhkov and Prosecutor General Yury Skuratov. Each of them had his eye on the presidency, but the small detail of which of them should become the main candidate was put on ice until nearer to the election. Skuratov launched a massive attack on Yeltsin's closest associates and his family, instigating several criminal cases simultaneously, including some relating to officials speculating in the government bond market immediately before the default, and the Mabetex Case.

This involved a Swiss company belonging to Behgjet Pacolli, the future president of Kosovo, who paid bribes for contracts to reconstruct the Kremlin. Skuratov was actively collaborating with Carla del Ponte, the attorney general of Switzerland, and his investigators became frequent visitors to the Alpine republic. It became evident that what particularly interested the prosecutor general was Fyodorov's 'testimony' (a downright lie) about Victor Chernomyrdin. By discrediting Chernomyrdin, Skuratov hoped to sneak into the Kremlin.

National Reserve Bank, which the valorous tax inspectorate and law enforcement agencies had been battering for two years, which had had all its records removed, and whose managers spent more time at the prosecutor's office being interrogated than at the bank negotiating with clients, proved to be one of the few private (and honest) banks to survive the default. You could count on your fingers the number of people who decided to fight to save their businesses. Alfa Bank, for example. Most of the 'strategically important' banks chose to spirit away assets and declare themselves bankrupt.

Among those who departed this life in 1998 were such 'too-large-to-fail' banks as Khodorkovsky's Menatep, Smolensky's SBS-Agro, Inkombank, Oneximbank and Natsionalny Kredit, which between them serviced the entire federal bureaucracy. We had to resort to extraordinary measures to remain solvent ourselves, while settling up with clients in a frenzy to withdraw their money. We sold personal property and renounced salaries.

The situation was not helped by a sharp conflict with the French Crédit Agricole Indosuez (CAI). NRB refused to execute fourteen suspicious forward transactions that the French bank alleged were concluded before the 1998 crisis in Russia. All the instances of the Russian Court of Arbitration, including the very highest, recognised that these deals had not been concluded, given the absence of any written documents confirming them, and forbade CAI to take action aiming to debit funds from our accounts in Russia and abroad.

In spite of that, the Supreme Court of the State of New York found in favour of a writ lodged against us there by Crédit Agricole and ordered us to pay the approximately $120 million claimed. On the basis of that verdict, CAI sought to seize a total of some $400 million of our funds in foreign accounts. The war with Crédit Agricole lasted four years and ended only when the new President of Russia, Vladimir Putin, intervened. He wrote to the President of the French Republic, Jacques Chirac, and an expert intergovernmental group was established to review the matter.

NRB was not able to defend all aspects of its position, but the dispute was settled. We were forced to pay by Russian government officials who had secret accounts in the French bank and lobbied its interests.

'Rest in peace, dear comrade. Our suspicions proved unfounded'

By the spring of 1999, our bank had managed to overcome the liquidity crisis caused by the default. The situation of the unsinkable prosecutor general, whom the Kremlin had been unable to dismiss because of a clique headed by Luzhkov in the Soviet of the Federation (the governor of a province was at that time automatically a member of the Duma's 'upper chamber'), changed in the blink of an eye.

On 18 March, during an evening broadcast on the Rossiya television channel, Mikhail Shvydkoy, director general of the Russian National Television and Radio Broadcasting Company, suddenly asked television viewers not to allow children to watch the following news item. A secretly filmed video was broadcast to the entire nation in which 'a person resembling the attorney general' had sex with two 'young women with a deficient sense of social responsibility.' Shortly afterwards Skuratov was facing criminal charges and was dismissed from his position.

So ended the career of this 'campaigner against corruption' and would-be president of Russia. A year after that the case against me was dropped, having turned my hair grey and cost me several years of being called in like a negligent parent for questioning.

After reading the following document, I was reminded of a joke about the epitaph on the grave of an old Bolshevik shot during the purges of 1937:

'Rest in peace, dear comrade. Our suspicions proved unfounded'. The fates of the people and organisations implicated in this saga worked out variously. Mosbiznesbank lost its licence in July 1999 and six months later was declared bankrupt. The depositors, to whom Victor Bukato owed more than 10 billion rubles [$330 million],[5] were traumatised, but Mr Bukato, celebrating his sixtieth birthday at the time, did not appear greatly troubled.

Less than six months later, he was appointed deputy chairman of Vneshagrobank, and in July 2002 chairman of its board of directors. A short time after this bold staffing decision, which was approved by the Central Bank, something magical began happening in Vneshagrobank. In the course of a month, all its liquid assets, totalling over 1 billion rubles [$33 million], were withdrawn just as casually as they had been from Mosbiznesbank.

The interim administration from the Central Bank, when it arrived at Vneshagrobank following the declaration that it was insolvent, discovered that the office had been stripped of all its computers, the server on which all the financial details of money transfers, payments and assets were recorded, as well as a large quantity of its paper documentation. The inspectors were nevertheless able to establish the following:

> V.I. Bukato, by signing purchase and sale agreements in the period from 29 September 2004 to 1 October 2004, acquired illiquid promissory notes issued by organisations which had no real assets. The notes acquired, issued by more than fifteen organisations variously registered in Moscow, Moscow Region, Ryazan, Tula, Penza, Cheboksary, St Petersburg and other cities, are identical printed forms with continuous numbering, which indicates that all these securities were produced at the same time and in the same place.
>
> From this it can be concluded that the promissory notes are false. In this manner, V.I. Bukato created and increased the insolvency of Vneshagrobank; that is, he was guilty of deliberately planning bankruptcy by withdrawing assets from the bank in his own personal interests and the interests of other individuals to a total amount of 1,228,158,000 rubles [$41 million] thereby causing loss to the shareholders of the bank.

---

5 Owing to the volatility of the ruble–dollar exchange rate, approximate dollar equivalents are calculated prior to 6 November 2014 at a rough and ready rate of 30 rubles = $1 and thereafter at 60 rubles = $1. Other currencies are converted at the rate obtaining at a particular time.

Those who suffered from Bukato's actions included such depositors as the University of Friendship of the Peoples, the National Union of Theatre Managers, and the Administration of Omsk Province. Charges were brought under Article 196 of the Russian Criminal Code on 'Planned bankruptcy'. The newspapers reported that in all this Bukato had been merely the figurehead, while the main beneficiary was Ilya Khaikin, the principal shareholder and chairman of the board of directors. However, as is usually the case, it was our hero who had to take the rap.

Victor Bukato made Russian banking history by being the first chairman of a credit institution to be convicted of planned bankruptcy. In December 2007, the Khamovniki District Court gave him a two-year suspended jail sentence. Additionally, to satisfy a claim by the Deposit Insurance Agency, he was obliged to pay compensation of 951 million rubles [$32 million] and all his property was seized, including 180 square metres of real estate in the affluent Gorki-2 development in Moscow region.

The fate of our heroic submariner also bears a moral. The money Fyodorov stole from us brought him no joy in his life abroad, neither in business nor in his personal life. Only Russia, which Skuratov had been so intent on trying to expel me from, would take Fyodorov back (*see overleaf*).

To: Mr V.V. Ustinov, Prosecutor General of the Russian Federation
cc: Mr V.V. Gerashchenko, Central Bank of the Russian Federation

From Mr I.I. Fyodorov
Postal address: 573 Virginia Dare Dr., Virginia Beach, VA, 23451
25 February 2002

Dear Mr Prosecutor General,
It has been difficult for me to decide to write this letter, because it completely repudiates my communication addressed to your predecessor, Mr Skuratov, of 19 November 1996, and refutes the facts therein. I am doing so, nevertheless, in order to make amends for my offence against people I have defamed and to restore my good name through repentance.
I officially declare that the facts contained in my letter of 19.11.06 concerning illegal acts allegedly committed by A.Ye. Lebedev, president of National Reserve Bank and A.L. Kostin, chairman of Vneshekonombank are entirely without foundation and are fabrications resulting

from my regrettable moral condition during those years.

I am obliged to admit that the allegations I made against these Russian bankers of 'machinations' with the fifth, sixth and seventh tranches of the RF Ministry of Finance's currency bonds, of threats against me and members of my family, and also of other unlawful acts of which I accused Messrs Lebedev and Kostin are at variance with the

Генеральному прокурору
Российской Федерации
Г-ну Устинову В.В.

Копия:
Центральный Банк Российской Федерации
Г-ну Геращенко В.В

От гр-на Федорова И.И.
Почтовый адрес: *573. Virginia Dare Dr.*
Virginia Dare Dr, Virginia Beach, VA 23951

2.5. февраля 2002 года

Уважаемый господин Генеральный прокурор,

Написать это письмо было для меня нелегким решением, ибо оно абсолютно дезавуирует мое послание в адрес Вашего предшественника г-на Скуратова от 19 ноября 1996 года и опровергает содержавшиеся в нем факты. Тем не менее я иду на это, чтобы искупить вину перед оболганными мною людьми и восстановить покаянием свое доброе имя.

truth. I very much hope that on my return to Russia I will be able
personally to apologise to the above-mentioned gentlemen for the
harm I have done to their businesses and reputations and that I shall
be able to tell the full story about the people who exploited me in this
dishonourable game.
  Yours truly,
  I. Fyodorov

Fyodorov did indeed come and tell the full story. The kitchen in which that criminal case was concocted proved to be in the same apartment of ill omen in Bolshaya Polyanka Street where the home video was shot of 'a person resembling the prosecutor general' cavorting with prostitutes. The 'den' belonged to Suren, the brother of Ashot Yeghiazaryan, and had been bought with Unikombank's money. Ashot regularly organised such themed entertainments for Skuratov. He paid for everything himself, and provided other services besides.

The middleman linking them was Khapsirokov. In intervals between his amorous exploits, they 'resolved issues'. It was here they came up with the idea of crippling NRB and it was from here that they directed it. Gangsters – prostitutes as a bribe for the prosecutor general – racketeering. Nothing complicated.

According to Fyodorov, he turned to Yeghiazaryan as a potential source of gangland backup when he conceived the idea of taking us for a ride. For Ashot, Fyodorov's pathetic $7 million were hardly worth going after, so he and Khapsirokov decided to help themselves to a jackpot called National Reserve Bank. To carry out the plan, they brought into play the prosecutor's office, tax inspectors and police, corrupt journalists and the Orekhovo Gang. They expected that those subjected to criminal prosecution would, as usually happens in such cases, emigrate and leave them free to help themselves to the bank.

As regards Yeghiazaryan, in 1998 both his financial ventures, Unikombank and Mosnatsbank, crashed into bankruptcy. More accurately, they were wilfully bankrupted. As Unikombank sank beneath the waves, everything it still had of any value was removed, including the Daev Plaza business centre not far from Bolshaya Sukharevskaya Square. One fine day it transpired that the 16,000 square metres of apartments built by Unikom for its own offices now belonged, not to the bank, but to Daev Plaza Ltd, which was owned by Wyndham Ltd, a company registered in Bermuda and run at that time by two agents of Ashot, Konstantin Merzlikin, deputy chairman of the Unikombank board, and Mikhail Ananiev, the head of the bank's securities section.

There was a curious tale in respect of Mosnatsbank also. The government authorised it to keep the accounts of Rosvooruzheniye (now Rosoboron-export), a state monopoly for the export of Russian defence industry production. When Mosnatsbank went bankrupt, it was discovered that $120 million in Rosvooruzheniye's account had disappeared without trace. Actually, not completely without trace: the money had been issued in the form of bogus loans to two offshore banks, Veksnark Bank Inc. and AKO Bank Corp., both registered in the Republic of Nauru. Arriving on that coral island in the Pacific Ocean, these financial resources of the Russian defence industry instantly evaporated.

Criminal files were opened on both cases and many of Yeghiazaryan's minions fled abroad. One of them, Konstantin Koloyan, accidentally got himself caught ten years later. He was living in Moldova and decided to marry, but found he had only a Soviet-era passport. In order to replace it he flew to Moscow, where he was arrested and sentenced to four years in a prison camp.

Yeghiazaryan himself, like Konstantin Merzlikin and Mikhail Ananiev, continued his endeavours in the political arena. In 1999, as a candidate of Zhirinovsky's 'Liberal-Democratic' Party, Ashot was elected to the State Duma. Konstantin Merzlikin first worked in the secretariat of Yury Maslyukov, the first deputy of Prime Minister Yevgeny Primakov, and later, when Mikhail Kasianov was prime minister, rose to be head of the Russian civil service. In 2000 Mikhail Ananiev became deputy chairman of the Federal Property Fund of Russia.

Moskva the Golden

The paths of Yeghiazaryan and me crossed again several years later, when I too became a deputy of the State Duma. Unlike me, however, Ashot did not do battle with the gambling business or the Luzhkov-Baturina juggernaut with its policy of infill urban development, made no attempt to amend the Criminal Code and Criminal Procedural Code by introducing the possibility of plea bargaining, and did not raise the issue of welfare payments for larger families. He simply did not attend plenary meetings.

On the other hand, he had a fine view from the windows of his office on the seventh floor of the old parliament building of Okhotny Ryad ('Hunter's Row'), where the renowned Hotel Moskva was first razed to the ground and then completely rebuilt. That became Ashot Yeghiazaryan's principal occupation.

The construction project was Yeghiazaryan's, so it was very convenient for him to observe how work on site was progressing. In 2005, when the hotel was demolished, I and the Stolitsa [Metropolis] group of deputies opposed rebuilding it. Alexey Shchusev's historic building, dating from the 1930s, had been destroyed, but after the demolition the huge space it had vacated opened up a staggering view of the Kremlin. Even Mayor Luzhkov on one of his Saturday tours admitted the sight was breathtaking.

I got colleagues to sign a petition to the mayor and the president appealing for a Park of Concord and Reconciliation to be laid out on the site of the former hotel, and decided to hold a press conference. There was an attempt to disrupt it by a group of young people purporting to represent those of unconventional sexual orientation, who noisily asked questions about a gay parade. They were unsuccessful: the provocateurs were escorted from the hall.

The whole 'protest' had been organised on the instructions of Ashot Yeghiazaryan by his press secretary, Anna Zayarina. Here is the detail:

Anna: Everything went just ... anyway, I'll tell you about it now. There were difficulties getting them in. We resolved them on the spot ... we dragged the guys in, we had enough of our backup people on the ground. So, the first question was asked by that guy in the scarf, yes, the one we wrote ... He didn't answer it, and then there was a rumpus, like 'No, you answer my question!' It was being filmed by all the cameras [...]. ORT [*Public Radio and TV*], and NTV, then our 'queens' too, so ... he began to smile [*me, that is – AL*], still didn't reply, they went after him again: 'No, we are going to ask you this question again, where do you think we're going?' Anyway, then there was like a slight scuffle ... by now everyone in the hall was hooting with laughter ... so, anyway, it was all being filmed. I think that probably, if things go right, it should even get on the news.
Ashot: Ah, it's all holding ...
Anna: Yes, everything went off really well, the guys themselves really, they, you see, it was good they're actors, they crushed him, I mean they know it's like acting. Yes, but ... there was, of course,

some dreadful pornography, just dreadful, some kind of people in scarves, pederasts they wouldn't allow in. Well, really just awful, so anyway that's how it went.

Ashot: We need to say thank you to the guys for their work.

Anna: Yes ... well, you decide, let's you know ... so, we need really to slip the guys a little money, just something quite modest.

Ashot: We'll do what you decide.

Anna: Well ... there were, you know, these two actors pretending to be queens, one wearing the scarf, really, well, I would give them each a grand. If we give the rest two hundred or three hundred dollars, that'll be fine.

Ashot: Let's give the rest of them five hundred.

Anna: Yes, sure, whatever, well, let's make it five hundred ... and look, I need to know, I had some journalists there who were asking serious, topical questions, and I need to know, we need to place stuff, because I want it on skandaly.ru, it would be best to get it on skandaly.ru now, say, and post it somewhere on dni.ru. That's two sites ... so as then to get it reposted from there. What d'you think?

Ashot: Yes, of course, we should do that. Let's do it, and check what else we've got, separately, as a second line of attack, that that gay raised their flag in the Duma and now he's setting the pace and we're rooting for him [...]

Anna: Yes. But we can post it on scandals now this story.

Ashot: Go for it, go for it, now he's no longer afraid to come out of the shadows!

Anna: And we'll string this one to dni.ru, with our 'orange' guys.

Ashot: I know him, we just need to make it so he can't take any more of all this crap. [...]

Anna: Well, you know, there was such a commotion that really nobody was interested any longer in serious questions, everybody had, like, got so stirred up, you know ... Like, at first everyone thought it was fun, had a laugh, swore, but our friend, he effectively disrupted the press conference. [...] Really, everything went off well.

Ashot: And results, will we get results in other agencies?

Anna: I think so. I'll start monitoring, let's keep an eye open, there might even be something on the radio or television. We'll keep an eye on what develops on its own, and after that we can add to it. [...]

Ashot: Well done!

Ironically enough, it was on Hotel Moskva that Yeghiazaryan's dazzling career eventually came unstuck. In 2009 he had a conflict over the project with his long-standing partners, Mayor Yury Luzhkov and his wife, Yelena Baturina. Then his old pal Mikhail Ananiev went to see the law enforcement agencies. At this time the former official had retired, and he accused Yeghiazaryan of having stolen from him eighteen million fiduciary dollars used for constructing the Europark retail complex and reconstructing Hotel Moskva.

According to Ananiev, while working at the Russian Federal Property Fund he was unable to engage in business, but Yeghiazaryan offered to 'simply give him money', and after he retired from government service to return his share 'in the form of a percentage of the authorised capitals of the companies'. As a result, Ananiev ended up with only a four per cent holding in Europark. When the company owning the complex was subsequently, in the best traditions of financial jiggery-pokery, reallocated to different people, the ex-bureaucrat's share disappeared altogether.

A criminal investigation was opened into Yeghiazaryan's conduct. The State Duma did not believe there was anything political about the accusations levelled at their eternally absent colleague and stripped him of his parliamentary immunity by an overwhelming majority. By this time Ashot had fled to the United States. He settled in Los Angeles, hired lawyers at considerable expense, and they began applying for him to be granted political asylum, claiming, needless to say, that their client was a 'victim of the bloody regime of Putin'.

In autumn 2010, I prepared documents for submission to the FBI, demanding that Yeghiazaryan be brought to justice in the United States. His activities were a perfect fit for the letter of the 1971 anti-mafia law known as RICO (the Racketeer Influenced and Corrupt Organizations Act). New, turbulent events obliged me to lay that aside, however. Which was a pity.

PART II

The New Hunting Season, Ten Years On

CHAPTER 8

Learning from Mistakes

The Promised Land of Crimea

In the first half of the noughties, I had assets worth a billion dollars and had resolved all my personal, legal and business problems. At that moment I took a trip to Crimea that was to change my whole attitude to money. I was there for the first time in the company of my intelligence colleagues. It was autumn, there was a storm. What an unbelievable spectacle! We were staying in Professors' Corner, the western part of Alushta, in an old Soviet-style boarding house that was rusty and musty, with broken windows and without hot water. We drank Crimean port all night with girls.

At some point I went out on to the balcony of this 1938 building. In the autumn, the charge of energy there is phenomenal, a mixture of cold mountain and sea air. When you go fishing, you see Alushta spread out before you in the hollow between the rounded volcanic Mount Kastel and the Demerji ridge. Why not try settling here and live life no worse than on the Côte d'Azur?

When we were flying back to Moscow, the plane got caught in a lightning storm. We hit air pockets several times and plunged 100–200 metres. Our flimsy aircraft was hurled up and down as if the laws of gravity had ceased to operate. I could think of nothing more sensible to do than address myself to the Almighty, debating with Him what I had done wrong, what I would have to pay for, and why my life should have to end at this precise moment and in this precise manner. I think I may have deviously mentioned a plan to build a church in Malorechenskoye, which I had not actually yet decided on. I promised to do it. The plane was damaged, but an hour later landed safely in Moscow.

After that episode, I embarked on many years of building projects in Crimea. There was absolutely no economic calculation in this, and indeed could not have been, both because of the shortness of the holiday season there and the obstructiveness of the authorities. I also had an opportunity to invest in the Maldives, but settled for Crimea. I liked that. Altruism as construction, when business creates something good for people.

This was not entirely normal behaviour. Businessmen prefer to buy a huge pile in the south of France and then slave away on it. Moor a yacht nearby, or preferably two. That is as far as their imagination takes them. My Hotel Morye (The Sea) was built not for me, but for the hundreds of thousands of people who have subsequently stayed in it. It is a hotel in a park, which embodies my childhood dreams of a happy, carefree life. In the course of ten years, this place has changed out of all recognition: dozens of villas, hotels, swimming pools, restaurants, an aqua park …

Using my own money, I reconstructed the embankment. A 65-metre-high church-cum-lighthouse has sprung up and become one of the landmarks of Crimea. The ruined Anton Chekhov Theatre in Yalta has been restored and international festivals are held there now. We recently opened a Nature Clinic – the largest in Europe – and cinema concert halls with seating for thousands. It remains for us to establish an eco-settlement, to erect a 'Sails of the Motherland' tower that will eclipse Dubai's Burj Al Arab, a marina for yachts, and an open-air museum of modern art. There is no shortage of work still to be done.

I made a political mistake in connection with Crimea. Not even a mistake, more an act of stupidity born of arrogance. In April 2004, a summit meeting between the presidents of Russia and Ukraine was held in Crimea. The event was taking place on the eve of a presidential election in the Ukrainian Republic, so Leonid Kuchma brought his successor, Victor Yanukovych, for 'inspection'. Together with Vladimir Putin, a whole delegation flew in, all the top people of the Russian Federation – the government, the Administration, businessmen, State Duma deputies under its then chairman, Boris Gryzlov. There was a lot taking place within the framework of the visit: summit-level negotiations in Yalta, and a meeting at our guest house Hotel Morye in Alushta, where the presidents and speakers all planted a palm tree in the park near the symbolic Arch of Concord.

Then all the entrepreneurs, seven from each side, were taken in buses with curtained windows to Stalin's secret dacha in the mountains for a confidential meeting. Kuchma, who had awarded me the Order of Merit for my work in Crimea, said we must support Yanukovych's election campaign and put up $10 million a head. The money would be accepted in any form by Viktor Medvedchuk, who at that time was head of the Administration of the president of Ukraine.

'Yanukovych with his criminal past and inclinations is a bad bet,' I decided. 'Ukraine deserves a different candidate.' It seemed to me that the president of Russia also was not particularly taken by this candidate, and perhaps even found him unsuitable, avoiding personal contact with him: an FSB officer's understandable attitude to a representative of the 'negative sector'. Kuchma nevertheless carried on pushing and eventually got him accepted.

At that I declined to hand over the money. I would prefer to restore the Chekhov Theatre, which would be costing more, and said as much to Dmitry Medvedev, who was then head of the Presidential Administration. I was not to be forgiven for that, as I am well aware. When the 'Orange Revolution' occurred in Kiev and Yanukovych was toppled for the first time, there was a campaign to determine whose fault it was, and some of my 'well-wishers' wrote me down as a sponsor of Yushchenko. Things only got worse. My relations were hopelessly marred.

One's personal wool and the state's wool

At that moment I was not, formally, any longer an entrepreneur. Elected to the State Duma in December 2003, as a law-abiding citizen I resigned all my business positions and plunged headlong into legislative and social projects. Shortly before that, I had arranged to invest the money I had earned in the financial markets in the real sector, namely, aircraft construction and air transportation, mortgage lending and construction of affordable housing, and agriculture.

The philosophy behind these investments was to take on the most challenging sectors and use my resources to modernise everyday life. National Reserve Corporation was built on the foundation of National Reserve Bank, an industrial group that was to initiate new projects, with the managers of the bank and the corporation being granted mandates to manage the assets independently, in return for an undertaking to pay 'bonuses' to the directors in the form of minority shareholdings.

Do you know what the main contradiction of capitalism is in its current phase? It is the conflict between owner and manager, between the principal and the agent. There is a phrase in the film *The Captive of the Caucasus*, 'Don't confuse your personal wool with the state's wool!' It is expressed by Jabrail, a driver, to his boss, Comrade Saakhov, to whom he is selling his niece, Nina. Saakhov is the local state official. In large private corporations, managers often start confusing their wools, because they are handling huge amounts of money and taking decisions about specific managerial issues.

I appointed Anatoly Danilitsky as chief executive officer of the National Reserve Corporation. He had worked as a diplomat in the Ministry of Foreign Affairs and I knew him from London. Danilitsky was an educated, well-trained and honest man, but very fond of 'a piece of skirt'. Once when a little flushed on a flight, he asked me, 'Do you tell them you love them?'

'You mean, when I feel nothing for them?' I asked, just to be clear.

'Yes.'

'No, I don't say that.'

'It's all right for you, you're good-looking,' Anatoly said and became pensive.

I have all my life had doubts about whether I am attractive, as well as about other merits, but do not get hung up about it. Danilitsky compensated for his complexes by being highly knowledgeable about yachts, villas, hotels, restaurants and amusements, including dancing half-naked on the table. I had to leave him entirely on his own with large sums of money – hundreds of millions of dollars. That was a mistake. Four years later, I discovered a hole in the balances that, alas, could only partly be explained by the 2008–2009 financial crisis.

Danilitsky once introduced me in Paris to an entertaining citizen who introduced himself as Sanchez. He offered me his services to buy a bank in Bahrain – we had just sold our subsidiary bank in Zurich to Lukoil. I did not like the idea, but without an intermediary Bahrain was closed to us. We decided to sign using Sanchez, under the watchful eye of our lawyers in Switzerland. Three months later, Sanchez stole all the money from our bank account in Bahrain. Danilitsky urged me to forget it, on the grounds that Sanchez was threatening to blame me for his being 'hunted by the KGB'.

I was unrelenting and hired detectives in the United Kingdom who, within a few months, found Sanchez had been murdered some time before in Thailand. It was revealed that this was the pseudonym used by Francisco Paesa, wanted by the Spanish police, a former officer of the intelligence services and an adventurist on an international scale. In 2006, Paesa had returned $10 million he had stolen from me, but still owed another $15 million. His niece, Beatriz García Paesa, who laundered the money stolen by her uncle, lives in Luxembourg.

I have been conducting this lawsuit for fourteen years now, and it is the accumulation of episodes like these that has led to my writing this book. The director of my projects in Ukraine, Vyacheslav Yutkin, was tidier. He 'spent' twice the actual cost on building my hotels, and got the same contractors to build the same again for him with the difference. In reality, they were all resolving the same task of how to transfer money into their own pockets in the process of investing, and getting kickbacks from subcontractors. And sod the result. As Eduard Bernstein, one of the founders of the Second Socialist International, put it, 'Movement is everything: the end goal is nothing.'

An example of this process is my experiment with low-rise private housing. In 2005, academician Alexander Nekipelov and I published 'Low-Rise Housing as an Archimedean Fulcrum' in *Izvestiya*. It was a manifesto. The main idea was that building private, individual houses at affordable prices on a massive scale could be the locomotive that would pull the economy forward and make possible the formation of a genuine middle class.

Moreover, we wrote, 'real success can be achieved only through a genuine partnership between the state and business. It is up to business to provide the factories and the construction; it is up to the state to provide the land and to de-bureaucratise the entire process of relations between the partners. And also to provide the engineering and social infrastructure.'

At this time was born the National Housing Corporation, an affiliate of National Reserve Corporation. It set about implementing the project of building quick-construction individual houses using the latest timber frame technologies. This type of housing has proved very successful in such subarctic countries with a very severe climate as Canada, Norway and Finland. It is the standard approach everywhere that has its own forests. It seemed it should have no problems in Russia.

The results were mixed. On the one hand, in a matter of five years it proved possible to create a whole mini-sector with ten factories producing components, and to build well-designed villages in Leningrad, Moscow, Rostov, Volgograd, Tula, Belgorod and Voronezh provinces. These consisted of several thousand individual homes, and were the most ambitious project of their kind in Russia.

On the other hand, it has to be admitted that we failed to generate any genuine partnership with the state. We ourselves had to buy the land for building on (more precisely, to buy it back, because all land suitable for building had long ago come under the control of local officials and their relatives) at astronomical prices.

Our National Housing Corporation tried to take part in tenders put out by the Housing Development Assistance Foundation, but had no success. One such competitive tender was to construct the Vostochny microdistrict in Istra. The winner was a firm controlled by Andrey Shishkin, deputy chairman of the HDAF itself, who was subsequently arrested for extorting bribes. Just getting the paperwork approved could take a year. There was no question of getting low-cost provision of infrastructure – roads, water, sewerage, gas and electricity.

The end result was that the price for which it was possible to sell the houses without going belly-up proved a good deal less affordable, although I tried everything I could to drive it down. In the village of Blagovo in Moscow province, for example, we gave the houses away for next to nothing, and with a twenty-year loan repayment period.

On top of objective problems in implementing the affordable housing programme, there were plenty of 'subjective' ones. At every construction site, at every stage, the managers, together with fraudulent subcontractors, were stealing money. There were some spectacular instances.

For example, in the guise of a wood processing plant, a loss-making sawmill with rusty equipment, which was already impounded under a lawsuit, was bought in the forests of Novgorod for no less than €11 million. The money was transferred from one offshore company to another to someone called Igor Skvortsov, who was listed as a vice-president of Vneshtorgbank. I invited him to a discussion at my office where he refused to return a penny. For good measure he lodged a complaint with the Interior Ministry and departed for Angola, where he headed a bank partnered with Vneshtorgbank. Today, of course, he lives in London.

The Blue Wings crash

The biggest business fiasco was not waiting for me in Russia, however. It was an air transportation project in Germany. In 2006, National Reserve Corporation acquired the German airline, Blue Wings. Although the company was worth barely the couple of million euros we paid for the certificate, my managers contrived to value it at €15 million but paid, of course, €20 million. For Blue Wings we bought not only second-hand

Airbus A-320 aircraft, we also ordered new airliners.

Our partner in the project was General Electric Company's aircraft leasing subsidiary, GE Capital Aviation Services (GECAS), which has the largest fleet of aircraft in the world (neck-and-neck with the, also American, International Lease Finance Corporation). In part the contract was paid for with our money, in part by loans from GECAS, issued through the specialised PK AirFinance in Luxembourg.

I was slightly uneasy about the fact that the leasing company did not offer to lease us the planes and acted as a lender, but at first everything went well. At least, to judge by the auditors' reports from KPMG and the graphs and presentations I was shown by the boards of directors. By early 2008, Blue Wings was the fifth largest air passenger carrier in Germany, serving 1.1 million people and squeezing Lufthansa on its routes to Russia.

Then came the financial crisis, which seriously hit the industry. Many global airlines went bankrupt. In 2009, the German regulator Luftfahrt-Bundesamt (LBA, the Department of Civil Aviation) unexpectedly suspended Blue Wings' licence, quibbling over late payment of airport fees in Düsseldorf. This was despite the fact that, on all indicators, the company's financial position was more stable than that of Lufthansa, which had suffered losses of $1 billion. One possible explanation was wire-pulling by a competitor in the shape of Lufthansa, the more so because LBA is described in Germany as a 'department' of that monster aviation company. The licence was renewed a few months later, but Blue Wings had lost market share and customers.

In early 2010, I suspected the company's management of embezzlement. In answer to my enquiries, the director of Blue Wings himself filed a petition for bankruptcy of the carrier with the local authorities. PK AirFinance immediately seized the aircraft it held as security. I was confident they would sell the planes at an open auction, pay off the debts and return the difference – about $100 million – to us. Suddenly, however, the planes were to be found in a variety of countries (from Israel to New Zealand), and nobody discussed anything with us.

After this, PK AirFinance announced that the aircraft were in poor technical condition and in need of a major overhaul, but did not allow us to have their condition assessed. The repair of each side was estimated at $10 million. Repairs simply do not cost that much. For that money you could make a new plane out of bits of junk. Here almost new aircraft, which had been operating in Germany under strict supervision, had suddenly been reduced to a lamentable state and needed huge investments to put them right! The company rejected our proposal to have an independent assessment conducted.

The planes were supposedly repaired, and we were told to get lost. They had allegedly spent all our money restoring the aircraft to airworthiness, so thank you and goodbye. After that there was a rigged auction in London at which the planes were bought by – GECAS! – for $171.5 million, although in reality they were worth vastly more than that. In this manner, with the aid of repairs and a rigged auction, my money was transferred from the pocket of one GE affiliate to the pocket of another. GECAS then leased the planes back to the American airline jetBlue, from whom we had originally bought them, and since then they have been delivering the fraudsters a stable income.

We discovered that this is common practice with the Americans. They used much the same methods to tear Indian, Chinese and Pakistani airlines to pieces. Aeroflot too suffered from their adroit marking up of repairs. When the now defunct Aeroflot-Cargo returned two Boeing 747s to the leasing company, GECAS first estimated $1.5 million for repairs, but later raised the price to $4 million for each side. Aeroflot paid up.

We decided to sue GE in the High Court in London. Preparing the claim took several years, and the trial itself lasted more than a year. As time passed, we discovered that the New York-based international law firm Debevoise & Plimpton, which was representing us, was working for both sides. There was a conflict of interest, and the lawyers accordingly refused to prepare our case. This is standard practice for global corporations: they bind themselves contractually to well-known legal companies, so that they cannot act against them in court. Because of these conflicting interests, we were unable to get any of the best, the very good, or even just good lawyers to take on our case. I had to settle for average.

In the course of the hearings, cross-examination of GE officials brought to light details of fraudulent tax evasion schemes in the US on the part of GECAS. In the end the judge gave a verdict unprecedented in legal proceedings against General Electric – in our favour. The compensation was less than we had anticipated – only $17 million – but in this case it was not only the financial, but also the moral and ethical dimensions that mattered. We wanted to create a precedent and end the impunity.

Alas, GECAS filed an appeal and won the case three years later. The judge in the appeal court admitted that we had clearly been ripped off, but pointed out that this was not against the law. There we have a classic example of the pursuit of truth and justice in the Western judicial system.

Our losses on this project totalled over $250 million. It was probably the biggest Russian business disaster in Europe. This 'air crash' would not, however, have happened but for the corrupt collusion of our top managers with the founder of Blue Wings, Jörn Hellwig, and representatives of GECAS. That is how they behave.

As was later discovered in the course of an investigation carried out by American detective agencies, Anatoly Kashirsky, the head of Alpstream, our Swiss subsidiary, and Hellwig had come up with a wheeze in 2004 to ship aircraft to Iran, evading the sanctions imposed by the US and EU over the Islamic Republic's military nuclear programme. Blue Wings legally leased A-330 airbuses and transferred them to Mahan Air, a company owned by former Iranian President Ali Akbar Hashemi Rafsanjani.

The deal was managed on his behalf by Tahmasb Mazaheri, a former Iranian finance minister, and the Swiss bank Credit Suisse provided financial services for the entire project. The ayatollahs used these planes as they saw fit, to transport arms, fighters of the Islamic Revolutionary Guard Corps and terrorists of the Lebanese Hezbollah group, all under the cover of an entirely civilian European airline. Hellwig, himself an experienced pilot, personally flew to Tehran and undertook the most sensitive flights.

These, as it were, 'partners' decided not only to foist a German air transport company on National Reserve Corporation and buy second-hand aircraft using loans, but in addition to sign a contract with the European aircraft construction giant EADS for twenty new Airbuses for a billion dollars! All the contracts were from the outset drawn up to favour GECAS. Purchasing aircraft on their terms would have made it impossible for the company ever to be profitable. The entire business plan was a cover for fraud.

When there was a danger that information would surface about their business dealings with Mahan Air, the 'concessionaires' simply decided to bury the evidence. They wilfully set Blue Wings up to have its licence revoked and made bankrupt, handed a fleet of aircraft to their American 'partners', and shared the 'commission', blaming everything on the financial crisis and the machinations of the Luftfahrt-Bundesamt.

It is quite amazing that there is no interest in the information about dark dealings with the Iranians from the US authorities, to whom I communicated the results of our investigation. Although perhaps there is nothing surprising about it: this story implicates a huge corporation whose boss, Jeffrey Immelt, was in charge of the President's Council on Jobs and Competitiveness under Barack Obama.

National Reserve Corporation's losses resulting from the activities of a number of employees in key positions in our group amounted to several hundred million dollars. Part of the money the fraudsters stuffed into their own pockets, part they invested in a 'business' they knew could never become profitable. For their scams, they knocked together hundreds of offshore firms in different jurisdictions and pushed money around them.

In this tax fraud and evasion scheme, they were assisted by the world-famous consultancy and auditing group, KPMG. It was responsible for the returns of NRC Group's holding in Cyprus and turned a blind eye, regularly giving its stamp of approval to bogus reports to me, the owner, about 'outstanding' business successes. I had no choice in the matter because, as mentioned, I was now a deputy in the State Duma and could only follow my business by means of documents from the auditors.

In 2008, I left the State Duma and found numerous violations in the corporation. Until then I had often criticised the Russian government's 'pyramid of power' for failing to combat corruption. Now I very much understood the Kremlin's predicament: if I myself had been unable to forestall embezzlement, what chance had those with a 'business' on an incomparably greater scale? Neither the owner of a large business, nor the person in charge of a large country can personally delve into every issue and manage everything: he has to trust people. And here some very unpleasant surprises await him.

The Kremlin has everything yet to do, although the first swallows of spring, like Vladimir Yakunin, have already taken to the skies. The crisis that befell the global financial system in 2008–2009 hit business hard, but crises also have a beneficial, cleansing effect. Like a storm at sea, they force the ship's crew to mobilise and dump ballast. The petty crooks fell off by themselves, while the major crooks have had to be driven out. I launched a special dossier on my website, 'Graveyard of Lost Reputations', where potential partners and employers of these people can obtain an insight into who it is they are dealing with.

The scoundrels are still knocking at the door and pleading, 'Let us back in.' But, as Ilf and Petrov's character Ostap Bender said at the grave of Panikovsky, 'I was often unjust to the deceased, but was the deceased a decent person? He was not a decent person. He had been blind, an impostor and a goose thief. He put all his strength into trying to live off society. But society did not want him to live off it. Mikhail Samuilovich could not endure this contradiction, because he was very volatile. And so he died. There is no more to be said!'

CHAPTER 9

Déjà vu

Masked Performance: the favourite genre
of the *siloviki*

On the morning of 2 November 2010, I drove to the head office of National Reserve Bank. It is situated in the upper floors of the Principal Plaza business centre on Sixtieth Anniversary of October Avenue, opposite the Sberbank Savings Bank. The site, which I bought from Ukrainian oligarch Ihor Kolomoyskyi, and the building, which was undertaken by Turks, cost far more than the going rate – thanks to the managers of National Reserve Corporation.

It is no surprise that in September 2008 the drivers of Anatoly Danilitsky were detained with a suitcase containing rubles in small denominations to the value of $1.5 million at the International Trade Centre on Krasnopresnenskaya embankment, where the main contractor for the building of Principal Plaza, Sengir Mehmet Rasim, a Turkish citizen, had his office. Danilitsky engaged lawyers from the firm of Zhidkov & Zharova and 'sorted' the incident at the level of the management of the Moscow Municipal Directorate of Interior Affairs, explaining that he had once lent Sengir money to buy an apartment.

Back in February 2010, we wrote to the FSB about this (*see p. 128 top*).

It needs to be mentioned that I worked mainly at my personal office in Vrazhsky Street and it was not every day that I put in an appearance at Principal Plaza. That is, it was necessary to be on the lookout for me to find me there. When I took the lift to the eleventh floor and went into the office, the bank security officer reported that armed men in masks had just burst in, blocking all entrances and exits. An investigator in civilian clothes came into the office and showed me a judicial warrant to conduct a search (*see p. 128 bottom*).

As is customary, no coherent explanation was offered as to why it was necessary to arrange this national pantomime, known as the Masked

НАЦИОНАЛЬНАЯ РЕЗЕРВНАЯ КОРПОРАЦИЯ

ООО «НАЦИОНАЛЬНАЯ РЕЗЕРВНАЯ КОРПОРАЦИЯ»
Россия, 117036, Москва, пр-т 60-летия Октября, 10 А
Тел.: +7 (495) 646 5151, факс: +7 (495) 646 5152
ИНН 7728896690   КПП 772801001

№ _____
на № _____

В Федеральную Службу Безопасности
Российской Федерации

107031, г. Москва. ул. Большая Лубянка, д. 1/3

ЗАЯВЛЕНИЕ
о преступлении

Компания Cavenham Limited[1] (Кипр), входящая в холдинг Национальной Резервной Корпорации (далее - НРК)[2], 10.03.2006 заключила с другими офшорными компаниями Tolido Limited (Кипр) и Cytherian Limited (Британские, Виргинские о-ва) договор купли-продажи российского ООО «Принципал плюс», которое на тот момент, выступало заказчиком-застройщиком земельного участка, расположенного по адресу: г. Москва, Проспект 60-летия Октября, владение 12.

Кроме прямого перевода 32.557.802 долл. США фирмам-продавцам за 100% долей уставного капитала ООО «Принципал плюс», Cavenham Limited выкупила права требования к ООО «Принципал плюс» по двум займам у швейцарской компании Interoil Trading S.A. на сумму 2.755.000 долл. США. По имеющейся информации Interoil Trading S.A контролируется[3] Коломойским И.В. (бывший губернатор Днепропетровской области Украины, обвиняемый органами Следственного комитета Российской Федерации в организации особо тяжких преступлений), он же на момент сделки являлся собственником ООО «МКБ «Москомприватбанк».

Помимо этого, в соответствии с условиями данного договора купли-продажи, ЗАО «Национальная резервная корпорация» выкупило 12 векселей у ООО «МКБ «Москомприватбанк» на общую сумму 109.364.195,61 руб. и 1 вексель у ООО «Торговый дом на ходынке» на сумму 65.264.686,98 руб. (всего: 174,628,882.59 руб. или 6.236.745,8 долл. США по курсу ЦБ России). Общая сумма сделки составила 41.549.547,81 долл. США.

Руководство холдингом НРК в период с 2004 по 2009 г.г. осуществлялось Данилицким Анатолием Антоновичем[4], который также являлся генеральным директором ОО «НРК» - управляющей компании ЗАО «Национальная Резервная Корпорация».

Вместе с тем, стоимость компании ООО «Принципал Плюс» на момент её приобретения была существенно завышена, поскольку Общество не осуществляло хозяйственную деятельность, а основными составляющими его актива, являлись затраты в незавершенном строительстве, расходы на приобретение права аренды земли и авансы, выданные подрядчикам. Основной составляющей пассива Общества являлась задолженность по привлеченным займам, а строительные работы финансировались за счет привлеченных займов.[5]

[1] Конечными собственниками Cavenham Lim... Кудимов Юрий Александрович – 15% и Дани...
[2] Неформализованная группа компаний, объ...
[3] По имеющейся информации Данилицкий_v...
http://gazeta.ru.ua/ECONOMICS/privatbank_ve...
Франции и Украины.
[4] Из «Отчета о результатах проведения и... исследования текущего состояния активов о...

ПОСТАНОВЛЕНИЕ

гор. Москва   21 октября 2010 года

Тверской районный суд гор. Москвы в составе:
председательствующего судьи Неверовой Т.В.,
с участием прокурора отдела прокуратуры гор. Москвы Григорян Г.Б.,
при секретаре Магомедовой С.С.,

рассмотрев в открытом судебном заседании постановление старшего следователя 2 отдела СЧ ГСУ при ГУВД по гор. Москве Крылова П.П. о возбуждении перед судом ходатайства о производстве выемки документов, содержащих охраняемые федеральным законом сведения, относящиеся в соответствии со ст. 26 Федерального закона «О банках и банковской деятельности» к банковской тайне, путем проведения обыска в помещении АКБ «Национальный резервный банк», по адресу: гор. Москва, проспект 60-летия Октября, д. 10 «А»,

УСТАНОВИЛ:

В производстве 2 отдела СЧ ГСУ при городу Москве находится уголовное дело № 89280, возбужденное 03.08.2010г. по признакам преступления, предусмотренного ст. 159 ч. 4 УК РФ, в отношении неустановленных лиц.
Срок предварительного следствия по данному делу продлен 01.10.2010г. руководителем следственного органа до 04 месяцев 00 суток, то есть до 03.12.2010г.
Предварительным следствием было установлено, что неустановленные лица, находясь в городе Москве, в помещении ОАО АКБ «Российский капитал», расположенном по адресу: город Москва, ул. Б. Молчановка, д. 21 «А», 07.10.2008 года, действуя от имени ОАО «ЦентрЛизинг» ИНН 7701569912, фактически являющейся фиктивной и не ведущей финансово-хозяйственной деятельности, с целью хищения денежных средств указанной кредитной организации заключили кредитный договор № 00-303/К-08 на сумму в 450 млн. рублей, не имея намерений на его исполнение.
После получения указанной суммы на расчетный счет ОАО «Центр Лизинг», денежные средства были похищены неустановленными лицами путем их последующего перечисления на расчетные счета иных подконтрольных неустановленным лицам юридических лиц.
В ходе расследования настоящего уголовного дела было установлено, что в АКБ «Российский капитал» (ОАО) действовала группа из сотрудников банка и иных привлеченных лиц, которые в указанный период времени осуществляли хищение имущества банка.
Преступная группа осуществляла хищение следующим способом: соучастники, используя собственные возможности, привлекали в банк компании, в том числе и фиктивные, которым выдавались заведомо невозвратные кредиты. В последующем кредиты выдавались членами преступной группы направлялись на приобретение векселей, эмитированных АКБ «Российский капитал» (ОАО), а кредиты так и оставались непогашенными.
Также в ходе расследования настоящего уголовного дела было установлено, что большая часть указанных выше векселей впоследствии была сосредоточена в АКБ «Национальный резервный банк».
В целях избегания уничтожения и порчи вещественных доказательств, в связи с тем, что интересующие следствие документы содержат охраняемые федеральным законом сведения, относящиеся в соответствии со ст. 26 Федеральным законом «О Банках и банковской деятельности» к банковской тайне, старший следователь 2

Performance. Why do people wearing balaclavas and bearing assault rifles have to block the security desk, jump over turnstiles and herd the bank staff away from their workplaces when, if so requested, any bank will provide the security agencies with all documents of any conceivable interest to them without having to be asked twice?

Within an hour, Russian and foreign journalists were thronging the street outside the entrance, where our press secretary Artem Artemov did his best to reassure them. On the Internet there was discussion of the news that Lebedev had been arrested. For the moment, however, no arrests were planned. As the performance continued, it became evident that several dozen officers, under the direction of Senior Interior Ministry Investigator Pavel Krylov, with backup from the special forces, were participating in it. Their visit, the warrant stated, related to embezzlement at the Russian Capital bank.

Whatever happened to Russian Capital?

The tale of Russian Capital deserves a digression. It began in autumn 2008, when the global financial crisis, sparked off by the collapse of one of the world's largest investment banks, Lehman Brothers, boomeranged on the Russian economy. In Russia, the situation was more threatening than in 1998. The stock market went into freefall, shares of blue-chip companies lost their value, and banks began to experience liquidity problems.

The state decided to intervene, but no systemic actions to contain the crisis were taken initially. The law 'On measures to stabilise the banking system', which made the Deposit Insurance Agency responsible for giving financial support and rescuing 'problematic' banks, was passed only in November 2008. The government's decisions were taken case by case, as firefighting measures.

One such case was Russian Capital. This major bank had an extensive branch network and several tens of thousands of depositors. In September, it ceased processing customers' payments or, in the parlance of the accountants, 'battened down the filing cabinets'. Bankruptcy. In 'peacetime' conditions, the Central Bank was obliged in such cases to impose an interim administration and subsequently revoke the bank's licence. The Deposit Insurance Agency had to repay depositors. In the present situation, however, the bankruptcy of a major bank would certainly have had a domino effect, with the depositors of other lending institutions rushing to withdraw their money, and the entire financial system would collapse.

The authorities therefore decided to bring us in to take over the failing bank and oversee a bailout. Our National Reserve Bank was, at that time, the most solvent in Russia, and probably in the world, with a ratio of capital to assets of over fifty per cent. The top officials at the Ministry of Finance and the Central Bank asked us to take temporary loans on preferential terms and sort out the mess.

The technicalities were that National Reserve Bank bought Russian Capital from its owners for a nominal 5,000 rubles. The Central Bank deposited $300 million with NRB (for some reason they were out of rubles, and before long we got a bloody nose from the exchange rate, because we were bailing out Russian Capital with rubles). NRB was to repay the loan to the Central Bank with interest of six per cent per annum. We had no realistic opportunity to assess the hole in Russian Capital's balance sheet, being given just three days to study the bank's records and assess the state of its finances. It was a complete speculation.

The owner of Russian Capital was fifty-year-old Alexey Ivashchenko, a former economist in the credit planning department of the Ulianovsk branch of the State Bank of the USSR, who subsequently worked in the State Bank's central office and at Zhilsotsbank (the USSR Bank of Housing and Utilities Infrastructure and Social Development). In the 1990s, he was for a time vice-president of the Mosbiznesbank, so energetically plundered by its new 'effective managers', with Bukato leading the charge. Ivashchenko successfully transferred the skills he acquired there to his next challenge.

In 2005, he was again in the media spotlight, because he had been used as bait in an FSB special operation: during a meeting with him at the Hotel Baltschug in central Moscow, officials of the Federal Tax Service and of the Moscow headquarters of the Central Bank were arrested. They were trying to extort over $5 million from Ivashchenko in return for halting a prosecution of the bank for failure to pay taxes of two billion rubles [$67 million]. (The tax service was seeking to charge Russian Capital VAT on operations that had involved precious metals.)

The outcome was that the 'commissioners', caught red-handed, were sentenced to significant terms of imprisonment: ten and eight years respectively. The bank did not in the end contribute anything to the budget. After this, Ivashchenko developed a cosy relationship with the FSB's Economic Security Service (K Directorate – 'Counter-intelligence Support in the Loan Finance Sector').

No sooner had we started familiarising ourselves with Russian Capital's affairs than we began to suspect that all was not what it seemed at the bank. Nevertheless, the request from the Ministry of Finance and the Central Bank was very pressing and we agreed to it. NRB flooded the crippled bank with our own money via an interbank loan. Its operations were unfrozen, deposits were returned, accounts were serviced, promissory notes were honoured, and so forth. We also had to bail out a proportion of Russian Capital's loan portfolio, which was partly in default.

In other words, our bank's money was used to pay off another bank's debts. NRB's losses from the rescue operation totalled more than 1.2 billion rubles [$40 million]. We had accepted a cat in a bag and paid through the nose for it.

We could soon see that Russian Capital was a factory for siphoning off and laundering money. The bank's top employees were paid an inflated salary and contributed part of it (as much as $1.5 million a month) to a secret account. This money was used for bribing the senior management of a number of 'state unitary enterprises' and 'municipal unitary enterprises' in return for paying low interest on their balances.

Separately, the bank kept a second ledger for lending: while officially the rate was six per cent, the actual rate was twenty per cent. The money was laundered through Cyprus or Latvia, and Russian Capital did not turn its nose up even at Northern Cyprus ($4.5 million), which is usually the resort only of 'businessmen' from Colombia. It came as news to us that Belarusian banks were also involved in money laundering.

We discovered that the bankruptcy of Russian Capital had nothing to do with the 'unfavourable situation in the world financial markets', or because of 'errors in investment policy': it resulted directly from the theft of clients' and depositors' money by the former owners and management of the bank. In total, under a number of schemes, they transferred 5.4 billion rubles [$180 million] to offshore companies. It was because of this breach in its side that the bank sank. It was a straightforward case of fraud and embezzlement and I sent a request for an inquiry to the law enforcement agencies (*see overleaf*).

Before long I was receiving kiss-offs from all directions, informing me there were no grounds for initiating criminal proceedings.

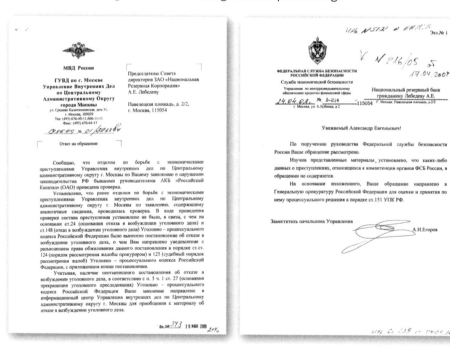

General A.I. Yegorov, deputy head of K Directorate of the Economic Security Service of the FSB, wrote to me that my communication 'contained no information about crimes falling within the competence of the agencies of the FSB of Russia.'

Our suspicions grew when pressure began to be put on the Central Bank in the commission for monitoring the spending of state funds allocated to support banks, with demands that it should 'take Russian Capital away' from Lebedev on the grounds that he was not concentrating on enabling it to recover. In spring 2009 the Central Bank, bowing to pressure from the would-be enforcers of the law, insisted that we should transfer Russian Capital to the Deposit Insurance Agency and return the money lent to us before the time agreed. The Central Bank and DIA did conduct an inspection, which confirmed that NRB had done everything correctly.

The upshot was that we rescued a bank, adding money of our own to the funds we had been lent and spent on the bailout, and then the bank was taken from us. We were forced to return after five months loans we had been promised for ten years. We took the Central Bank to court, but were unable to recoup our losses. The Deposit Insurance Agency took advantage of the renewed solvency of Russian Capital and used it as a supporting bank. The state, in the form of the DIA, made no attempt to investigate the embezzlement schemes and bring the bank's former owners to justice.

The pay-off (and punishment) for my efforts to obtain justice was that, a year and a half later, the security forces invaded my office with their masked performance. The moral to this story is that you really ought not to go investigating embezzlement in Russian Capital and other banks.

Redirecting the finger of suspicion

The 'search by seizure' was over by evening and our uninvited guests departed. Shortly afterwards we appealed against the legality of the search warrant and our lawyer gained access to the documents that had served as the basis for the masked performance. The conductor of the orchestra was not in fact the police, but K Directorate of the FSB (which, the reader will recall, had assured us all this was outside its sphere of competence).

Here is the report of the officer in charge of the First Unit of its Second Division, Captain Yevgeny Volotovsky, dated 8 October 2010 and addressed to the head of the directorate, General Voronin:

To Deputy Director of the Bureau, head of K Directorate of the Economic Security Service of the Federal Security Bureau of Russia, Lieutenant General V.G. Voronin.

REPORT
I have to report that in the course of the operational support of Criminal Case No. 89280 information has been obtained that during 2007–2008, a group of employees of Russian Capital Bank Ltd and other involved persons embezzled the bank's resources.

The criminal group acted in the following way: the culprits, using available opportunities, brought in companies, including fictitious companies, to the bank and issued loans to them which it was known would not be repaid. The culprits made use of the following companies in their criminal activities: Eleksbrokers Ltd, ElitN, a private company, and Ob Engineering, a limited liability society.

In 2007–2008 large loans were made by Russian Capital to these companies, on the basis of which financial resources were subsequently forwarded to them to purchase promissory notes from Russian Capital for the full amount of the loans. No collateral was provided for these loans, because the companies were known to be insolvent.

In the course of our work, it has been established that most of these promissory notes were concentrated in National Reserve Bank, to whom since October 2008 8 billion rubles [$267 million] have been allocated for the financial rescue of Russian Capital (of which 5 billion rubles [$167 million] were actually transferred to the Bank).

Using funds allocated for the financial rescue, in late 2008 National Reserve Bank repaid the promissory notes issued by Russian Capital, paid for by the loans granted, to a number of borrowers, including Eleksbrokers PLC, ElitN and Ob Engineering, in the amount of approximately 750 million rubles.

At the time of redemption of the promissory notes, the said borrowers were experiencing considerable financial difficulties, and at the present time obligations in respect of the loans have not been met and are classed as overdue.

Thus, while outwardly performing the functions of financial rescue, representatives of National Reserve Bank were, contrary to the legitimate interests of Russian Capital and for the purpose of deriving benefit for National Reserve Bank, damaging a credit institution by replacing liquid assets with assets known to be illiquid.

Even to a non-professional it will be obvious that what the secret policeman had glued together was a complete con. The text is replete with undisguised nonsense. At the time of the actions complained of, Russian Capital was owned 100 per cent by National Reserve Bank: that is, it could have no 'legitimate interests' other than those of its parent organisation. Volotovsky opines that we caused damage to ourselves. As for the 'replacing of liquid assets with assets known to be illiquid,' the liquid assets referred to are those promissory notes the former owners and managers of Russian Capital had issued to themselves in order to camouflage their siphoning off of billions of rubles to Cyprus.

Could our rescuers in Russian Capital refuse to honour properly executed promissory notes? Especially when the person presenting one such promissory note for 130 million rubles [$4.3 million] was no less than the high-ranking head of the banking department of K Directorate?

In December 2010, an individual claiming to be Mikhail Fradkov, the Director of the Foreign Intelligence Agency, phoned National Reserve Bank office and asked us to receive one of his generals. Our security officers checked out the phone number and it genuinely was emanating from the mother ship in Yasenevo. That being so, there were no grounds to disbelieve him. The visitor duly appeared, flashed his FIS ID and introduced himself as Konstantin Yakovlev.

For a start, the stranger asked us to sell him a cut-price apartment. He had noticed that National Reserve Bank had an apartment on Leninsky Avenue with a long-term mortgage. Next he suddenly announced that K Directorate of the FSB, together with the Interior Ministry, had cobbled together a criminal charge whose ultimate target was me. He claimed that the Central Investigation Department of the Moscow Interior Affairs Directorate had instigated an extraordinary inspection of National Reserve Bank by the staff of the Central Bank and, to authenticate his words, presented the associated document (*see overleaf*).

The letter asserted that National Reserve Bank had embezzled the deposit we had returned to the Central Bank back in 2009. Seeing the incredulity in my eyes, 'Yakovlev' asked for a piece of paper, on which he wrote a proposal to resolve the problem through none other than the chief of the Central Investigative Directorate of the Moscow Directorate of

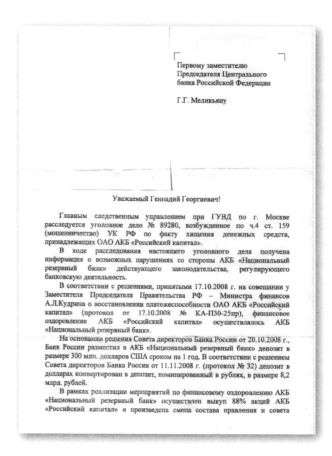

Первому заместителю
Председателя Центрального
банка Российской Федерации

Г.Г. Меликьяну

Уважаемый Геннадий Георгиевич!

Главным следственным управлением при ГУВД по г. Москве расследуется уголовное дело № 89280, возбужденное по ч.4 ст. 159 (мошенничество) УК РФ по факту хищения денежных средств, принадлежащих ОАО АКБ «Российский капитал».

В ходе расследования настоящего уголовного дела получена информация о возможных нарушениях со стороны АКБ «Национальный резервный банк» действующего законодательства, регулирующего банковскую деятельность.

В соответствии с решениями, принятыми 17.10.2008 г. на совещании у Заместителя Председателя Правительства РФ – Министра финансов А.Л.Кудрина о восстановлении платежеспособности ОАО АКБ «Российский капитал» (протокол от 17.10.2008 № КА-П30-25пр), финансовое оздоровление АКБ «Российский капитал» осуществлялось АКБ «Национальный резервный банк».

На основании решения Совета директоров Банка России от 20.10.2008 г., Банк России разместил в АКБ «Национальный резервный банк» депозит в размере 300 млн. долларов США сроком на 1 год. В соответствии с решением Совета директоров Банка России от 11.11.2008 г. (протокол № 32) депозит в долларах конвертирован в депозит, номинированный в рублях, в размере 8,2 млрд. рублей.

В рамках реализации мероприятий по финансовому оздоровлению АКБ «Национальный резервный банк» осуществлен выкуп 88% акций АКБ «Российский капитал» и произведена смена состава правления и совета

Interior Affairs, Ivan Glukhov (who was subsequently dismissed for corruption and figured in a criminal case), and department head Gabyshev. For a consideration, of course, of $1 million that, if I preferred, could be paid after the case was closed.

Needless to say, we saw the fake general to the door. Unfortunately, it soon became evident that the letter was not fake.

Innocent as charged

A delegation from the Central Bank arrived at our bank to perform an 'unscheduled targeted audit'. On 3 February 2011 the deputy head of the Central Moscow Territorial Directorate, Konstantin Galustian, who had begun his career in Ashot Yeghiazaryan's Mosnatsbank and supervised his already mentioned very special Louis d'Or bank in Barbados, assembled the members of the working group conducting the audit.

Towards the end of the meeting, in the presence of everyone, he informed the chairman of the board of National Reserve Bank, Andrey Manoylo, that everything happening to the bank was related to personal instructions from 'the Boss' (at which point Galustian gave a nod in the direction of the office portrait of Putin) to 'bury NRB' in retaliation for certain cartoons published in our British media.

I am reminded of a story once related by the Soviet writer and journalist, David Ortenberg, editor-in-chief of the Soviet Army newspaper, *Red Star*. During the Finnish war the newspaper came out with an unfortunate typo. 'Our Red Army soldier sexpelled the White Finns from the village.' That morning everyone was scared rigid, anticipating, at the very least, that they would be arrested. Instead, Stalin himself phoned the newspaper and, laughing, asked for nobody to be punished.

The complicating circumstance here is that my British newspapers do not publish cartoons. Ever. The president would probably have been surprised if he heard that some of the heirs of Lieutenant Schmidt were exploiting his name to eliminate their business rivals. That was a common technique of the Argentinian anti-Communist junta which, from 1976 to 1983, reclassified as Communists anybody they wanted to steal from. Referring to the same mythical 'order', the FSB officers attached to a number of state enterprises and agencies 'urgently requested' them to close their fixed-term accounts with our bank.

Clients began leaving us even if it meant losing cash: the interest rate on deposits had fallen sharply, as a result of which the directorate at the Ministry of Foreign Affairs that serviced the diplomatic corps in Moscow, AvtoVAZ, Gazprom and the Residential Mortgage Agency suffered significant losses. The state Vneshtorgbank for foreign trade withdrew from a deal with us to raise $250 million through convertible bonds, thereby sacrificing a $2 million-dollar profit and suffering major reputational damage. And that despite the fact that it was Vneshtorgbank itself that had initially persuaded me to give them the mandate for the deal.

It was only a matter of time before the firefighters turned up – where would we be without them? – and ordered us to close the office because there was supposedly some problem with the way the fire alarm system was installed (and that in a top class business complex built to the latest standards and equipped with advanced fire-extinguishing systems). They declared it was only necessary to close the floors occupied by National Reserve Bank: there was no problem with the premises of Rusnano, the government's nanotechnology development company, although the fire safety infrastructure of the entire building was a single unit and serviced by our engineers.

There followed a succession of obvious efforts at entrapment, where some scruffy-looking provocateurs urged the bank to engage in illegal transactions with every appearance of money laundering, and so on. We informed the Central Bank and the competent authorities every time.

Things got worse. In December and January there were dozens of documented incidents of harassment and intimidation of our staff and their relatives in the provinces. At an official meeting with me, a colonel from K Directorate turned up accompanied by Yury Sagaidak, involved in the Magnitsky case, and urged me at great length to emigrate and entrust my business to 'reliable people' if I didn't want to end up in 'the Bastille'.

The disinformation news backup to the attack on my business was not long in coming. The artillery softening up for the special operation was provided by, among others, *Kommersant*. At first, when reports began appearing in the newspaper about embezzlement of state bailout funds and a criminal case against NRB, which was under investigation by the police, I tried talking to the newspaper. *Kommersant* greatly cherished its reputation as a respectable business publication. To no avail.

By chance I had an opportunity to talk to the paper's then editor, Mikhail Mikhailin, when I bumped into him at a conference. Mikhailin listened and promised to find out what was going on. However, the reports, which appeared to be carbon copies of each other, continued. I wrote Mikhailin an open letter, pointing out that there was no criminal case against the bank, although attempts were being made to fabricate one. Zero effect. *Kommersant* continued to spread disinformation, including a fairy tale that I was about to sell NRB 'to Uzbek investors'!

The haemorrhaging of clients' deposits from the bank in the first two months was over 5 billion rubles. The loss of deposits rose to 7 billion [$233 million]. Those behind the attack were intending to provoke a liquidity crisis and then, using the pretext of insolvency, to send outside administrators into NRB. The task of that temporary administration would be quite simple: to sell off the bank's best assets for next to nothing, primarily our shares in Aeroflot and Gazprom, and our mortgage portfolio, while at the same time accusing the bank's owner of what he had for many years, and publicly, been suspecting of every other Russian banker. After that the choice would be emigration or prison.

Fortunately for us, the flight of capital took longer than expected: six months rather than one or two. The Central Bank's investigation, which lasted three months, found no illegality. An almost 500-page-long document was compiled, whose final conclusions were that NRB had been functioning solely within the law. There had been no violations. Slowly but surely, however, Edgar Allan Poe's pit and pendulum did their work: we sold assets at a discount, customers withdrew their money.

After a year, all that remained of the bank was its proud name. We had repaid our clients all their money. I had been deprived of my banking business, but had proved by my example that an honest banker was not an oxymoron.

Banking gangs: crime without punishment

Unfortunately, neither Alexey Ivashchenko nor Irina Kireyeva, who had run Russian Capital, answered properly for what had happened. Not only that, soon a similar bankruptcy was declared at their new place of work, the Lipetsk Provincial Bank. The state compensated the depositors through the Deposit Insurance Agency. It is a familiar story for Russia's banking 'business', in which criminal groups operate and move on from one bank to another with the same invariable result, afterwards preferring to live abroad.

I had to deal with such gangs on more than one occasion. I remember the career path of Vladmir Romanov, a citizen who became famous as the director of Elektronika Bank when it went bankrupt in 2008. National Reserve Bank at that time, again at the request of the government and senior management of Rosatom (a state-owned corporation that, I intuited, had had a special relationship with Elektronika), took over its obligations to private investors.

After analysing the activities of the previous management, we sent all the materials of our investigation to the law enforcement agencies, and on 1 July 2009 the Central Investigative Directorate of the Moscow Interior Affairs Directorate initiated a criminal case. The investigation was obliged to admit that between 29 October 2007 and 20 October 2008 the bank had issued unsecured loans to the tune of 9 billion rubles [$300 million].

In my statements to the law enforcement agencies, I noted that

Elektronika Bank had been the victim of an organised crime gang specialising in illegal financial asset-stripping. In my view the organisation was created in the early 2000s by Alexander Altunin, the former director of stock market operations at the Sberbank savings bank, abetted by Vladimir Romanov.

Some time later, Pavel Luchkin (a former executive vice-president of Elektronika) and Igor Rechister (the co-owner of Multibank) joined the gang. Companies controlled by these types issued huge loans that were subsequently not repaid. Surprisingly, the investigators never did succeed in finding out where the companies receiving loans from Elektronika Bank were registered.

After stripping the assets of Electronika, the gang moved on to Multibank. According to the investigation, in summer 2010 Vladimir Romanov applied to Matvey Urin, a notorious bank fraudster currently serving a jail sentence, for a loan of half a billion rubles [$17 million] 'to acquire a controlling interest in Multibank through proxies'. Mr. Urin, the investigation believed, gave Romanov the money, which was subsequently withdrawn from the bank by buying shares in the Forward Capital investment company. This company had figured in an earlier criminal investigation of Urin as a means of siphoning off funds. It later became known that a further 750 million rubles [$25 million] had been stolen from the bank.

In March 2013 the criminal case against Elektronika was dropped. The press service of the Investigative Directorate reported that its enquiries had found no evidence of criminal wrongdoing in the actions of the bank staff. But then, just a year later, the Bank of Savings and Credit (S Bank) was declared bankrupt. Romanov (perhaps coincidentally) was also involved there.

On 18 March 2014 the bank had its licence revoked. On the verge of bankruptcy, large-scale operations were carried out to sell and transfer assets subject to seizure, without any actual funds being received in return. As the website of the Central Bank reports, the scale of these operations, identified by the bank's provisional administrators, amounted to at least 2.5 billion rubles [$83 million].

According to our sources, money from S Bank was withdrawn by issuing loans secured by assets (both the borrowers and the pledgers being companies controlled by Romanov). The pledge agreements were cancelled by the bank unilaterally, with the result that the bank was left without the loan capital and without collateral.

The provisional administration also established the almost total depreciation of the bank's loan portfolio, whose real value was put at 300 million rubles [$10 million]. The value of assets was not more than 1 billion rubles [$33 million], while the extent of liabilities to its creditors was 10.5 billion [$350 million]. As was noted in the Central Bank's report, the financial operations carried out by the bank's former managers and owners showed evidence of criminal activity.

The Bank of Russia forwarded its materials to the Prosecutor General's Office and the Interior Ministry to consider and take the appropriate procedural decisions. As far as I know, however, no action to investigate the matter was taken. The Deposit Insurance Agency won a case in which Romanov personally was the defendant and the court ruled that he must reimburse the DIA approximately 1 billion rubles, but this was rescinded on appeal.

That was not the end of the story. After the bankruptcy of S Bank in 2014, Romanov acquired Rinvest bank in Ryazan, which in July 2016 also went bankrupt, leaving a hole in its budget of over 6 billion rubles [$100 million].

CHAPTER 10

A Financial Black Magic Performance, and How It Was Done

How Unified Energy System was taken to the cleaners

After the saga of Russian Capital, I might have been expected to lie low and keep quiet, but I wanted society to learn a lesson from it. After counting up my irretrievable losses, I wrote reports to the country's leaders and the law enforcement agencies detailing the actions taken against my bank. Events impelled me to reflect on those.

The nature of the work I had started off doing meant that I felt most at home investigating corruption among high-ranking officials (in particular, studying the life and deeds of Moscow's ex-mayor Yury Luzhkov and his wife, the 'successful businesswoman' Yelena Baturina) and embezzlement in the financial system. The latter topic has only recently begun to be discussed publicly.

This variety of criminal activity is very complex, and specialised knowledge is needed to understand the mechanisms of fraud. Corrupt officials and fraudsters in the banking sector contrive intricate schemes that to the uninitiated look perfectly legal. These invariably involve cross-border operations, and the globalising world order creates an ideal environment for the financial mafia to operate in.

In December 1996, one of National Reserve Bank's stock market operations was the purchase in an open auction of 8.5 per cent of the shares of Unified Energy System of Russia. For the first time in the history of Russian privatisation, there was no fixing of the result, no under-the-counter payments. The auction was open to all comers on a basis of sealed bids. We beat Credit Suisse First Boston, who were expected to win. A consortium led by National Reserve Bank offered 350 million dollars, while

Credit Suisse offered 340 million. The group of comrades in the government who were conducting the auction were defeated, although the liberals were firmly on the side of Credit Suisse. Alexander Voloshin from the Presidential Administration, who later became chairman of the board of directors of UES, viewed us favourably.

The share price began rising very rapidly, and by summer 1997 had risen 600 per cent. The asset we owned had virtually zero liquidity. It was impossible to sell such a volume on the stock exchange, but in theory we had a mountain of money in the accounts. I was elected to the board of directors, and for several years observed the interesting process by which a vast state monopoly of fundamental importance to the national economy, no less important than Gazprom, was split up and carried off piecemeal by the 'members of the team' literally for pennies. My voting 'against' had no impact: the management of UES invariably carried the vote.

Among the decisions I voted against was one phenomenal deal, the very apotheosis of circuitry design. At the beginning of this book, I spoke about the trillion dollars of dirty money that accumulates every year around the globe. This scam, like many others mentioned here, is one of the components of that trillion.

The Russian Federation owed the Czech Republic some $3.6 billion. It no longer matters now that the debt was an artifice. After the collapse of the USSR, the government of the Russian Federation, prompted by some concerned individual, recognised the debt, despite the fact that it had developed because the USSR, as part of its policy of giving economic assistance to countries of the socialist camp, supplied Czechoslovakia with gas and oil at below global market prices, and took in return engineering products at above global market prices which were, in many respects, of lower quality than those available in the West.

Evidently someone paid someone, and I can even guess who. In the early 1990s, there was an episode involving Noga, a company owned by the Sudanese-Swiss swindler Nessim Gaon. He was supposed to supply foodstuffs to Russia in exchange for petroleum products. Having received $680 million on his contracts, Gaon brazenly raised his prices and the Russian side terminated the deal.

Then this swindler, together with his lawyer Alexander Dobrovinsky, came up with a debt of $1.5 billion he claimed he was owed and began harassing the Russian government in various jurisdictions, having the sailing ship *Sedov* impounded in Brest in France, then Russian aircraft at the

Paris air show in Le Bourget, then paintings from the Pushkin Museum at an exhibition in Switzerland. A group of people was working within the Russian government who, for a modest recompense, signed documents recognising non-existent debts for billions of dollars.

But to return to our deal. In 2002 Prime Minister Kasianov of Russia and Prime Minister Zeman of the Czech Republic announced that the debt problem had been resolved through a tangled scheme under the supervision of Russian Deputy Finance Minister Sergey Kolotukhin, Kasianov's representative. The Czech authorities sold to a firm called Falkon $2.5 billion of the $3.6 billion of debt for $547.5 million, that is, at a discount of seventy-eight per cent.

Falkon immediately sold the debt claim to UES that, in turn, sold it on to the Russian government. The Czech Ministry of Finance received less than $400 million under this scheme (Falkon was subsequently granted an additional $150 million discount), while the Russian Ministry of Finance wrote off the tax liability of UES.

The trick was that UES remained in debt to Falkon to the tune of $2.5 billion, which it continued to repay without any discount. The result was that some $2 billion were 'accidentally lost' to an offshore company and were split between officials (including some at the most senior level) who had had some involvement in the scheme. The money was placed in a special trust, from which it flowed through the German Deutsche Genossenschaftsbank into a big Russian investment fund that owns a large number of office properties in our capital city.

In other words, money does not disappear, it just gets transferred from one person's pocket to another person's pocket. In this case it left the pockets of the citizens of the Russian Federation without ever reaching the pockets of the citizens of the Czech Republic. In the Czech Republic, incidentally, all those involved in this scam were arrested and jailed. In Russia too, it would be a simple matter to unravel the tangle and at least confiscate the real estate bought with stolen money, but no one could be found to undertake the task.

Aviaprom is bled dry

In the mid-noughties, as a deputy in the State Duma, I investigated the scam of the Financial Leasing Company (FLC). This state-owned agency was created in 2001, with a controlling stake owned by the Russian Federal Property Fund and the government of Tatarstan. Its official purpose was to support the building of aircraft. I had proposed to the Russian government that, in order to rescue our aircraft industry, we should establish an air leasing company called Ilyushin Finance (IFC). The government was present in the form of Vneshekonombank (the Bank for Development and Foreign Economic Affairs).

The idea was that private business and the state should invest capital in the company with which it would commission aircraft and lease them to airlines. I invested a total of around 6 billion rubles [$200 million] in cash. The aircraft factories in Ulianovsk and Voronezh were given orders and production revived. Dozens of new Russian aircraft were built and Ilyushin Finance became the largest aircraft leasing company in the Commonwealth of Independent States.

At this point some fraudsters, supported by Kazan [the capital of Tatarstan], created their own phoney company, supposedly in the interests of the Kazan Gorbunov Aircraft Factory. I surmised that this was for the purpose of embezzlement ($15 billion rubles [$500 million] was 'successfully' stolen), but the matter proved more serious than that. The Financial Leasing Company, like Ilyushin Finance, received money from the budget in 2002–2006, but the managers of FLC and the officials behind them (and, as it transpired, there was also someone standing behind *them*) had their own ideas about where the money should be spent.

For a start, they bought a mansion in the centre of Moscow, where repairing the floors in the office of the CEO alone cost … $12 million. Instead of manufacturing aircraft, FLC issued loans to fly-by-night subcontracting firms, which were then transferred to a company called FLC West in Luxembourg, or simply spent.

This scheme was devised by the deputy director of FLC, Andrey Burlakov, his civil wife Anna Etkina, who was deputy chairman of the board of Mira-Bank, and a certain Yevgeny Zaritsky. The criminal 'protection' was provided by the leader of a gang of hitmen, Aslan Gagiev, nicknamed Jacko the Bloody, who appears in the FLK accounts as Sergey Morozov, a shareholder of the company. Gagiev was famous for having cemented Oleg Novoselsky, the chairman of the board of Kutuzovsky Bank, in a barrel and tortured him for several days in the summer sun. The barrel, together with the banker, was then dropped in the Moscow Canal.

A number of victims were despatched to the next world actually in the offices of FLC, in a room next to the boardroom where meetings were held with government officials. It proved possible to find a list of the officials who received kickbacks for the plundering of FLC. All this continued unabated from 2001 until 2008.

Around $500 million was stolen from FLC, but that was evidently felt to be insufficient and, with the assistence of a protective *krysha* of 'law enforcement' officers, a criminal case was fabricated against Ilyushin Finance for supposedly improperly having a secondary issue of shares. The audit was at first conducted by the Voronezh Prosecutor's Office (where IFC was registered). They found no evidence of wrongdoing, so in July 2005 the materials were called for by the Prosecutor General's Office in Moscow.

The same day, a criminal case was opened, and that same day Judge Solopova of the Basmanny Court, at the request of Deputy Prosecutor Biryukov, seized shares belonging to a private shareholder, namely, me. The company's operations were paralysed. The case duly collapsed, the court recognising that the secondary offering had been legitimate, but it left a bad taste, and not only with me, I hope.

Part of the money embezzled from the state, over $300 million, was spent on Burlakov's purchase from a Norwegian company, Aker Yards, of shipyards in Germany and Ukraine. Based on these assets, a company called Wadan Yards was created. Burlakov took the position of chairman of the board of directors, with Etkina as vice-president for finance. The swindlers spent a further portion of the money on 'living'. Burlakov, for example, collected expensive cabriolets.

In 2006, the Russian Audit Office conducted an inspection of FLC that revealed 'misappropriation of funds' (although all the company's assets had disappeared long ago). It took the law enforcement agencies two years to wake up and realise that, instead of Russian aircraft, German shipyards had been bought, and not on behalf of a state company but of its former managers. FLK itself owned nothing: even its office furniture was found to be hired.

The fraudsters had succeeded in issuing several bond-secured loans in the form of credit-linked notes.[6] They were bought through Dresdner Bank by credulous Western investors who believed a fairy tale about a trustworthy

---

6 A credit-linked note or credit bond is a type of bond tied to a loan agreement. It is issued by the lender; the payment of the principal and/or interest is contingent on whether a particular adverse event (for example, bankruptcy of the borrower) occurs.

leasing company backed by the state. That money too was stolen, and investors naturally addressed their claims to the Russian government and began publishing open letters in *Vedomosti*.

Criminal proceedings were instituted in connection with the goings-on at FLC. A number of officers in K Directorate, whose job it was to keep an eye on the company, were dismissed from the service (this after hundreds of millions of dollars had disappeared without trace). Then there was the next financial crisis and Wadan Yards went bankrupt. These shipyards were economically crucial for the city of Wismar in the federal state of Mecklenburg-Vorpommern, which happens to be Angela Merkel's consituency, and in September 2009 elections to the Bundestag were being held.

No doubt purely out of a sense of social responsibility and concern for local jobs, the Federal Chancellor immediately flew to Sochi and asked Dmitry Medvedev, who was currently president, to resolve the matter. By this time *Novaya Gazeta* and *Der Spiegel* had published several investigative articles about embezzlement at FLC, and we can rest assured that they would have been read by the government of the Federal Republic of Germany.

The issue was resolved by the president's special representative for international energy cooperation, Igor Yusufov, whose son 'bought' Wadan Yards (later renamed Nordic Yards) for €40 million. How surprising that this company, which was on its way to being declared bankrupt, emerged unscathed a month later. It would usually have taken years. Two years after that, in 2011, the shipyards were again caught up in a regrettable business spat in respect of the purchase for $1 billion of the minority stake in the Bank of Moscow of its former director Andrey Borodin, who fled to London.

What do you think of the scenario? First Borodin, while still the director of a bank, gives Yusufov a billion dollars against the security of the shipyards (which, truth to tell, would not sell for a bent euro). With the money Yusufov then buys Borodin's nineteen per cent of the bank's shares, and ultimately sells them at a premium to the new owner of the Bank of Moscow, the state-owned Vneshtorgbank. As a result, Vneshtorgbank has to ask the government for a record 300 billion rubles [$10 billion] to rescue the bank Borodin had plundered.

The fate of the defendants in the FLC case proved tragic. They would have done better never to have left Matrosskaya Tishina prison on bail. On 29 September 2011, a hitman shot Burlakov and Etkina at the Khutorok restaurant on Leningradsky Avenue, where they were meeting NTV journalist Maxim Gladky. Burlakov was killed and Etkina (now in hiding in Israel) was severely injured. The tally of the gang of their 'business partner' Gagiev, who is accused of commissioning the hit, is over 100 victims, including the mayor of Vladikavkaz, Vitaly Karaev, bankers, investigators, and other gangland bosses.

What is the upshot? The theft of money from the Russian budget through FLC exacerbated the problems of Russia's aircraft construction industry, harmed the investment climate, and caused a crisis in north Germany that was discussed at the highest level. So what if they stole $500 million – that's not so much spread over seven years. After all, as I have said, globally a trillion gets stolen every year. But what are we to make of the fact that this state company (it is interesting to see who was chairing its board of directors at the time), which had received huge injections of cash from the state budget, turned out to be a cover for criminal activity, effectively controlled by a gang of throw-backs with a hundred murders to their name?

All these stories serve as a vivid illustration of how the mechanism of embezzlement and money laundering works. We see that such operations are cross-border in nature, and that combating fraud and corruption is one of the most urgent items, not only on Russia's agenda but on the international agenda too. However, the efforts of the civilised world to address this problem too often run into a lack not only of cooperation but even of elementary understanding between the governments of the leading economic powers.

Setting the standard: the tale of Mezhprombank

The most surprising fact is that standard and, to some extent, legal schemes are employed in embezzlement. There are two ways commonly used to siphon off money. The easiest is to make loans to your own companies, preferably offshore. That was the technique favoured, for example, by Sergey Pugachev, the owner of one of the top ten Russian banks, Mezhprombank. Even more surprising is that, of the money stolen, $1 billion was an unsecured loan from the Central Bank.

The tale of Mezhprombank is a classic, standard-setting example of a large-scale swindle involving the theft of money from the Russian banking system. Pugachev was a senator from Tuva, whose image was that of 'a

Russian Orthodox banker' and 'a person close to the emperor'. When the financial crisis began in 2008, the Central Bank deposited 30 billion rubles [$1 billion] with Mezhprombank 'for stabilisation'. (Naturally, no one at the Central Bank was aware that the bank had no actual assets.)

The bank made two hundred loans to Russian fly-by-night and offshore companies owned, through nominees, by Pugachev. The total amounted to 3 billion rubles [$100 million]. That was all the money there was in the bank, including the Central Bank's deposit. After that, Pugachev sailed off in the same direction as the money had gone, and periodically reminded everyone of his existence in the gossip columns of London and Monaco, where he had mansions, yachts and VIP jets. The strategically important shipbuilding enterprises of Severnaya Verf (Northern Shipyard) and Baltiysky Zavod (Baltic Factory), which were part of the Mezhprombank group, were on the verge of bankruptcy.

Vladimir Putin and Dmitry Kozak had personally to go there and sort out the rescue of the factories, pouring government funds into them. Wicked rumours assert that, before making his escape, Pugachev ruined Defence Minister Anatoly Serdyukov. They had agreed that the 400 billion rubles [$13 billion] allocated in the budget to build ships for the navy, would be deposited as a 100 per cent advance in Mezhprombank. The 'commission' was to be a cool $2 billion. This detail was one of the reasons for the subsequent troubles of the former section head of scandal-struck Furniture Store No. 3 of Lenmebeltorg.

As it happens, I was the first person to look into Pugachev's activities and draw them to the attention of the law enforcement agencies. I wrote to the then Interior Minister in June 2011 (*see opposite*).

Besides issuing fake loans to yourself, another way to rob a bank is to buy land or some other useless asset (like junk bonds of mutual investment funds) from yourself at vastly inflated prices. After stealing the money, you can declare bankruptcy. Your 'protector' inside the regulator recognises the bankruptcy as due to the vagaries of the market ('Well, that's just how it goes: the guys made some dud investments'), and the government's Deposit Insurance Agency repays the cheated depositors at the taxpayer's expense.

Sergey Ignatiev, the former chairman of Central Bank, gave a long interview on the eve of his retirement in 2013 to *Vedomosti*, in which he honestly admitted that of the several hundred banks whose licences the Central Bank revoked while he was in charge of it, the vast majority were planned bankruptcies. In the banking sector there were whole gangs who

НАЦИОНАЛЬНЫЙ РЕЗЕРВНЫЙ БАНК

Акционерный коммерческий банк
"НАЦИОНАЛЬНЫЙ РЕЗЕРВНЫЙ БАНК"
(открытое акционерное общество)
Россия, 117036, Москва, пр-т 60-летия Октября, д. 10а
Тел.: (495) 213 32 20 Факс: (495) 956 32 30
info@nrb.ru www.nrb.ru
ОКПО 29296062, ОГРН 1027700458224
ИНН/КПП 7703211512/775001001

____ 0 8 ИЮН 2011 № 2299/0000004

на №

Министру внутренних дел
Российской Федерации

Нургалиеву Р.Г.

Уважаемый Рашид Гумарович!

В течение последних нескольких месяцев я неоднократно обращался в различные правоохранительные органы с заявлениями о выводе активов на сумму свыше 5 млрд. рублей бывшими руководителями учредителями АКБ «Российский капитал» (Банк РК), который по просьбе Правительства и Центрального Банка санировал АКБ «Национальный резервный банк» (НРБанк).

Следствием этих обращений явились обыски и проверки самого НРБанка, основанные на сфальсифицированных документах некоторых сотрудников и руководителей правоохранительных сотрудников, в том числе начальника ГСУ при ГУ МВД России по г. Москве Глухова И.А. о якобы имевших место многочисленных нарушениях со стороны НРБанка во время санации Банка РК.

Проведенная Центральным Банком многомесячная проверка НРБанка не выявила ни одного нарушения, в том числе и якобы имевшего место хищения кредита, выделенного НРБанку Центральным Банком на санацию Банка РК.

Подтверждено самое главное – НРБанк успешно санировал Банк РК, не допустив его банкротства.

Фактически же со стороны недобросовестных сотрудников правоохранительных органов и Центрального Банка была предпринята попытка рейдерского захвата НРБанка, которая по причинам от них независящим, не увенчалась успехом.

На этом фоне и в это самое время происходили события, которые не привлекли внимания ни сотрудников правоохранительных органов, ни многочисленных чиновников Центрального Банка, призванных по долгу службы осуществлять надзор за банковской деятельностью.

Я имею ввиду ситуацию вокруг теперь уже печально известного Межпромбанка.

Она практически идентична той, ко...
большим ущербом:

- высокорискованная, без обеспечен...
- отсутствие адекватных резервов,
- недостоверная, а, точнее, фальсиф...

В итоге, по предварительным данным, причиненный ущерб может составлять свыше 60 млрд. рублей.

И в это же самое время Межпромбанк на беззалоговом аукционе получает 34 млрд. рублей от Центрального Банка.

Не вызывает никаких сомнений, что подобные действия были возможны либо при полном попустительстве со стороны чиновников Центрального Банка, либо при «крышевании» сотрудниками правоохранительных органов.

Мне как кредитору Межпромбанка причинен ущерб. Прошу Вас провести проверку и дать юридическую оценку действиям руководителей Межпромбанка, Центрального Банка и других лиц.

Одновременно, был бы признателен за ответ на мои обращения по поводу Банка РК, которые, по имеющейся информации, приобщены к материалам уголовного дела № 89280, находящегося в производстве ГСУ при ГУ МВД России по г. Москве.

С уважением,

Президент АКБ
«Национальный Резервный Банк»   А.Е. Лебедев

owned several banks at the same time. Matvey Urin, currently in jail, owned six banks simultaneously, and Alexey Alyakin owned five. Money was slipped from one bank to the other, like the pea in guess-the-thimble.

How to launder a trillion dollars in the West

Efforts to stop illegal activity and return embezzled funds invariably run up against the same obstruction: corrupt officials and fraudsters move the money they have stolen into foreign jurisdictions and then move abroad themselves, where they often have the temerity to claim political asylum (like the above-mentioned Andrey Borodin). Every time the fraudsters state they are being persecuted in their home country for their oppositional views, although until that moment nothing had been heard of their holding any such views and indeed, as a rule, they fully supported the policies of the current government.

In the countries of the European Union and in Switzerland there now reside Sergey Pugachev; the former mayor of Almaty in Kazakhstan, Viktor Khrapunov; Yelena Baturina, the wife of former mayor of Moscow, Yury Luzhkov. The president of the East European Finance Corporation, Alexander Gitelson, was arrested in Austria, while Mukhtar Ablyazov who, as chairman of TuranAlem Bank, misappropriated billions of dollars, was arrested in France. The fraudsters and swindlers hiding in Europe have joined forces in various self-proclaimed 'anti-corruption committees', acting in accordance with the familiar pattern of the thief who shouts, 'Stop thief!'

Besides Europe, the United States of America is often a safe haven. For a long time, the former minister of finance of the Moscow region, Alexey Kuznetsov, who organised multibillion-dollar embezzlement of budgetary funds allocated for construction of social infrastructure facilities, including schools and day care centres, evaded justice there. The case against him included murder charges. It was only when he came to Europe that this corrupt official was arrested while using false passports and is now awaiting the decision of a French court on whether to extradite him to Russia.

Or take Ashot Yeghiazaryan, whose career has been described in some detail in the earlier part of this book. He lives in California today and is seeking political refugee status. Will the law on combating organised crime be applied to him? Doubtless the question is rhetorical.

Imagine the situation if Calisto Tanzi, founder of the Italian company Parmalat, or the American megafraud Bernie Madoff, had thought to provide themselves with an emergency landing site, then siphoned off the money they stole from investors to a country with strained relations with their home country – Venezuela, say. Then, when they were declared bankrupt, they could have fled there, declared themselves victims of political persecution and 'opponents of the Obama regime'. Who can doubt that, instead of now serving their time in prison, they might have been living the life of Reilly?

Let me recall that, according to international monitoring organisations like the Tax Justice Network, business fraudsters, in conjunction with high-ranking corrupt officials, have misappropriated and laundered some $60 trillion around the world over the past twenty years. Russia's share of this dirty money is around $100 billion, that is, only three per cent. The main flows of illegal capital originate in China and Africa.

The most iconic crimes of this type in the West were the corporate frauds at Enron and Parmalat, complex financial scams like those of Bernie Madoff and Allen Stanford, rogue traders like Jérôme Kerviel of Société Génerale and Kweku Adoboli of UBS, manipulation of the London interbank offered rate (LIBOR) perpetrated by Royal Bank of Scotland and Barclays Bank, the sub-prime mortgage crisis, scandals involving HSBC, Standard Chartered Bank, Goldman Sachs, Credit Suisse, and so on.

Global corporations have long placed themselves above the law, declining to pay tax on multibillion-dollar profits. They do this through the use of offshore schemes, including some in European jurisdictions. We have only to recall the scandal surrounding the technological giant, Apple, a company that, thanks to its 'subsidiary' in Ireland, was able to 'optimise' its tax base to the tune of $44 billion.

A *New York Times* investigation by Pulitzer Prize winner David Kocieniewski into the tax capers of the US company General Electric demonstrated that, having made a net profit in 2010 of $10 billion, instead of paying tax at thirty-five per cent, GE claimed a tax benefit of $3.2 billion.[7] Obviously, with such a fiscal approach, the US budget is bound to be heavily in deficit. General Electric, a 'global' (i.e., offshore) corporation, an icon of US business, has numerous 'subsidiaries' and 'sub-subsidiaries' in Luxembourg,

---

7 David Kocieniewski, 'At G.E. on tax day, billions of reasons to smile', *New York Times*, 22 September 2015. https://www.pulitzer.org/winners/david-kocieniewski.

Ireland, Switzerland, the British Virgin Islands, and so on, and is also part of the criminal financial oligarchy.

Corruption and fraud on an international scale would not be possible if the culprits did not have, working on their behalf, an entire industry dedicated to siphoning off, concealing and laundering dirty money. They have at their disposal numerous offshore jurisdictions, tax havens, special 'investment banks', tens of thousands of the best lawyers, and nominee directors of companies. If someone has embezzled more than a billion dollars and emigrated to such a tax haven, it becomes all but impossible to hold them to account.

There is a principle that, the more you steal, the less the probability that you will be unable to evade punishment. The trial of such a person will cost at least fifteen per cent of the amount embezzled, will require proceedings lasting many years, and a successful outcome is by no means certain.

'Dirty money' is a time bomb placed under the global financial system. The financial oligarchy is a threat to the stability of the world economy. It 'protects' global corruption that, like apartheid, deprives whole nations of Asia, Europe and America of a future. Hillary Clinton, then US Secretary of State, once borrowed my simile for a speech she gave at a university. So far, at least, no actions have followed those words.

I firmly believe that this global apartheid can be faced down only through the joint efforts of the world's leading nations, although some of them, alas, have become a safe haven for corrupt officials and swindlers from all over the world. It is essential to stop granting refuge to dirty money and to clean up the Augean stables of the offshore tax havens by making it illegal to possess resources through nominees.

There is nothing dangerous about this. Indeed, the effective termination of money laundering on Cyprus did not destabilise the world economy. This is precisely what the commission on global corruption, set up at the G20 summit meeting in Seoul, was supposed to do, but so far it has nothing to show for itself. Neither have the UN Convention against Corruption or the efforts of the Organisation for Economic Cooperation and Development had the necessary impact.

One way out of the impasse would be the creation at international level of an organisation with broad powers to investigate crimes of corruption and fraud involving the transborder movement of individuals and capital. This should be an effective body resembling Interpol that, incidentally, costs its member countries only $70 million a year to run. A financial

Interpol should make the return of embezzled and laundered money both speedier and cheaper. Efforts to combat corruption and the international financial oligarchy would become genuinely international and, most importantly, efficient.

The task is to return to peoples the wealth stolen from them and to strike at corruption from an unexpected angle, namely the ultimate beneficiary resources in offshore jurisdictions. Am I the only person who understands this? In summer 2011, I set out my ideas in appeals to the leaders of the G20 and in an article in the *New York Times*, which was titled 'A World Anticorruption Police'. It evoked no response from the Western elite. Next, I recorded two video lectures about global corruption and embezzlement in the banking system, a kind of master class for law enforcement officers. When these lectures were posted on my YouTube channel, they collected hundreds of thousands of views.

CHAPTER 11

'In Compliance with the Instructions of the Chairman of the Investigative Committee of the Russian Federation ...'

The NTV Show: an unexpected brush with the turbulent Mr Polonsky

In early autumn 2011, I returned from Belovodiye, the Shambhala in the Altai Mountains, to the restless anthill of the metropolis and plunged again into routine matters. The country was crawling into the marathon of the propaganda campaign preceding elections to the State Duma and later the presidency. Nobody wanted me as a Duma candidate: the minders had had quite enough trouble in the fourth convocation, and this election put the final nail in the coffin of independence in electoral politics.

I had a phone call from NTV asking me to take part in a recorded talk show called *The NTV Show*. The topic was 'The Global Financial Crisis'. There was plenty I wanted to say about that. I asked who else was invited, and they told me Mikhail Prokhorov, Irina Yasina and Olga Romanova. I agreed. I wanted to put out on air an idea I had discussed with Maxim Trudolyubov from *Vedomosti*. This was that there should be a free handout of shares, through special accounts, to the public in such state-owned companies as Rosneft, Sberbank, Vneshtorgbank, and the like. We believed such a measure could compensate the people for losses suffered as a result of the privatisation of the 1990s and lead to formation of a real middle class.

There had been a special section devoted to this at a conference *Vedomosti* held at the Hyatt Hotel, at which we tried to argue that, in the first place, not everyone would sell the shares on the day they received them and drink themselves silly, and that, in the second place, restrictions could be placed on the purchase and sale of the shares, so that they were not all instantly dumped on the market. I wanted to bring this specialised discussion to a broader public.

I arrived at Ostankino. NTV talk shows are recorded on the first floor and follow a certain ritual. While preparations are being made in the main studio for the recording – the audience are being shown to their seats, the lighting is being checked, and the camera operators are planning their interaction – the guests assemble in adjacent premises. There are dressing rooms, the wardrobe, plates of fruit, water, and even bad brandy for those who wish to imbibe. I immediately spotted Yasina and Romanova in this green room and went over. At that moment someone behind my shoulder said rather loudly, 'What is this dickhead doing here!'

Beside me stood a robust, two-metre-tall, pink-cheeked thug with a scrawny, dishevelled sparse beard and curly hair. He turned away, as if his remark had not been directed at me, although it clearly had. 'Sergey Polonsky, the developer,' the smiling young lady accompanying me informed me.

We had not met before, but I had heard a few things about Polonsky, like probably most Russians who did not have a billion dollars, and who, at a reception and presentation of his company Mirax during a real estate exhibition in Cannes, he had suggested could go stuff themselves. This gala event was held in early 2008, before the financial crisis.

It is worth mentioning that before the crisis, the business of certain developers (which, incidentally, included Yeghiazaryan) was run very simply. They received a development site and approval of the project through patrons in Mayor Luzhkov's town hall. For the prospective construction, they obtained loans from the state bank and money from investors. The amount of money obtained was several times more than the actual building costs, so they insouciantly siphoned off the greater part and moved it without hindrance to foreign countries, where they made 'investments'.

For example, Polonsky paid over $200 million for the Sungate Port Royal hotel in Turkey. They financed piss-ups on yachts in Cannes. They brought pop diva Madonna to Montenegro for $15 million. Then there were projects in the UK, Switzerland, the US and Cambodia for hundreds of millions – all paid for with money collected in Russia.

In total, Mirax received no less than a billion dollars from shareholders and creditors. Some was used for building, it is true, although only about twenty to thirty per cent of it. They paid no taxes anywhere. More than half the money collected was siphoned off and laundered. Some they squandered or sank in various 'projects', some they hid (for example, a 'loan' of $70 million from the plundered Lithuanian Snoras Bank, in connection with which a criminal investigation is underway involving the well-known bank swindler, Vladimir Antonov). Like the FLC fraudsters, they issued CLN and other debt instruments to the tune of $400 million for unrealised projects.

For several years, banks and investment funds that had bought these 'risk-free' securities looked on open-mouthed as the signboards outside the office of 'Horns and Hooves' changed to 'No Title', to 'Infinity Stream', and so on and so forth, and registered default after default. This, however, did not bother the financial oligarchy, because money is no object. It is not coming out of the pocket of the investment bankers, and is mostly also dirty money. If it gets written off, it will not be for the first time. But who does it really belong to, and who is behind it?

Here is a typical Mirax project. The story closely resembles Charles Perrault's *Puss in Boots*, with its change of ownership of land and real estate, only in Moscow. In 2002, the warm-hearted and socially concerned Moscow local government authorities gave away free of charge to the All-Russian Physical Culture and Sports Organization for the Disabled a 1.5-hectare plot of land for building a 'centre for the social and physical rehabilitation of the hearing-impaired'. This was the Trud [Labour] Stadium in the city centre, near Paveletsky railway station and with access on to Derbenevskaya embankment.

According to the resolution of the Moscow authority, the site and the project itself were being donated for a specific purpose. The future 55,000-square-metre building was to be 100-per-cent owned by the Union of the Deaf and used specifically for the rehabilitation of hearing-impaired people. The deaf, however, with apologies for the questionable pun, heard nothing about this largesse.

Mirax now takes the stage in the form of two companies, Stroymontazh and Lenstroymontazh. In 2003, those in charge of the Union of the Deaf sign an investment contract with them, under which, when the centre is completed, only thirty per cent will be for use by the disabled. In 2006, a supplementary agreement is signed, whereunder the representatives of the Union give their undemanding 'partners' a full ninety-six per cent of the floor space of the future centre. The agreement was actually signed after the building had been completed.

This violation of the resolution of the Moscow local authority did not stop Pyotr Biryukov, the then prefect of the Southern Administrative District, from commissioning the facility in the same year as a rehabilitation centre for disabled people. Never mind the fact that the hearing impaired did not even get into the building.

Needless to say, nobody at the prefecture knew anything about that, because it would be easier to travel to the moon than from Derbenevskaya embankment, which is a stonking one and a half kilometres away. Admittedly, if you looked out of the prefect's window, you could see the building's facade and note that there was not a word on it about disabled people. On the other hand, MIRAX GROUP was emblazoned on it in metre-high letters, together with the group's telephone number, so that potential buyers and renters should know where to apply. And thus was a social amenity, which in all the documents is still listed as the Centre for Social and Physical Rehabilitation of the Hearing-Impaired, transformed into the Pollars Business Centre. Some sleight of hand, you may agree.

Polonsky, before the financial crisis, had received planning approval from the Moscow authorities to build over twelve million square metres of residential accommodation and offices. The only person with a more extensive portfolio was the mayor's wife. The situation concerning Yelena Baturina, now present at every modish party in London, could not be clearer. Her husband, famously a connoisseur of the art works of Zurab Tsereteli, dismissed all suspicions that his wife's business was receiving preferential treatment by remarking, 'My wife is a successful entrepreneur, I only get in her way.'

A meaningful contribution to her success probably came from Shalva Chigirinsky, another darling of Moscow's construction industry, who in 2003 formally made over half the share capital of the Moscow Oil Company to Baturina through the Swiss bank of Wegelin for, as was said in an earlier informal agreement, 'administrative assistance' on the part of her husband.[8] Chigirinsky's business at the time, which controlled half of the Moscow City international business centre, was embarking on a project to renovate the Rossiya Hotel on Varvarka, next to the Kremlin, and was estimated to be worth $1.5 billion.

---

8 Natal'ia Golitsyna, 'Moskva dlia dvoikh', *Kommersant*, 7 September 2009. https://www.kommersant.ru/doc/1228839.

Left: *With opera singer Galina Vishnevskaya at a performance in the Russian Cultural Centre near Paris*

Right: *Chekhov Dinner in Moscow: Nikita Mikhalkov, my wife Elena, son Evgeny, Kevin Spacey and John Malkovich*

Left: *Charity Gala to raise funds for children with cancer: son Evgeny, Mikhail Gorbachev and Ralph Fiennes. London, 2008*

Above: *With Sir Elton John and my wife Elena*

Above: *With Hugh Grant*

Left: *With Nayalia Vodianova at a charity event*

Above: *Botswana, 2008. On the eve of the global financial crisis*

Left: *In Botswana National Park*

Right: *In the Egyptian desert, on the way to Siwa oasis*

Above: *Oasis Siva. Here Alexander the Great talked with the oracle*

Left: *Fascinating views of Mongolia*

Right: *Expedition to Mongolia is not an easy walk*

Above: *Near Lalibela, Ethiopia*

Right: *With Botswana Bushmen*

Left: *My friend - patriarch of the Dani tribe, Papua New Guinea*

Clockwise from top: *Fishing on the Shantar Islands in the Pacific Ocean, the Far East of Russia*

Preparing to dive in the Arctic, on the former Soviet submarine base in Linahamari. Murmansk region, Russia

Working as a waiter in the cafe 'Petrushka'. London, 2016

The biggest lion population in Europe is in the Crimean nature park 'Taigan' - 75 predators

Above: *Learning to obtain a pilot licence*

Left: *In the courtroom with my lawyer Henry Reznik at the trial on accusation of 'hooliganism for political reasons' for the incident on a TV show. Moscow, 2013*

SIR ELTON JOHN & DAVID FURNISH

5ᵗʰ March, 2013

To Whom It May Concern:

I have known Alexander Lebedev for fifteen years. He is a decent, generous, kind and thoughtful person and a man of integrity.

He has been very supportive of the Elton John AIDS Foundation, a charity which I founded, and I consider him to be a good friend.

Yours sincerely

Elton John

1 BLYTHE ROAD, LONDON W14 0HG
TEL 020 7348 4800 FAX 020 7348 4830

Ian McKellen

7 March 2013

To whom it may concern

ALEXANDER YEVGENIEVICH LEBEDEV

The charge against my friend, Alexander, is a serious one. I wanted to put it into the context of what I know of the man whom I count as a friend of some years.

The impact of Alexander Yevgenievich's commercial interests in the United Kingdom have been considerable and entirely beneficial. I am one of many people who respect and rely on his publications for accurate and insightful reporting of national and international affairs.

In private, I have always found him to be correct in his manners, utterly charming and gracious. He is a true man of the world, critical of the hypocrisy and unsociable attitudes of others. The incident which has led to the current charges seems to me entirely uncharacteristic and worthy of leniency.

I very much hope Alexander Yevgenievich will be allowed freely to continue his important work at home and abroad.

Ian McKellen

Professor Sir Ian McKellen CH CBE

Clockwise from above:
'Character reference on accused person' by Sir Elton John, presented in Moscow Court

'Character reference' by Sir Ian McKellen

'Character reference' by John Malkovich

LE PAVILLON DE LA REINE
PARIS

To Whom it may concern;

I am writing on behalf of my friend Alexander Lebedev to ask the court for leniency in his case. I do not wish to interfere in the decisions the court is charged to make. I can only ask the judge to take into account that Alexander is a person of fine character, of a refined culture, and with a generous nature. Though he may have acted unwisely to a deliberate and egregious provocation, he is neither a violent nor dangerous man. He is a man who has done many charitable deeds in Russia and beyond, and is an emissary for Russian culture of an inestimable value. I hope that the court will see fit to release him and let him carry on his fine work. Thank you for your time.

Sincerely,
John Malkovich

HÔTEL & SPA ★★★★
28 Place des Vosges - 75003 Paris - T. +33 (0) 40 29 19 19 - F. +33 (0) 40 29 19 20 - www.pavillondelareine.com

SNC Pavillon de la Reine - Siret 506 303 164 000 22 - APE 5510Z - TVA FR 01 506 303 164

I took an active interest in these issues, so already had a long-distance conflict with Polonsky well before our encounter in NTV's green room. In 2006, I and a group of my fellow deputies in the Stolitsa [Metropolis] coalition group, held a press conference about problems in the town-planning policies of the Moscow mayor's office. The day before, Maria Stroeva, then a presenter at Russian Business Consulting TV, sent me a message through Live Journal: 'Yevgenievich, we are being relocated to the Federation Tower in City of Moscow and we are all scared. We've heard there is a crack in the foundation.' I had that checked out by engineers and they confirmed the information.

At the press conference, I dutifully reported the suspicions of problems with the tower and sent a request to Rostekhnadzor, the building regulations inspectorate. It transpired that Polonsky had a presentation on the tower scheduled for the following day. Investors and creditors were anxious, and Polonsky sent an angry fax to my office in the State Duma demanding I should attend the presentation. He promised to give a million dollars to anyone who could find a crack. The crack could only be detected by a complicated technical examination, and I had only insider information from the builders to go on.

Rostekhnadzor, the Ministry of Emergency Situations and the Prosecutor General's Office continued to talk with the developer. It transpired that in February 2006, when the foundation of the tower was being laid, there were forty-degree frosts in Moscow, traffic jams resulted, and cement-mixer vehicles were unable to deliver cement at the right time. The technical requirements were not met and the builders concreted over the entire foundation of the prospective skyscraper.

This was subsequently admitted by the chief designer of the Federation Tower, Vladimir Travush. Incidentally, he also designed the Transvaalpark water park in Yasenevo, which collapsed two years before the events described with many casualties. In view of infringements in the design of the fire safety systems, the Ministry of Emergency Situations ordered closure of the building site, but this decision was overruled judicially, perhaps because Vneshtorgbank was the biggest investor and had bought office space in the already built West Tower.

Pre-crisis, the construction industry was one big pyramid. The greater the scale of the building project, the more money you could borrow for it and, with a flick of the wrist, misappropriate. The financial crisis took the feet from the real estate market, and it was the builders of pyramids who first found themselves standing beside the broken trough. By the time *The NTV Show* was being recorded, Polonsky had announced the closure of the Mirax brand (earlier, when it seemed to him that he had God by the beard, he had called his son Mirax) and asked reporters not to call him a businessman.

When a journalist, Nikolai Mikhalyov of RBC Daily, questioned Polonsky's motives, he invited him to his office, pushed him into the toilet and began forcing his way in, filming the whole episode on a camcorder. Polonsky posted the video on the Internet and caused a great commotion. In his Twitter account he presented himself as a Pavlovian dog that reacted reflexively. In short, he was widely regarded as a person with issues.

Evening TV stops being soporific

By the second hour of recording at NTV, Polonsky had managed to toss several barbed comments in my direction, while apparently talking only to himself. What viewers subsequently got to see was less than half of what actually occurred in the studio. We were sitting on three rotating chairs that skated about on the podium, with me to the left of the audience, Sergey Lisovsky on the right, and Polonsky in the middle. During the recording, Polonsky tried several times to get into an argument with me. He clung to Lisovsky, stood up, ran around the studio, and offered to give Herman Sterligov, who was sitting in the second row, a massage. Herman was probably right when he said the fellow was high on drugs.

For an hour and a half, I put up with these absurdities. I talked about a people's privatisation and a special tax on oligarchs' 'windfall' income. This one-off levy was introduced in 1997 by the Labour leaders Tony Blair and Gordon Brown for businessmen who had made unjustified profits during the Margaret Thatcher privatisation programme of the 1980s. Their government raised £5 billion that way and channelled it into social programmes. Alas, all my pronouncements were subsequently edited out.

I kept strictly to one principle: under no circumstances talk to Polonsky about anything. I spoke only to the presenters and did my best to avoid looking at my neighbour. At this point the microphone was passed to a woman in the audience. She was a single mother, and asked us as we sat there on the podium in front of her how she was supposed to feed her four children on a salary of 15,000 rubles [$500] a month.

Polonsky grabbed the microphone and started yelling that in Russia only losers earned that little. He turned to Lisovsky, who was sitting on his left with the words, 'There you've got a chicken farmer' (Sergey owns the Mosselprom chicken farms), then to me, 'and here you've got an airman,' and concluded by saying, 'I'd like to punch them in the face!'

At that I lost patience, stood up and said, 'Do you want to try?' Polonsky was taken aback. 'Just control yourself, pal!' I remarked, sitting back down. At just that moment I heard him say, 'And this is the man who was talking about the Federation Tower,' and out of the corner of my eye (my shortsightedness is -6) I saw an arm moving towards me.

Thinking a punch was about to land, I moved to fend it off. Using my left hand, I covered my opponent's jaw. The chair on its little wheels disappeared off stage from where, shortly afterwards, Polonsky's frightened face appeared. The best response I could think of at the time was, 'Well, do I have to take my glasses off, you halfwit?'

Leaving Ostankino, I was sure NTV would cut the incident out or ditch the programme altogether in the two days before it was due to be broadcast. Even before I had reached home, however, Aram Gabrelyanov had already uploaded a 'sensational post' on his Lifenews portal, and an hour later Polonsky had a photo on Twitter holding his jeans, which for some reason were torn at the crotch.

I made my position clear immediately and unambiguously: if some lout insults and attacks you on the tram the only thing you can do is put him in his place. Tussles of this kind are no great rarity, not only in television studios but even, let's face it, in the chamber of the State Duma.

The broadcast of *The NTV Show* was inexorably approaching. The station featured it in every hourly advertising break. The result was that a rather ordinary programme about the financial crisis, from which all I had to say about a people's privatisation was cut, beat all the ratings records. Did the management of NTV know they were setting me up for a criminal prosecution?

Polonsky could come up with nothing smarter than to write the following appeal:

To the President of the Russian Federation, D.A. Medvedev
To the Chairman of the Government of the Russian Federation, V.V. Putin
To the Patriarch of Moscow and All Russia, Kirill

Esteemed Dmitry Anatolievich! Esteemed Vladimir Vladimirovich! Your Holiness! There are moments in the life of every person when they need the counsel of their elders. Today is one such for me. I request your advice.

Non-businessman Sergey Polonsky

The victim of this 'brutal assault' was for a long time reluctant to involve the law enforcement agencies. There was, in reality, nothing for him to complain about: a torn pair of jeans and a bruise on his rear trochanter, registered a full four days after the incident, do not add up to evidence of a crime. At most, this could have served as the pretext for bringing a private case for compensation in a magistrate's court.

There are thousands of such episodes in Russia every day. Someone fills in someone's face. How many times has Vladimir Zhirinovsky got into a scrap right in the chamber of the Duma? One might have expected people to laugh and move on. Public opinion seemed to be on my side. Polonsky's provocative behaviour had earned him such a bad reputation that the public saw his little setback as a triumph of justice.

The general feeling was expressed by an anonymous commentator, who wrote to me on LiveJournal: 'Alexander Yevgenievich, your hand was powered by all the suffering people of Russia who are derided by such chancers as Polonsky.' Dmitry Rogozin, at that time Russia's representative at NATO, wrote on Twitter, 'Well done, Lebedev! Although it's naughty to fight, you gave him a lesson he deserved. Good man.'

On 21 September, however, on the birthday of the then senior helmsman of interior affairs policy, Vladislav Surkov, a meeting of the Coordinating Council of the All-Russian Popular Front was held, during which Alexander Shokhin, president of the Union of Industrialists and Entrepreneurs, unexpectedly decided to raise this burning issue with the leader of the APF, Vladimir Putin.

'We have a Front and don't fight anyone, while they don't have a front and go boxing each other's ears. It's hooliganism,' Putin joked and asked Shokhin whether the Russian Union of Industrialists and Entrepreneurs had an ethics committee.

'We do,' Shokhin responded, 'but fortunately these two squabbling businessmen are not members of the RUIE, and neither has complained about the other.'

'Well, we do have veterans in the APF, not very young but very strong,' the prime minister remarked with a laugh. 'There are organisations of veterans of the military operations in Afghanistan. They could give our squabblers' hide a tanning they wouldn't forget in a hurry.'

'The lessons from *The NTV Show* programme could be analysed,' Shokhin suggested.

'Good luck to them,' Putin said, ending the discussion. 'Imagine how they fight over money. They'd tear each other's throats out.'

It needs to be said that Mr Shokhin was being disingenuous. Firstly, because both National Reserve Bank and National Reserve Corporation were members of the RUIE and regularly paid their dues towards its upkeep. Secondly because, at Shokhin's suggestion, I had invested $100,000 in a company called The Russo-Chinese Centre for Trade and Economic Cooperation, which was run by Sergey Sanakoev.

A hooligan 'motivated by political and religious hatred'

It was ten days after this categorisation that Polonsky's epic statement was sent to the head of the Investigative Committee:

To the Chairman of the Investigative Committee of the Russian Federation, A.I. Bastrykin.

Application for the initiation of criminal proceedings under Part 2, Article 116 and Part 1, Article 213 of the RF Criminal Code in respect of Alexander Yevgenievich Lebedev, born 1959. (According to information obtained from the Internet, A.Ye. Lebedev is a deputy for the Sloboda District Duma of Kirov province of the Russian Federation).

In connection with the widespread public outcry in Russia and abroad over the incident described below, I request you to instruct the director of the Investigative Directorate of the Investigative Committee of a subject of the Russian Federation to initiate criminal proceedings, to conduct a thorough inquiry, and bring criminal charges against Alexander Yevgenievich Lebedev for hooliganism and battery motivated by hooliganism.

On 16 September 2011, at approximately 18:00 hrs (plus or minus 5 minutes) in the Ostankino television studio (located at 12, Academician

Korolyov Street, Moscow), during the recording of a broadcast of 'The NTV Show', in which A.Ye. Lebedev, S.F. Lisovsky and I were taking part as experts, A.Ye. Lebedev, who was sitting to my right, having special training and martial arts combat skills, knowing that we were watched by numerous people in the television studio, unexpectedly struck me three heavy blows to the head with his fists after I had uttered the incomplete sentence, 'Three years ago this very person ...' (I pointed with my hand to the right where Lebedev was sitting).

On account of the unexpectedness of the attack by A.Ye. Lebedev and the heavy blows to which I was subjected, I fell together with my chair into a gap behind the podium. Fortunately, thanks to my physical fitness and army training in the parachute troops, I avoided serious injury from the blows in the region of my head, from falling into the gap, and from colliding with hard, protruding parts of the stage structure, otherwise resultant consequences in the form of my suffering trauma threatening to life and health would have been inevitable.

It can now be confirmed that the blows by A.Ye. Lebedev were intentionally inflicted on me by his fists to the vitally important temple region of the head, and these targeted blows were intended to lead to all manner of consequences, including my dangerous fall head first with unforeseeable consequences.

Witnesses to the incident were the citizens present in the studio, and also the presenter of the NTV programme, Anton Krasovsky.

Everything that occurred is objectively registered on the video recording, which I am also providing to the investigative authorities.

The conformity of the actions of A.Ye. Lebedev to the offence provided for in Point 'a', Part 2, Article 116 of the Criminal Code of the Russian Federation, is obvious: while present at a public event, he attacked me, motivated by hooliganism, and inflicted blows on me which caused me physical pain, including as a result of my subsequent fall. The presence of 'motivation by hooliganism' is confirmed by the awareness of him (Lebedev) of the public nature of his unlawful actions.

Assaulting me in front of numerous members of the audience as a person participating in a discussion on a television programme is not only a violation of my physical privacy, but also a grave challenge to public order. And disregard of the interests and tranquillity of the many citizens present at the recording of the television programme is a manifestation by A.Ye. Lebedev of ostentatious ignoring of generally accepted norms of behaviour in public places.

Moreover, having professional training and possessing combat skills of attack and defence, A.Ye. Lebedev during the attack on me used his skills, which are qualified as 'the use of weapons' in the definition of evidence of hooliganism (Point 'a', Part 2, Article 213 of the Criminal Code of the Russian Federation). However, let the final legal definition of the unlawful actions of A.Ye. Lebedev be determined by the investigative agencies.

After his publicly committed act of physical violence, A.Ye. Lebedev continued to violate public order by unlawful acts, provoking me to conflict, but I did not yield to this provocation. The hooligan doctor of sciences, A.Ye. Lebedev, was well aware that a large number of spectators were watching the proceedings.

Later I learned that, when preparing his attack on me, some six minutes before the planned attack, A.Ye. Lebedev performed special warm-up exercises of his fingers and hands, before the cameras, in front of many people, after which he 'leaped up and ... delivered three lightning-fast blows to the head' (see the printout of the online publication and attached video).

It should be noted that the targeted blows inflicted by A.Ye. Lebedev, aimed at the easily damaged temporal region, are, according to the Regulations for Determining the Severity of Physical Injuries and in forensic medical practice, agreed to be life-threatening and injurious to health at the time of the inflicting of such blows.

These wilful actions of A.Ye. Lebedev, applying the skills of professional inflicting of blows, fall within the remit of Point 'a', Part 1, Article 213 of the RF Criminal Code.

After the incident, A.Ye. Lebedev not only showed no repentance for what he had done but admitted his initiative in committing an unlawful action and boasted, 'I struck first because I see no reason to allow a punch to land if you know you are about to get it. But there was no fight and no one got beaten up. I did no more than slightly freshen him up. I neutralised him.' (See the attached printout of the Internet publication.)

Yes, there genuinely was no fight (that is, no exchange of blows). But I was assaulted, and that there were no serious consequences was no thanks to the offender. The main point is that A.Ye. Lebedev, motivated by hooliganism, using his fists, inflicted three targeted blows to my head and the adjacent part of my body. And everything occurred in the presence of a large gathering of people.

Lebedev's claims aimed at justifying himself, that he was supposedly acting in a state of necessary self-defence and attacked first in order 'not to allow a blow to land', are untenable. The claim is refuted by the video recording and the statement of NTV presenter Anton Krasovsky that 'Polonsky did not provoke anyone and behaved appropriately. In this programme Polonsky behaved absolutely appropriately. One could sense that he had come to discuss serious matters' (see the attached printout of the online publication).

On the contrary, provocative remarks impugning my dignity were constantly being made throughout the whole broadcast by A. Lebedev sitting on my right, and by S. Lisovsky to my left. However, having mastered the relevant practices of self-discipline (including Chi Kung, the ancient Chinese practice of managing energies), I did not succumb to provocation and did not go beyond the limits of what is permissible.

In conclusion I wish particularly to emphasise that this crime was perpetrated by a doctor of science, a parliamentary deputy who is perfectly aware of the harm his misconduct does to the prestige of Russian politicians. Of course, he (Lebedev) has partly achieved his goal – he will now go down in history. As a black stain on Russian television broadcasting, as a doctor of science and a deputy who committed an act of bare-faced hooliganism.

The foregoing testifies to the great danger to society of the personality of A.Ye. Lebedev, since behaviour of this kind shows open contempt for Russian society and fosters the propagandising within it of a cult of violence and indiscipline. The criminal nature of the act is aggravated also by what was perpetrated, exploiting one of the most popular Russian television channels, namely NTV.

What occurred in the television studio has received a great deal of publicity and, in particular, Vladimir Putin, the Prime Minister of Russia, at a meeting with representatives of the All-Russian People's Front, characterised A.Ye. Lebedev's actions as hooliganism.

On the basis of the above, in the light of Article 140, Part 1, Point 1, Articles 141, 144, 146, 447, and 448 of the Code of Criminal Procedure of the Russian Federation; Articles 213, Part 1, 116, Part 2 of the Criminal Code of the Russian Federation, and also Point 11 of Directive of the

Plenum of the Supreme Court of the Russian Federation No. 45 of 15.11.2007 'On judicial practice in criminal cases of hooliganism and other crimes motivated by hooliganism'

I REQUEST:

If information about the election of A.Ye. Lebedev to the post of deputy of the Sloboda District Duma of the Kirov Region of the Russian Federation is in fact the case, that a criminal case be opened against Alexander Yevgenievich Lebedev in respect of Article 448, Part 1 of Article 11 of the Criminal Procedural Code of the Russian Federation on the perpetration against me of hooliganism and battery.

In connection with the widespread public outcry in Russia and abroad at what occurred in the NTV studio, to conduct an inquiry and take a procedural decision to institute criminal proceedings directly by the Investigative Committee of the Russian Federation.

I am prepared to provide all further clarification on the substance of the attached materials when explanations are received from me in connection with my complaint about a crime. [sic]

Sergey Polonsky

Yes, Polonsky really did claim the hands of the 'hooligan doctor of science' were weapons. But even more interesting is the following document, which appeared three days later:

To Deputy Head of the Investigative Directorate of the Northeast Administrative Region of the Central Investigative Department of the Investigative Committee of the Russian Federation for Moscow, D.S. Trubin.

In connection with a request from the chairman of the Investigative Committee of the Russian Federation, I ask you personally to carry out an inspection in accordance with Articles 144, 145 of the Criminal Procedural Code of the Russian Federation in respect of deputy of the Sloboda District Duma of the fourth convocation for the Ilyinsky Constituency No. 5 of Kirov province A.N. [sic – AL] *Lebedev who on 9/16/2011, being present at a recording of 'The NTV Show' television programme, in gross violation of public order, expressing manifest disrespect for society, publicly beat S.Yu. Polonsky with his fists.*

In the course of the enquiry, objectively establish all circumstances of the incident, visit the television station where the recording took place, request a copy of the relevant videorecording, inspect it, establish the contact telephone numbers of S.Yu. Polonsky and A.N. Lebedev, take measures to have them summoned to the Investigative Department and questioned on the circumstances of the incident, after which, no later than 10/6/2011 submit to the Central Investigative Department of the Investigative Committee of Russia for the City of Moscow a draft directive on the instigation of a criminal case under Article 213 of the RF Criminal Code.

> *Director of the First Department*
> *of Procedural Control,*
> *S.V. Bessarabov*

A report was immediately compiled:

To the Director of the Investigative Department for the Northeast Administrative District of the Central Investigative Department of the Investigative Committee of the Russian Federation for Moscow, Colonel of Justice, S.V. Frolov.

REPORT
on the detection of evidence of a crime

I have to report that on 18 September 2011 at approximately 22.30 hrs on the NTV television channel, being a mass news medium, a television programme, The NTV Show, was broadcast, during which one of the participants of the programme, A.N. Lebedev [sic], in gross violation of public order, expressing manifest disrespect for society, beat with his fists S.Yu. Polonsky, another participant in the programme.

In connection with the fact that in the actions of A.N. Lebedev there is detected commission of a crime under Point 'a', Part 2 , Article 116 of the RF Criminal Procedural Code, taking account also of the fact that A.N. Lebedev, as a deputy of Sloboda District Duma of the fourth convocation for Ilyinsky Constituency No. 5 of Kirov province as an elected member of an institution of local government falls into the category of persons in relation to whom a special procedure for the conduct of criminal cases applies, I consider it necessary in respect of the above incident to carry out an inquiry in accordance with Articles

144–5 of the RF Code of Criminal Procedure by forces of the Investigative Directorate of the Northeast Administrative Region of the Central Investigative Department of the Investigative Committee of the Russian Federation for Moscow.

> *Deputy Director of the Investigative Directorate of the Northeast Administrative Region of the Central Investigative Department of the Investigative Committee of the Russian Federation of Moscow, Captain of Justice, D.S. Trubin.*

And immediately, on the basis of that report, a directive was issued:

DIRECTIVE
on initiation of a criminal case
City of Moscow, 4 October 2011
13:50 hrs

Director of the Central Investigative Directorate of the Investigative Committee of the Russian Federation for the City of Moscow, Major General of Justice V.V. Yakovenko, having considered a report on the detection of evidence of a crime of 3/10/2011, registered in the Criminal Acts Registration Book of the Investigative Department for the Northeast Administrative District of the Central Investigative Department of the Investigative Committee of the Russian Federation for Moscow, Reference No. 66pr-2011 of 3/10/2011,

HAS ESTABLISHED:

Alexander Yevgenievich Lebedev, being a deputy of Sloboda District Duma, Kirov province, on 9/16/2011, at approximately 18:00 hrs, being located at 12 Academician Korolyov Street, Moscow, at the premises of the Ostankino Television Technical Centre, during the production of the television programme 'The NTV Show', did publicly, in gross violation of public order, expressing manifest disrespect for society, inflict several blows with his fists in the region of the head on S.Yu. Polonsky, causing the latter physical pain as a result of which the latter fell from a chair.

In view of the fact that in the actions of A.Ye. Lebedev there is detected commission of a crime under Point 'b', Part 1, Article 213 of the RF Criminal Code and in accordance with Articles 140, 145, 146, Part 1 of Article 156, Part 1 of Article 447 and Part 1 of Article 448 of the RF Code of Criminal Procedure,

HAS RESOLVED:

1. To instigate a criminal case against Alexander Yevgenievich Lebedev on suspicion of commission of a crime under Point 'b', Part 1, Article 213 of the RF Criminal Code.

2. To assign to the criminal case the Reference No. 693852, to delegate the conducting of the preliminary investigation to the head of Babushkinsky Interdistrict Investigative Department of the Northeast Administrative District of the Central Investigative Department of the Investigative Committee of the Russian Federation for Moscow, Major of Justice Roman Dmitrievich Sirotin.

3. To send a copy of this directive to the Prosecutor of the City of Moscow.

Director of the Central Investigative Department
Major General of Justice V.V. Yakovenko.

The lawyers could not believe their eyes: without any pre-investigation checks, without even interviewing those involved in the incident, overnight a criminal case is instigated under Article 213, Part 1, Point 'b', 'Hooliganism, that is, gross violation of public order, expressing manifest disrespect for society, committed on the grounds of political, ideological, racial, national or religious hatred or hostility or on the basis of hatred or hostility towards any social group'. Up to five years imprisonment. This is the same article under which members of the Pussy Riot group were convicted, only they came under Part 2: 'as part of an organised group'.

What evidence was there of my harbouring 'racial hostility' or 'religious hatred'? Indeed, what had the Investigative Committee got to do with any of this? How did Bastrykin come to be involved in it? If a citizen believes he has unfairly received a punch in the face but has no injuries to show as a result, he goes to the local policeman, and from there to a magistrate, where he himself acts as the prosecution. Instead, to investigate this crime that had been dreamed up over the course of several days, the entire Babushkinsky district department of the Investigative Committee, where the television centre was located, was brought in.

Later, the case was taken further up the ladder to the Department for Investigation of Especially Important Cases of Crimes Against the State and

Economy. A seven-man brigade of investigators was taken away from investigating murders and other serious crimes falling within the purview of the Russian counterpart of the FBI to pick over something not worth a hill of beans. Among other things, they conducted a search at Ostankino and seized a recording of the programme, but it was the edited version that was broadcast, not the studio original.

The difference between them was that we were sitting in the studio for over two hours, while what was broadcast was only forty-eight minutes after being cut by the editors. The full record, from all twelve cameras, which entirely clarified the incident, was of no interest to the investigators. The questioning sessions, to which I was dragged every week, were like a bad theatre performance.

'Were you in Ostankino on 16 September?'

'Yes.'

'Did you beat Polonsky?'

'No, I defended myself.'

'Did you intend to kill him or cause him grievous bodily harm?'

'Are you taking the piss?'

Advocates and Acrobats

Soon Alexander Dobrovinsky got in on the act as Polonsky's lawyer, an individual well known in certain circles. The fact is that Dobrovinsky is not exactly a lawyer and not exactly Dobrovinsky. He was previously known by the name of Kusikov, his grandfather, Ruben Kusikov, having been the younger brother of poet Alexander Kusikov; a member, along with Sergey Yesenin and Anatoly Mariengof, of the 'Order of Imaginists'. At what is described in documents issued by the military recruitment office as conscription age, he decided he would prefer to go to France, where his mother, a former ballerina, lived.

There Kusikov became Aivazyants and drove a taxi. In those years, Aivazyants supposedly completed his higher education, although we have been unable to find information about him in any European educational institution.

In 1992, at the age of thirty-eight, this gentleman, by now under his third surname of Dobrovinsky (I have yet to meet a woman who changed her surname twice), returned to Moscow and opened a legal office. Among his clients were both 'business bosses' like the Chernoy brothers, who once controlled aluminum production; Semyon Mogilevich, who figures on the FBI's list of most wanted criminals; and Yevgeny Rybin, who fought YUKOS. In the record of Dobrovinsky's career there are other episodes about which further information is required. Here we will merely mention them.

In spring 1998, Rashit Sharipov, chairman of the board of directors of Magnitka, disappeared together with thirty per cent of the company's shares. These surfaced shortly afterwards, strangely enough in the possession of Dobrovinsky, who explained he had bought them on behalf of a foreign company. In 2008, when Vladimir Nekrasov, the head of Arbat-Prestige, a chain of perfume and cosmetics stores, landed in jail, Dobrovinsky took the helm of the company.

Then in 2013, this gentleman acquired the notorious Pushkino Bank, from which its former owner, Alexey Alyakin, had by then withdrawn all the assets. A few months later it went bankrupt, leaving the state to deal with a black hole of 15 billion rubles [$500 million] and more than 60,000 depositors. Dobrovinsky's name was linked in the press with Vyacheslav Ivankov (Yaponchik) and other gangland bosses.

Dobrovinsky appeared as a player in my 'lawsuit' on Vladimir Zelensky's talk show on the Russia channel, where the Ostankino incident was being discussed. He announced that he intended not only to see me punished with the assistance of Russian law enforcement, but also to sue me in a British court, claiming compensation in the amount of £10 million for 'moral harm' caused to his client. That this was not an empty threat I soon found out.

Mikhail Fridman, the owner of Alfa Group, invited me to speak at his Colour of Night club in Bolshoy Kozikhinsky Street. The format was that they would invite somebody interesting to an informal charity evening. They announce the event, people reserve tables, and there is then a question-and-answer session. It would be a sin to shirk contributing to a talk show in which Dmitry Bykov, Kseniya Sobchak, Chulpan Khamatova and many other genuinely interesting people had participated!

After an hour of conversation, a young woman popped out of the semidarkness of the hall. She had the demeanour of a provincial model and shoved a packet into my hands. Thus did I learn of the existence of the British law firm of Carter-Ruck. This is a well-known office specialising in media and defamation cases. Among British journalists it is considered a badge of honour to be sued by Carter-Ruck. Certainly, the firm's reputation as a go-to for claimants led to it being christened, by the satirical magazine *Private Eye*, 'Carter-Fuck'. In his later life, the firm's founder, the late Peter Carter-Ruck, asked if the magazine would drop this moniker. Instead, they started calling him 'Farter-Ruck'.

The handing of documents to a defendant is a standard stage of British judicial procedure. A London court will not accept a claim until the defendant has been formally notified (which is why the late Boris Berezovsky pursued Roman Abramovich for several years, finally cornering him in an Hermès store). The touch of vaudeville in my case had all the signs of classic Dobrovinsky, who had heard about my talk from announcements on the club website. I was not hiding from anyone and had not refused to see Polonsky in court.

It hardly seems likely that Polonsky was serious about suing for libel. As far as this gentleman's business reputation in the United Kingdom was concerned, it was far from positive. He invested a portion of the money he had moved from Russia in the Beetham Tower project, a building in Bankside in London. It is a huge tower resembling an Australian boomerang. The idea initially provoked protests from the city's population, because of its negative impact on the historic setting. After the financial crisis, when Polonsky and his companions were unable to service the loans they had taken against construction, Royal Bank of Scotland took over the project itself.

Be that as it may, it felt to me that the focus was not on winning a court case, but on causing the defendant as much trouble as possible and trying to force him to settle out of court. There were several little dramas similar to the one at the Colour of Night, and each time it was claimed that 'Lebedev was trying to avoid justice'. The last occasion on which I was served with a writ was during a public lecture I gave on global corruption at Chatham House in London.

All this apparent hocus-pocus is standard legal procedure in England but anyone in my position might also feel it helps show the client that the law office is busy earning its fee. And its fee is not going to be small. I had no option but to spend several tens of thousands of pounds on lawyers in two years and I would be surprised if Polonsky paid Carter-Ruck any less.

After the softening up with heavy artillery bombardment, Dobrovinsky came forward with a 'peace plan'. Through my lawyer, Henry Reznik, he proposed we should 'settle our differences'. We met at the Not Far East, a restaurant on Tverskoy Boulevard. Polonsky arrived dressed in a style favoured by gangsters in the 1990s: Adidas tracksuit bottoms with a red windcheater. Dobrovinsky did the talking, and I had a sense that Polonsky was present purely as furniture. He was tense and gloomy, his thoughts elsewhere.

At the end of the meal, I asked to be left alone with Polonsky. I wanted to get a complete impression of him. He immediately started addressing me using the familiar 'ty': 'Sasha, I so much respected you, but after what you did it became impossible for me to stay in Russia. You ruined my karma. You know, for me this is now the most important thing in my life, because the whole country is on your side.'

I said, 'Well, if you think the whole country is on my side, perhaps it's not a good idea to carry on stirring things up? I've said publicly that I mistook your gesture in my direction for a threat and overreacted.'

Polonsky nodded. 'Well, fine. Of course. But I'll do what my lawyer says.' He meant, of course, Dobrovinsky.

Our encounter convinced me finally that it was not Polonsky who had initiated the criminal case. Just as previously with Submariner Fyodorov, this guy was a pawn in someone else's game. To tell the truth, I feel sorry for Polonsky. He has been in jail on a trumped-up charge for over two years now, and the prosecutor's office is asking for an eight-year sentence. He has obviously crossed swords with some highly influential businessmen, who have appropriated a proportion of his development projects. He is yet another victim of business predators and his own mistakes. Something tells me, though, that we have not heard the last of him.

A few days later, Dobrovinsky phoned my lawyers: 'Pay me five million.'

'On what grounds?'

'Those are my fees.'

In return his client would do us the favour of withdrawing his absurd statement to Bastrykin and stop the court case in London.

Polonsky sent me a text message: 'Sasha, you are cool. I understand you. I don't need this money, but we need to do as my lawyer says.' This overlooked the fact that the criminal charge was a public matter: it had been brought by the state in the form of the Investigative Committee. How was it supposed to be possible to settle the matter between ourselves? Dobrovinsky made no reply.

I know how much legal services cost. I seem to have rubbed up against every well-known legal firm in the world, and at this time the process of filing a lawsuit against General Electric was in its final stages. The total cost of preparing and pursuing the claim in a London court amounted to some

£7 million, but that was for several years of work, and here was Kusikov Aivazyants-Dobrovinsky retaining a prestigious London firm to do the real and above board work but then trying to get me to pay him a comparable sum for doing nothing, by intimidation. It was a common or garden try-on, an attempt at extortion, blackmail.

We tried to appeal against the bringing of a criminal case, but got nowhere. The investigation ground on. I was periodically summoned for questioning, asked the same questions, gave the same answers. For the umpteenth time in fifteen years it became an integral part of my routine. You become accustomed to anything, and all but forget that procedurally you are a suspect. All that changed was the Articles under which I was being charged. They became less serious.

In late 2011 and early 2012, the 'creative class' protested in Bolotnaya Square and on Sakharov Avenue. An important event occurred in my personal life when Yegor, my third son, was born. It became clear that the predators trying to seize my business were not going away and a new hunt began. That was the price I had to pay for the public investigations I had been conducting for over ten years. One morning I opened my eyes and realised I did not want to go on living. I had lost all interest. That was the most terrible ordeal that has so far befallen me.

CHAPTER 12

Faithful to the Legacy
of Dr Goebbels

A present for the New Year

The New Year is a national holiday when, by tradition, we give each other presents. In 2012, we found a very special surprise waiting for us under the New Year tree, but it was not Grandfather Frost who burst into National Reserve Bank, it was the Tax Inspectorate bringing us a 'comprehensive inspection', and inspectors from the Central Bank in numbers unprecedented in the history of the Russian banking system. Mezhprombank, mentioned above, where no less than 30 billion rubles [$1 billion] of unsecured loans from the Bank of Russia disappeared without trace, was inspected by sixteen people; the Bank of Moscow with its 172 divisions merited eighty people.

In both those cases, Russia's vigilant regulator embarked on an inspection only after everything had already been stripped from the bank, despite the fact that the regulator can see the problems of any financial institution online: banks report twice a day; everything is completely visible. In our case, it was a bare six months since the end of the last unscheduled, targeted inspection, when they had been unable to find fault with anything. Accordingly, the appearance of 130 inspectors, under the direction of a certain Yelena Pitukhina, looked like a barefaced hit.

The inspection was carried out as if it was a security forces' special operation. The inspectors descended on our head office and all nineteen of the bank's regional offices. The 'paratroopers' were most interested in my current account, as well as in documents relating to the financing of humanitarian and media projects: *Novaya Gazeta*, the *Independent* and *Evening Standard* in the United Kingdom, the Gorbachev Foundation and Raisa Gorbacheva Foundation, the Elton John AIDS Foundation, the charities of *Vogue* magazine and of Natalia Vodianova and Chulpan Khamatova.

I have never had any secret accounts. Ever since the memorable Skuratov Hunt I have made a point of keeping my finances as transparent as possible. In National Reserve Bank there is an account into which money I earn is paid: my salary and dividends as the bank's principal shareholder. These funds, minus spending on my family and personal needs (which are rather modest), I spend on charity and various socially useful causes. It was precisely this account that was subjected to the closest scrutiny.

Simultaneously, a massive disinformation attack was launched on me personally. I cannot remember so much dirt ever before having been flung at an entrepreneur or public figure. This time the main channel was the Internet. First, a dedicated anonymous site appeared, devoted exclusively to my humble self. This resource served as a matrix from which materials were reposted on hundreds of websites and repeated in thousands of blogs.

The following sites turned to publishing negative materials: moscow-post.ru, inright.ru, compromat.ru, flb.ru, stringer, wek.ru, the news agencies Interfax, Rosbalt, Novy Region, and Agentstvo politicheskikh novostei – Severo-zapad [Political News Agency – Northwest]. Also involved were highly 'respectable' publications, like the official mouthpiece of the Russian government, *Rossiyskaya Gazeta*, *Trud* [Labour], and *Tribuna*, and so on.

Black PR served, as before, to provide a background for administrative actions and operations by the security forces. The attack was mounted from several directions. The first was my business. The inspection of the bank was accompanied by periodic leaks of confidential information compromising bank secrecy. This was primarily information about the accounts of VIP clients. Here is a letter addressed to me from the executive director of the Interfax international news group:

To the President of National Reserve Bank, A.Ye. Lebedev

Dear Alexander Yevgenievich,

I offer my deepest apologies for publication on the finmarket.ru site of material entitled 'Are Reserve Finances a Song that Is Over?'

This item was published in the 'News from our Partners' section, which publishes commercial press releases rather than editorial texts. According to our house rules, items in this section, which are received from outside companies, must be agreed with the head of the Finmarket company and, where need be, with senior staff of Interfax. In this instance that procedure was grossly violated.

The director of Finmarket's advertising service and her subordinates have been dismissed and the director general of the Finmarket agency has been fined. We have closed the 'News from our Partners' heading on the Finmarket website. The item 'Are Reserve Finances a Song that Is Over?' was taken down from the site immediately we became aware of its existence.

At the present time we are continuing a detailed internal investigation, and will inform you of the results.

What occurred is a violation of the principles and standards of the editorial policy of Interfax and of our house rules, and we shall draw the necessary conclusions to ensure there should be no repetition of such situations in the future.

Yours faithfully,
Vladimir Gerasimov
Executive Director

The article referred to in this letter was on the subject of NRB. To the credit of the senior management of this respected news agency, they caught and punished staff who had condoned the placing of 'advertorial' material. That did not, unfortunately, help me a great deal. As a result of such publications, the impression was given that our bank was about to close and that I would be sent to jail. The flight of clients and investors, who were just beginning to get over their jitters after the last onslaught, resumed with renewed vigour.

Neither in Heaven nor on Earth

The bank was not the only prey of interest to the 'hunters'. As mentioned above, after being elected in 2014 to the State Duma, unlike many businessmen turned deputies, I left my leadership position at National Reserve Bank and instructed managers, to whom I transferred the business on trust, to invest money in the real sector of the Russian economy. The priorities identified were aircraft leasing and air transportation, agriculture and affordable housing. These are sectors where the state always plays first fiddle, but I decided to try to demonstrate that private business had a role to play there, too. That was how I saw my 'social responsibility'.

The fate of our aviation projects was far from smooth. I have written above about Ilyushin Finance, which was created to rescue Russian civilian aircraft production by placing orders with state-owned factories: Voronezh Aircraft Production Association and Ulianovsk Aviastar Aircraft Production. At first the company belonged 80 per cent to us and 17 per cent to Vneshekonombank: we contributed 2.5 billion rubles [$83 million], and Vneshekonombank contributed 500 million. Later Rosimushchestvo, the Federal Property Management Agency, appeared among the shareholders (its shares later being transferred to the United Aircraft Construction Corporation).

Up until 2006, the state contributed 9 billion rubles through a secondary offering and we contributed 5.5 billion. That left us with a 26 per cent holding. In all those ten years we received only 120 million rubles [about $4 million] in dividends.

That is two per cent of the money invested. For comparison, National Reserve Bank, of whose capital the Federal Property Management Agency owns 2.7 per cent, paid 870 per cent in dividends to the state budget over the same period.

In parallel, in order to support demand for aircraft, we created the wholly private airline Red Wings. It leased medium-range Tu-204s from Ilyushin Finance and became the largest operator flying new Russian aircraft. Moreover, we paid higher rates for leasing them than we would have for second-hand Boeing and Airbus aircraft, which all the other Russian air companies, including Aeroflot, were flying. Our investments in Red Wings added up to over three billion rubles. Thus, our modest contribution to the rescue of an entire state-run sector came to around 11 billion rubles in hard cash.

In 2010, the government had the idea of buying out our stake in Ilyushin Finance through Vneshekonombank (it was not a question of a deal, but of returning money we had invested). This was intended to enable us to buy (again through Ilyushin Finance) new aircraft for Red Wings from Ulianovsk Aircraft Production. At the same time, it was suggested to Aeroflot that it should buy a blocking stake in Ilyushin Finance from me at a discount. Vneshekonombank thus gained full control over Ilyushin Finance, and the company became its aircraft-leasing subsidiary.

The scheme was negotiated over several months and finally Sergey Ivanov, who at that time was deputy prime minister overseeing the aviation industry, sent a letter to the prime minister, which he endorsed 'Agreed'. At first everything went according to plan. Aeroflot bought almost seven per cent of the shares of Ilyushin Finance at a discount to the market price and our holding in the national air carrier fell below the blocking threshold. The stock market price rose sharply, and within a month of the deal Aeroflot had made two billion rubles [$67 million].

It was at this point that strange things began to happen. The proposal for Vneshekonombank to buy out Aeroflot's blocking stake in Ilyushin Finance was not, to my surprise, approved by the Supervisory Board of Vneshekonombank. Their justification was that 'the asset is overpriced'. The matter was then simply taken off the agenda. The end result of this saga was that we had lost our blocking stake to Aeroflot.

At that time there were discussions within the government over the fate of the new medium-range Tu-204-SM passenger jet project. This modern aircraft, which had already passed all the stages of certification, was to replace the Tu-204, which had been manufactured by the Ulianovsk factory since the 1990s and was analogous to the world's most popular models of this class, the Boeing 737 and Airbus A-320. The main problem facing Russia's civilian aircraft industry was the lack of supply in this segment.

All resources had been focused on a 'Superjet', in which billions of dollars were invested. The Superjet, however, was a short-range (regional) aircraft. It could replace the Soviet Tu-134 and Yak-42, but was no competition to Boeings and Airbuses. There was good reason why Boeing and the European Airbus corporation did not produce aircraft for this niche, where the global market had long been shared between Brazil's Embraer and Canada's Bombardier. Moreover, some seventy per cent of the Superjet consists of imported components. It is in effect a 'complete knock down' assembly, only put together in Russia.

Production of the wide-body, long-haul Ilyushin-96 had by this time stopped altogether; the medium-range Tupolev-154 was already aesthetically and technically obsolete (the last one was assembled by Aviakor in Samara in February 2013). To launch into mass production, an initial customer order was needed, an airline that would actually carry passengers on these planes.

The suggestion was then made that Vneshekonombank should extend a loan to Ilyushin Finance, which would give the Ulianovsk plant a large order for forty-four aircraft. Red Wings would lease and start operating these. In the government, everything was added up and it was realised that, not only would the loan be returned to Vneshekonombank with interest, but the state budget would receive billions of dollars through taxes on the whole chain from production to operation. That would be on top of a functioning production facility and new aircraft.

That would seem to have clinched the deal, and it could now be expected to go ahead. At this point, however, an 'analytical note' appeared in the government's White House, according to which the whole project had been devised solely to enable me to steal all the money allocated by Vneshekonombank. The most ridiculous thing about this was that, in the scheme as proposed, the money came nowhere near me. It went from a state bank to a state leasing company, and from there to a state aircraft factory.

The private company Red Wings got to play the least rewarding role in terms of revenue: it had to operate the aircraft, pay for leasing them, earn a profit and thereby contribute to the state budget through taxation. The 'note', however, had the effect its anonymous author evidently desired.

Next, a State Duma deputy from the 'A Fair Russia' party, Andrey Tumanov, editor of a newspaper called 6 Sotok [6 Hectares], who had not previously been known to have any connection with aviation, sent a request to the Prosecutor General that I be charged with criminal liability for 'attempting to destroy the Russian aircraft industry' and 'lobbying foreign manufacturers.' He quoted as the source of his information, Leonid Ryzhov, leader of the trade union at Voronezh Aircraft Production Association. These accusations were being made against someone who (in Ilyushin Finance and Red Wings) had invested some 11 billion rubles of his own funds in the Russian aviation industry!

The suborned media immediately picked up this 'news'. Ryzhov himself appeared and declared that he had never said anything of the sort and had had no contact with Tumanov. I wrote a letter to the Prosecutor General asking him to bring criminal charges against the parliamentary provocateur for his false denunciation. In vain. The upshot was that the project to build the Tu-204-SM was buried.

The handwriting was remarkably similar – first a Duma deputy's request, then publications – in the campaign to discredit an agricultural project we have been implementing since 2006 in the Tula and Bryansk provinces. In Russia most potatoes are grown as a subsidiary business or in smallholdings. There was no industrial-scale production at that time. On the basis of the Maxim Gorky state farm in the village of Popovka, in the Chern district of Tula province, we created the National Land Company, specialising in potato farming.

National Land Company acquired over 50,000 hectares of land, purchased the latest German equipment and built huge facilities for storage, sorting, washing and packaging the crop. Additionally, we opened a new plant in Popovka to puree and dry potatoes. It was at first fitted out with Dutch and subsequently also Russian equipment.

National Land Company has become the largest potato farm not only in Russia but in Europe, harvesting up to 250,000 tons annually, almost two kilograms per head for everyone living in Russia, including infants. We grow wheat, oats, barley, buckwheat, flax and maize. Our ultimate aim is not only to produce the raw material, but to create a genuinely Russian brand of Petrushka healthy food cafes, and feed people in the provinces at prices lower than those of McDonald's.

More than 1,500 people in the inveterately drunken depths of the provinces now have a well-paid job. National Land Company has participated in all the agricultural exhibitions, won awards and gained numerous certificates, both Russian and international, for the quality of our products.

One 'fine' day we learned from the mass media that a State Duma deputy belonging to the far-right Russian 'Liberal-Democratic' Party, Dmitry Litvintsev, representing the Volgograd region, had written a request to Gennadiy Onishchenko, the director of Rospotrebnadzor, the Federal Supervision of Consumer Rights Service, demanding an emergency inspection of our farm. The reason given was the deputy's suspicion that our potatoes were being grown on land 'contaminated by radiation as a result of the Chernobyl nuclear power plant accident in 1986.' In addition, it was alleged that NLC was using banned pesticides and that its products were a danger to health and life.

An inspection immediately arrived at the farm, paralysing our work at the height of the busy harvesting season. It was found that everything Litvintsev had written was a lie, but our reputation in the market, which had taken years to build, had been sullied. Not only we, but all the other agricultural producers in the region were affected − after all, it was not logically possible for the radioactive pall to have been confined only to land where National Land Company was operating.

The next target for attack was our affordable housing project. By 2012, the project was stalled: without supporting infrastructure from the state it was impossible to move forward, and claims against the bank limited the possibility of investing in it. At this point an open letter from seventeen incensed residents of the Moscow region was published in the government's official *Rossiyskaya Gazeta*. It was addressed to the prosecutor's office and the then governor, Sergey Shoygu. The signatories demanded I should be brought to book for not having built homes for them. I had promised to provide them with affordable housing and let them down.

In the letter I was compared to Sergey Mavrodi, the builder of the MMM pyramid scheme. From the text it might have appeared I had taken money from these people, but in fact, unlike Polonsky's Mirax and other 'developers', National Land Company never took deposits. We always built with our own money, and then sold the houses to whoever wanted to buy them.

Since officialdom had been sent a signal, it had to react. There were inspections and interrogations. The absurdity of the whole thing was blindingly obvious, and it soon became apparent that the supposed signatories of the letter had never signed anything of the sort. It was a straightforward forgery. It did, however, discourage me from trying to continue the project.

The Ukrainian 'Front'

Quite separately, the attack on my Ukrainian business interests was developing. Unlike other foreign investors, I did not take profits out of Ukraine but invested them in new facilities or spent money on charity. The main problems for investment in Ukraine have always been the ubiquitous corruption and grasping bureaucracy, who make the climate unfit for working in.

Unlike in Russia, where stability appeared with the arrival of Putin, the regimes in Ukraine were continually changing. Each new cohort of rulers brought with them a horde of senior managers, and the first thing they did was set about a redistribution of property.

The redistribution consisted, at the very least, of robbery. It was a cross between the musical comedy *The Wedding in Malinovka* and the soap opera *Santa Barbara*. It was particularly obtrusive under Yanukovych, when not a week passed without raiders with the nationalist trident on their cockades coming to demand bribes from our managers, threatening otherwise to make off with everything. Nothing deterred them, neither contacts with the high-ups nor the good work we were doing.

The most protracted conflict with the Ukrainian authorities arose over the renowned Ukraine Hotel (under the Soviet regime it had been the Moscow Hotel) on Independence Square in Kiev. In 2004, while Leonid

Kuchma was still in power, these authorities suggested I should invest in reconstruction of the hotel. A dilapidated pile built in 1961, it was to be transfigured into a five-star hotel.

A joint venture was established in the form of a private joint-stock company belonging fifty per cent to the Presidential Administration and fifty per cent to National Reserve Corporation. The Administration, which had the hotel on its books, contributed the building to the business capital, and we put in what in those times was a sizeable investment of $23 million. Thereafter, National Reserve Corporation was to reconstruct the hotel and begin operating it.

The project was agreed by all the top officials, including the then prime minister, Yanukovych. I had an official meeting with him and two other gentlemen. In order to fill in some spare time, the prime minister suggested a game of cards, and promptly took a pack out of his pocket.

In short, all the statutory procedures were observed. We invested our money in Hotel Ukraine, paid for the architectural design and were about to start on the preparatory work when the 'Orange Revolution' occurred. President Yushchenko came to power, and the first thing he did was try to take back the hotel on Independence Square. The prosecutor's office filed a lawsuit, and Prime Minister Yulia Tymoshenko issued a Cabinet directive with a plan to de-privatise the hotel. One of the points in this plan sounded very curious: 'Adoption by the Economic Court of Kiev of a ruling recognising as unlawful the decision to establish the Hotel Ukraine Company.' In other words, a 'correct' decision on the part of Ukraine's Themis was pre-planned.

The court battles – both economic and administrative – dragged on for years. All this time, the pile continued to fall apart, but its managers scrupulously carried off to Ukraine's Presidential Administration all the cash that passed through the hotel's accounts, and even the interest from National Reserve Corporation's financial contribution to the company's capital, which was deposited in the bank. In total $2–3 million annually found its way into other pockets.

A criminal case was fabricated against my friend and adviser in Kiev, Vladimir Tkach, a Russian citizen, and he spent four years behind bars, despite an appeal from the Russian State Duma in his defence, and the efforts of Vladimir Lukin, the Russian human rights ombudsman. When Volodya was finally released on bail, which I pledged, his health had been irretrievably undermined and he passed away shortly afterwards.

In the course of five years we won every court case, including litigation, in the Supreme Court of Ukraine. It seemed justice had triumphed and we should be able to resuscitate the reconstruction project, but the regime changed once more, Yanukovych became president and everything again began from scratch. The courts started, as if to order, to hand down completely contrary verdicts.

Yet another attack on our business was launched with the involvement of Sergey Kivalov, a former chairman of the Central Economic Committee of Ukraine and today a deputy of the Verkhovna Rada. He was assisted by his lawyer-daughter Raisa Bogatyryova, secretary of the National Security and Defence Council; the head of Yanukovych's secretariat, Sergey Levochkin; and the head of the Administration, Andrey Kravets. By 2012 all possibilities of defending our rights within the Ukrainian judicial system had been exhausted and we filed a lawsuit with the European Court of Human Rights, which accepted it as admissible.

My 'well-wishers' in Moscow evidently decided they could exploit the conflict with Yanukovych's entourage, and on 19 October 2012, I read the following news item:

> Russian oligarchs are secretly supporting candidates on the eve of elections to the Verkhovna Rada in the hope of recruiting lobbyists in the new parliament of Ukraine. This was announced by participants of a press conference in Kiev on Thursday.
>
> 'Today there is evidence of the influence of Russian transnational companies on Ukraine. It is being seen in such sectors as energy, the tobacco industry and others. Today, there is a definite influence from Russian oligarchs on the course of elections in Ukraine, this is manifested in the support of first-past-the-post candidates in Crimea, Kiev and Kiev region.
>
> 'This applies first and foremost to the Russian businessman, Alexander Lebedev, who is supporting candidates from such parties as Svoboda [Freedom], Udar [The Blow], and Batkivshchyna [Fatherland] parties. We cannot fail to be disturbed by this. The result might be that there are deputies in the newly elected parliament who will defend the rights and promote the interests not of the Ukrainian people, not of the voter, but of a Russian oligarch,' said Lyudmila Lukinova, a specialist at the National Academy for Public Administration.

'It would seem that Mr. Lebedev, having certain problems in Russia, has decided to engage in economic expansion in Ukraine,' comments Oleg Vernik, an expert at the Commonwealth of Independent States Election Monitoring Organisation. 'Although actually, in light of the news about Lebedev's visit on President Putin's birthday, the oligarch's oppositional credentials are in doubt, both in Russia and in Ukraine.

'The Russian businessman is putting his pre-election eggs in several baskets, financing and supporting candidates standing for election to the Rada from different parties, all the way from Svoboda by way of Udar to Batkivshchyna. It has been reported that Mr Lebedev is already buying up land in the Kiev region. Today that is possible only with the support of the local authority.

'Under Ukrainian law provision of finance and support by transnational companies to particular candidates is illegal. This is a direct threat, because in the end there may be deputies in the new parliament who are promoting the interests of transnational capital. We shall accordingly focus maximum attention on this issue,' Vernik warned.

In my blog I advised 'Ukrainian political analysts' to remember to eat pork fat when drinking their horylka in order not to talk alcohol-fuelled nonsense, which all the above suspiciously resembled. The next day, however, this drivel provided the basis for a dramatic performance played out at the gates of the Russian embassy on Vozduhoflotsky Avenue in Kiev. A crowd several hundred strong turned up with banners reading: 'We will not surrender Ukrainian territory to the oligarch Lebedev!', 'Lebedev get out of Ukraine!', 'Putin take Lebedev home!', 'Hands off the black earth of Ukraine!'

They brought along some brooms and a mini-belfry to whose tolling they chanted, 'Lebedev, this bell tolls for you!'. They hanged a dummy bearing the inscription 'Lebedev' on a gallows. Having made a lot of noise for an hour and a half, the anonymous 'civic activists' left in an orderly fashion, the time for which they were being paid having evidently expired. A week later, officers of the Security Bureau of Ukraine descended on my hotels in Alushta, and the usual 'inspections' began again.

'Nazi' and 'National Traitor' rolled into one

The ongoing 'hunt' was not confined only to my business interests. Someone had my good name in society in their sights, and the civil initiatives to which I have devoted a good deal of attention in recent years. There was no limit to the scurrilousness of what was written in numerous publications by the same few authors.

On the one hand it was argued that 'There is no such thing as a former KGB officer', and Lebedev was Putin's mole among the liberals in Russia and simultaneously in the English establishment. He was tasked with undermining the protest movement of Russia from within and freedom of the press in Britain. On the other hand, I was accused of being an agent of Western intelligence and the secret leader of a fifth column of 'national traitors' tasked with destroying Russia's sovereign independence.

Before the clamour of the 'protest' in Kiev had died away, a column of young people wearing surgical masks popped up on the nationalist 'March for Russia' on 4 November. (I suspect they were the same rent-a-mob as had demonstrated on Vozduhoflotsky Avenue) chanting 'Lebedev for Mayor!' Young people handed out leaflets with swastikas and the following text to anyone who would take them:

Stop a Rerun of the 1937 Purges!

Our country is rapidly sliding into a new totalitarianism. In just one year, searches have become commonplace, interrogations and the arrest of legal political activists just for daring to join demonstrations against the Party of Swindlers and Thieves. The number of criminal cases under Article 282 of the Criminal Code for blameless videos, texts and comments posted on social media is snowballing.

The church bureaucracy, which has long had nothing to do with spirituality is trying to drive our society back to medieval obscurantism, as the verdict in the Pussy Riot trial, founded on decisions of medieval Christian church councils, starkly illustrates. Again, as in 1937, no one who has an opinion different from the government line can feel safe.

The free press has been all but crushed. Alexander Lebedev, the publisher of the last remaining opposition newspaper *Novaya Gazeta*, is being prosecuted under Article 213 of the Criminal Code, officially for giving a well-deserved slap on a TV broadcast to that fat pig Polonsky, who has robbed and cheated hundreds of thousands of people who waited in vain for new homes, the man who openly said, 'Anyone with less than a billion can go stuff themselves.' The real reason is that Alexander Lebedev dared openly to speak out in defence of Pussy Riot, providing their lawyers with bail money and supporting them at the court hearing.

The system has not forgiven him for this.

We, autonomous nationalists, say: ENOUGH!

We are the youth of the street against the senility of the Regime.

We are civil society against the ossified, thieving bureaucracy.

We are the Russian people against international mob rule.

We are European freedom against Asian tyranny. We are the indigenous people against the hordes of foreign workers.

We demand:

Stop political repression: release immediately all prisoners of conscience, regardless of their political views;

Release the girls of Pussy Riot from jail;

Stop the criminal prosecution of Sergey Udaltsov and Alexander Lebedev;

Investigate the abduction and torture of Leonid Razvozzhayev, bringing in international observers and experts;

Observe your own Constitution! We demand freedom of speech and freedom of assembly in accordance with the Constitution of the Russian Federation;

Repeal articles 280, 282 and 205, Part 2 of the Criminal Code as politically based;

Dissolve the political police (the 'Centre for Combating Extremism');

Vet the members of United Russia and staff of the political police;

Dissolve the State Duma as not legitimately elected and hold snap parliamentary elections with access for all political forces;

For Rus! – Without swindlers, thieves, oligarchs, police brutality and immigrants!

The next day, the cesspits of the Internet were bubbling with postings of the following kind:

Is Lebedev Financing the March for Russia to Undermine Russia's State Sovereignty in the Interests of Western Intelligence Agencies?

As you will know, a double agent makes a living by working for two spy services simultaneously. He may work for two countries which are allies or two which are at war. Often, such a person only seems to be a double agent, because he is deliberately being used by one side to feed false information to its enemy.

'In 2003 Berezovsky said, "We will all be shot by lieutenants, but Putin personally will shoot Lebedev,"' Alexander Lebedev proudly recalled the other day in an interview with Oleg Kashin.

Why would Putin, the president and chief Russian secret policeman, soil his hands personally with ex-secret policeman Lebedev? It can only be because Lebedev has done something really monstrous, even in the eyes of an organisation as cynical as the KGB-FSB.

Alexander Lebedev was recruited by the KGB while studying at the Moscow State Institute of International Relations. In 1987–92 he was a spy in the United Kingdom, but the salary of a spy was evidently not enough for him. He registered a private company and, while pretending to be a spy, engaged in business (although in theory it is supposed to be the other way round). There was nothing distinguished about Lebedev's work in London, except that he accumulated a small amount of start-up capital. Nothing romantic, nothing heroic, and in 1991 Alexander retired and went into business.

But here is what is really interesting. Later, the UK authorities, having learned that Lebedev had been a spy, did not deny him re-entry or the opportunity to do business. They were exceptionally obliging to Lebedev and went out of their way to help him develop his business. Lebedev even bought up such highly authoritative newspapers of the Old World as the *Independent* and the *Evening Standard*, and his son, with tears in his eyes (literally!), adopted the citizenship of Great Britain, lives there and manages his father's business.

According to reports in the foreign media, the Lebedevs, father and son, are welcome guests in the most select aristocratic homes in London. Lebedev was allowed to organise a party, boastfully called a charity ball, on the estate of Earl Spencer Althorp [*sic*], the brother of Princess Diana (it was in this castle [*sic*] that the young princess spent her early years). At Lebedev's party, wolves and camels roamed the 8,500-acre estate, and this was only one of the bizarre entertainments offered to the guests.

* * *

What reasons could there be for London's high society to open its arms to an ex-Soviet KGB officer? To a person who in former times was paid £700 a month as a spy at the Russian embassy in London? The answer is only too obvious.

All Lebedev's doings in Great Britain during the Soviet period and his current political activity in Russia testify at the least to someone playing a dual game.

Let's face it, Lebedev's every step in Russian politics is in the interests of Western ideology and foreign capital. To put it bluntly, all the oligarch's so-called 'opposition' activities are directed at undermining the structure of the Russian state.

For example, in 2009 Lebedev attempted to become mayor of Sochi, and already during the election campaign began trying to destabilise preparations for the Winter Olympics – in the interests of their Western adversaries. Even after the refusal to register him as a candidate, he switched to supporting Boris Nemtsov. Then, three years ago, the whole 'liberal clique' living off foreign grants assembled in Sochi: there were Kasianov and Kasparov and Yashin, and countless directors of pseudo-charitable societies. Alexander Lebedev too spent time there, one of the cash cows of this pre-election commotion.

Incidentally, that same year of 2009 Lebedev's black Audi, escorted by a BMW X5 bearing three bodyguards, was several times to be seen in the compound of the British Embassy. What could this former secret agent of Soviet espionage have forgotten at the ambassador's? Or was he delivering new reports? Getting new instructions?

* * *

Last year Lebedev made media celebrities with a worldwide reputation out of ordinary hooligans – the Pussy Riot punk band. These young madams who had offended the feelings of believers became heroines in the West, not least thanks to reporting in his English newspapers.

By a deserved twist of fate, for assaulting Sergey Polonsky, Alexander Lebedev may today be given a real term in prison under the same Article as Pussy Riot, namely hooliganism perpetrated 'on grounds of political, ideological, racial, national or religious hatred or hostility, or on grounds of hatred or hostility towards a group in society.'

It is curious that Lebedev continued to incite hatred along these lines even while still unaware of which article he would be charged under for Polonsky. During the March for Russia journalists were astonished to see, and later wrote about, posters with the wording 'Lebedev for mayor of Moscow', 'Alexander Lebedev – our mayor', 'Lebedev, nation, freedom'.

In St Petersburg, framed by imperial black-yellow-white flags, those joining the March for Russia carried the selfsame posters. In addition, leaflets with the following content were observed: 'Alexander Lebedev, the publisher of *Novaya Gazeta*, the last remaining opposition newspaper, is being prosecuted under Article 213 of the RF Criminal Code.'

In fact, the criminal case against Alexander Lebedev is wholly unconnected with politics, but is connected only with the oligarch's aggression and psychological instability. Those on the March for Russia had no time for such details.

Naturally, nobody carries placards like that without being paid, and people do not hand out leaflets of that kind unless there is a 'consideration'. So it was only to be expected that the leader of the 'Lebedev' column in Moscow should astonish journalists by telling them that 'Alexander Lebedev is a unique type of Russian oligarch who stands up for the common people.'

Excuse me, but who are these 'common people' Lebedev is standing up for? Even after being elected the deputy for Sloboda District Duma in Kirov province, he had nothing but contempt for that depressed constituency. He has been seen there just three times: two of them during the election campaign when he promised the peasants to invest millions of rubles.

Instead of which Sloboda province sank into a deep crisis: more than a hundred cows died on the farms from starvation and the cold! Deputy Lebedev and his friend Belykh, the 'liberal' governor of Kirov province, do not give a damn about famine in the district: putting money into demonstrations by the nationalists looks far more worthwhile in reports back to the London 'Party Committee'.

* * *

After the wave of news reports about Lebedev financing the March for Russia, the oligarch's publications made a feeble attempt to defend him, claiming that those bearing placards in favour of Lebedev were agents provocateurs.

There were, however, far more placards than just one. Moreover, in St Petersburg huge banners reading 'Lebedev is Russia's Hero!' were spread out on the roofs of houses, beside which stood people with lighted flares. Their actions bore no resemblance at all to provocation.

It is clear enough why Alexander Lebedev appeals to the nationalists: they are hoping for financial support. According to *Forbes*, he is one of the top 100 billionaires. More puzzling is why Lebedev should be supporting people who give the Nazi salute.

Note that Alexander Lebedev participates in any ruckus. He does not just revel in any provocative actions designed to undermine Russia's sovereignty: he supports and instigates them.

Who has an interest in sowing in turmoil and instability in our country? These, after all, are not just actions intended to discredit the Government: they are blows struck against the underlying principles of our society, against morality and eternal ideals. Lebedev, no matter how rhetorical it may sound, is doing his utmost to destroy the love of Russians for their Motherland. He disseminates horror stories to the Western press, which is only too pleased to publish them.

By the way, Ukraine which is now only too painfully aware of the cost of interventions by the West, has already sent Lebedev off with a flea in his ear. A protest demonstration outside the Russian embassy in Kiev demanded Lebedev be 'given the bum's rush' out of the country, accusing him of financing national socialist parties in the Verkhovna Rada elections. The Ukrainian government, meanwhile, is reviewing the legality of how Lebedev acquired assets there.

Will Russia finally resolve to send this provocateur Lebedev off on a permanent business trip to Great Britain, or perhaps even further away than that? The sooner the better!

The idea of making me the nationalists' poster boy was, in my opinion, well targeted: it represented a serious threat to my reputation. It was only the execution that was forgettable. That last paragraph gave the game away, exposing the aim of the whole campaign of vilification. As during earlier broadsides, a succession of Helpful Henries appeared, all advising me to emigrate; as before, I flatly refused. That did not, of course, prevent rumours about my supposed emigration being spread. To this day many people believe I am based in London.

Below the belt

In Luc Besson's cult film *Léon*, twelve-year-old Mathilda asks the main character, a professional hitman, 'Can you do away with absolutely anyone?' Léon replies, 'Except women and children. That's the rule.' The criminal world has its own laws and ideas about honour, 'rules' under which families never get drawn in criminal disputes. Taking hostages and using family members to blackmail a victim is prohibited. No one observed this rule in my case. Realising they were getting nowhere with me, my adversaries decided to strike at my family.

I met my wife Yelena when I was a State Duma deputy. I received a letter from her father. (I read nearly all the letters I received, thousands every month.) Lena, who at that time was still a minor, had got entangled in criminal goings-on that all but deprived her of a future. She had fallen in with bad company. Her boyfriend, more than fourteen years her senior, turned out to be a drug dealer and forced her into selling drugs. Lena was caught in a sting. She agreed to cooperate with the police and helped them arrest the main drug dealer in Novosibirsk province.

In the course of the investigation, she herself took part in a sting operation, complete with a concealed microphone, car chase and shooting, which almost cost her her life. She was the key prosecution witness, and without her testimony the case would have collapsed in court. The defendants, by now in pre-trial detention, were continually sending her 'kites' through acquaintances, threatening her and demanding she should withdraw her testimony. Under the Criminal Code and Criminal Procedure Code then in force, Lena faced the same charges and a sentence of up to twenty years.

Formally, the law made no distinction between a person who had made it possible to bring an organised criminal group to justice and any other member of the gang. The officers promised to appeal to the prosecutor's office to take the help she had given the investigation into account at the hearing, but that proved to be just hot air. There is a saying that 'sincere confession is good for the soul but bad for the verdict.' Nobody was guaranteeing her anything.

I began studying the matter. Not being a lawyer, I brought in experts, including some from abroad. Russians are familiar from Hollywood crime movies with the concept of plea bargaining. It is common practice in the West, and one of the most important tools in combating organised crime. It arose because mafia families are highly secretive communities, and in a genuinely independent court system with adversarial procedures and good lawyers it can be impossible to prove the guilt of mafia chiefs.

For this reason, the key witness can often be a minor figure in the group, and usually one not involved in really serious crimes, who testifies in court. In return, not only are no charges preferred against such people, but they are put on a witness protection programme to prevent the mafia from taking revenge.

We held several round-tables about this in the State Duma and they led to proposals for amendments to the Criminal Code and Criminal Procedure Code. I had the support of a number of my fellow deputies: Andrey Makarov, a famous lawyer; Vladimir Vasiliev, the chairman of the security committee; Vladimir Pligin, chairman of the constitutional legislation committee; and Vladimir Gruzdev. What decided the matter was the view of the president. I argued for this change in the law at a meeting with Vladimir Putin, and he agreed to it.

The upshot was that Russian law now recognises pre-trial bargaining with the investigation. It is an innovation that has subsequently led to the detection of thousands of serious crimes, like contract killings and embezzlement, and to the destruction of networks for trafficking in human beings and drugs. As for Lena, the court hearing took place in 2007. The main defendants were given substantial terms of imprisonment, and she was given a suspended six-year sentence. After three years the sentenced was lifted.

In December 2012, Oleg Luriye, a journalist with a history, published an exposé in his blog in which he raged about the injustice of the universe. Lena, he claimed, had avoided prison only because she found an influential patron.

'According to the Constitution, the laws of Russia, as also the Articles of the Criminal Code, apply equally to everybody. Only in this country winds blow from different directions, and we surmise that if the person holding the fan is Alexander Lebedev, the billionaire and "fighter against corruption" who never tires of exposing in his media and Internet resources the bribe takers and embezzlers, the wind becomes a tornado, sweeping away laws, courts and penal codes,' Luriye wrote. Needless to say, Russia's 'media and Internet resources' instantly began a massive campaign to propagate his 'masterful investigation'.

We can sympathise with Luriye, no doubt; he had only come out of prison a year previously himself, having been jailed for blackmail (a tale analogous to that of Yulia Pelekhova – he had demanded money from a victim to induce him not to publish compromising materials). So the man needed money and this nice little earner came his way.

The problem was that in his blog he published copies of evidence from the criminal case and court hearings. This was a case involving a gang of drug dealers, one of whom was shortly to be released and that posed a serious threat to my wife's safety. Even that was evidently not enough for the people behind all this. Fake pornographic videos were posted on anonymous Internet sites, allegedly filmed in the Ukraine Hotel where, it was claimed, I was disporting myself with young women. Needless to say, this fakery had nothing like the impact of the video featuring 'a person resembling the prosecutor general' in Yeltsin's time.

The character assassins then adopted a different approach, and a woman from the Sloboda district was invented who was said to claim I had seduced her daughter, taken her to Moscow and turned her into a sex slave. Needless to say, the woman did not actually exist. It was a complete fabrication, generated in the mind of someone who was evidently not very bright. The fabrication found its way, however, not only to the usual cesspit websites, but even to the website of *Moskovsky Komsomolets*.

Sloboda district found its way into this libel because in 2011, at the suggestion of Nikita Belykh, the governor of the province, I stood in the elections for the Sloboda District Duma. There was no whiff of misuse of government resources in the campaign and the elections were entirely free and fair. Even here, however, black PR was in evidence. Leaflets were distributed in Ilyinsky multi-mandate constituency where I was standing as a candidate, asserting that Alexander Moiseyevich Lebeder [sic] had turned up in the fair land of Vyatka to get his hands on the whole of the forest.

When I was elected deputy, the newspapers wrote that this was a cunning ploy to enable Belykh to appoint me to the Council of the Federation. (Amendments had just been passed stipulating that only a regional, or at least local, deputy could become a senator.)

Nikita had no such plan in mind. He simply wanted, through me, to give a boost to the people in one particular district, at the same time as introducing me to the reality of how those in very remote places live. For my part, I did what I could to help my constituents: we renovated two schools, set up computer classes, provided ambulances for the village medical emergency team, and repaired the water mains.

I will never forget giving a talk in a village classroom about travelling with my son to Papua New Guinea, and showing our adventures on a big screen. The children clapped. I could never have imagined that shortly afterwards I would read the likes of this:

Oligarch Deputy Does Not Give a Damn about Famine in his District

On a state farm in Sloboda district, Kirov province, a hundred cows have starved to death. The farm's deficit was not all that terrible, only 5.5 million rubles [$183,000].

For comparison, in Perm region an agricultural enterprise has debts of almost 900 million rubles [$30 million], but the authorities are trying to rescue it.

'Oh, dear. We had such hopes of him, we thought he would help us, that's why we voted for him,' a former milkmaid from the village of Osintsy laments. And indeed, the residents of Sloboda district did, with an enthusiasm entirely understandable for voters in a remote rural part of Russia, elect a banker, someone who owned so many businesses, a billionaire for heaven's sake (!), Alexander

Lebedev to be the deputy for their district.

They were hoping, of course, for investment. They hoped that Lebedev, like Roman Abramovich, since he had come on the scene would support their district. He had promised a lot: 'tens of millions of dollars' (his words), investment in low-rise housing, in agriculture. Lebedev told the village people fairy stories about how he wanted to 'work the land'; he was really just like them, an ordinary, almost a country lad, only with lots of money, and he would not grudge it, he would share it with them.

Instead of that, Lebedev turned up only three times in a year to meetings of the Duma. Even when the deputies were electing the head of the district there was no sign of him – he flew off abroad. And the total amount of his, no, not investment, just a pittance! – was a little over a million rubles [$33,000]!

Instead of investments, of opening factories which would give jobs to people, instead of real help to local agriculture, Lebedev tossed an UAZ van to the hospital, a minibus to the school, a few computers and a little cash to repair a couple of classrooms. That was it. That was the extent of the oligarch's beneficence.

Nobody saw Lebedev solving the problems of the district's agricultural enterprises, nobody saw him working to develop or adopt programmes of socio-economic development. [...]

Alexander Lebedev became a deputy of Sloboda district for three reasons. The first was that nobody was going to let him, a businessman with a tarnished reputation, into national politics. Lebedev, a former KGB officer, built his business on dubious links with former officials and politicians under the influence of foreign states. Since the 1990s Lebedev had become accustomed to sucking money out of the state – his projects constantly received support from the budget. That is what Lebedev needs politics for: in order to move closer to the budget trough. But the state gets nothing in return.

In the capital, unlike the hospitable but naive back-of-beyond, everyone already knows this. The residents of Sloboda district had no idea, of course, why an oligarch was so eager to get into their Duma.

The second reason follows logically from the first: Lebedev wanted to use his position as a deputy to become a senator representing Kirov province in the Council of the Federation. By this time he had gained the support of Nikita Belykh, the governor of the province, but his senatorial ambitions came to nothing.

Some wretched Sloboda district and its problems (repairing the roads, street lighting, mains gas), with its cows starving to death, are hardly going to be of the slightest interest to the oligarch now. By the way, some experts have already suggested that Roman Abramovich should be taking issue with Lebedev, because he is discrediting the idea of representatives of big business giving support to particular territories.

Banker Lebedev's indifference to the woes of the territory to which he promised so much casts a shadow on serious businessmen in government positions. The voters will inadvertently begin tarring them all with the same brush: 'Oh, they promise the earth but the cows in their own districts are left to starve.'

The people living in the district are, by the way, very much insulted by Deputy Lebedev's take-it-or-leave-it attitude and are just waiting for the next elections to sort him out good and proper. 'It's just a pity it won't bring the cows back,' they say.

Having read my way through this masterpiece by an unknown soldier of the PR front, hiding behind the pseudonym of 'Marta Valieva', I reflected sadly that Krutakov, Ryazhsky, Pelekhova, and this Luriye were the mammoths of an era we thought we had left behind. They are incapable of emancipating their minds and thinking out of the box. This new generation of warriors are not only highly creative, but also very disciplined. They work in strict accordance with the maxim of that foremost ideologist of Nazi Germany, Josef Goebbels: 'The more monstrous the lie, the more willingly people will believe it.'

Inside the information war

My adversaries were acting in accordance with a clear plan of military-style operations which had been elaborated by an HQ. I was able to establish that this really was the case after reading a progress report on their 'special operation', which came into my hands:

Aims and Objectives of the Project

Throughout the entire period:

The *aim* is to achieve a critical level of discomfort for the Target on the territory of Russia, the Commonwealth of Independent States, Western countries and the USA by creating pressure in the public news, legal, corporate financial and personal spheres.

Overall Long-Term Objectives:

Create a negative social context and motivate the authorities and citizens to take action against the Target.

Create a negative business reputation and ostracism of the Target by business circles.

Deprive the Target of property and/or inflict maximum loss on him.

Current tasks for the initial period, 15 September 2012 to 31 January 2013:

Create an initial platform for instigating lawsuits, primarily on the territory of the CIS, gradually 'warming up' the news arena (the mass media, Internet) to that end. In circumstances where it proves impossible to instigate legal proceedings in a case for procedural reasons, publish facts to inflict maximum reputational damage.

Within this framework:

1. Demonstrate to the Russian and Ukrainian government authorities that the Target is extending financial support to marginal and extremist political forces.

Information has been disseminated associating the Target with the financing of objectionable opposition forces in Kiev province, Chernigov province and Crimea, as well as giving financial support to Svoboda, an extremist 'black hundred' movement. By the end of this period, provide supplementary coverage in the media associating the Target with the financing of extremists in Russia (the 'March for Russia').

A narrative of interference by a Russian pseudo-oppositionist in the affairs of Ukraine has been put out, and indications have been given that the accumulation of his start-up capital in Ukraine was predatory and corrupt.

By the end of the period, disseminate news about corrupt ties to Kuchma, including his dominant position (about 50 per cent) in the Gazprom securities market (financial surrogates in respect of payments due for Russian gas) and business privileges obtained thereby. Elaboration of the theme of illegal acquisition of real estate in Crimea and Kiev. Before the end of this period, a campaign in the mass media.

During the election campaign for the Verkhovna Rada, a panel discussion was televised in which political experts confirmed the Target's intention to interfere in the political and economic situation in Ukraine.

Within this period, exploitation as a media item of a protest rally against the Target conducted outside the Russian embassy with involvement of Ukrainian human rights activists and the media, as well as of Russian media.

Within this period, distribution of fact sheets relevant to subsequent media campaigns.

On the day of the March for Russia in Moscow on 4 November 2012, one of the columns carried placards and chanted slogans in support of the Target. There was also a demonstration by participants in the banned March for Russia in St Petersburg with placards in support of the Target.

Within this period, this will be further developed in the media. Agreement has been reached with the leaders of nationalist groups in Russia for small protest demonstrations by radicals with slogans in support of the Target in a number of East European and Western countries.

Within this period, several demonstrations will be held and reported in their media.

2. Establish and expand collaboration with government organisations responsible for counteracting the Target as an individual destabilising society and the state.

The issue of financing by the Target of opposition parties and radicals has been brought to the attention of the press services of the Administration of the president of Ukraine, and has been included in news summaries submitted to the top leadership.

Within this period, a monthly bulletin is being prepared for the newly elected Verkhovna Rada for distribution in the chamber of parliament.

The issue is being discussed with the Ukrainian Prosecutor General's Office of presentation of evidence by Major Melnychenko, who bugged President Kuchma's office, about the Target's corrupt relations with the first person of the state. News of his arrival and provision of evidence relating to the murder of Deputy Shcherban (connection to Yulia Tymoshenko) has been disseminated to the media.

Within this period, a media campaign on possible initiation of a criminal case against the Target based on Melnychenko's testimony.

3. Through individuals in authority and by direct contact, encourage official institutions in Russia and Ukraine to initiate criminal and civil proceedings against the Target. Provide them with ongoing support in conducting such proceedings.

Contact has been established with the Ukrainian Prosecutor General's Office in respect of illegal actions relating to the privatisation of the Ukraine Hotel, with a view to possibly initiating a criminal case of causing damage to the state.

Within this period, conduct an audit of Energobank (where funds of the company owned jointly by the Target and the state are deposited and used by the bank itself) with media coverage. Operational measures to establish complicity of the Target.

Contact has been established with the senior management of the United Trade Unions of Ukraine, with a suggestion they should ask President Yanukovych to conduct an audit of Energobank (owned by the Target), where a portion of the funds of the trade unions are deposited, as well as on the question of halting the activity of one of the Target's partners for illegal handling of the aforementioned funds.

Within this period, organise an audit of Energobank and the Trade Union Fund, with media coverage.

An audit has been initiated of European Insurance Alliance, an insurance company owned by the Target.

Within this period, detect infringements of the law, cause a gradual withdrawal of the client base and cause cessation of operations.

In Russia materials have been prepared for conducting an audit of two sets of real estate transactions in Moscow, with the prospect of instituting criminal proceedings.

Within this period, organise inspections by the tax authorities at the request of a Duma deputy, establish opportunities for instituting criminal proceedings, have the dubiousness of transactions covered in the media.

In Russia (Novosibirsk) negotiations are being conducted with two individuals involved in a case of drug dealing (Kholodkov, Karapetov) directed against the Target's civil partner, Yelena Perminova, with the aim of obtaining testimony from them about her real role in the case which was not reflected in the court's verdict.

Within this period, conduct a campaign in the media and establish the possibility of further criminal proceedings.

In Russia (Novosibirsk) a criminal investigation operation is being prepared in respect of drug traffickers using accounts in a branch of the National Reserve Bank.

Within this period, possible initiation of criminal proceedings, disclosure of information to the media.

4. Obtain and process information from publicly available and archived sources, recruit individuals willing to communicate information of interest which is not obtainable for analysis from official sources. Encourage former and current employees of the Target's corporate organisations to collaborate, also with a view to employing them operationally in later stages.

In the United Kingdom, Timan Oil & Gas is being examined by an auditor and lawyer to establish possible violations of the rights of the company's shareholders. (Results awaited.) Preparations have been made for the possible purchase of shares in the company by a professional able to supervise work with minority shareholders.

In Russia, confidential information has been obtained on the state of mining assets from a representative of Roskomnedr. In connection with a delay under the licence agreement the Target has 'resolved' the issue of extending missed deadlines by one year for two major deposits in the Komi republic. The deposit in Makhachkala is of little interest, and, in all probability, the Target is not prepared to engage with it. To comply with the licence agreement will require about $35 million, and as a result shareholders in Timan Oil & Gas are being advised to reduce their holdings in return for new investments in the company and to bring the company back to the stock market.

Within this period, prevent the company from attracting investment, create dissatisfaction among the minority shareholders, make the conflict with the company's shareholders public, and make it impossible to fulfil the licence agreement. Identify the Target with infringement of shareholders' rights. At the same time, organise audits in Russia and cast doubt on the legality of the decision to extend the licence agreement, examine the circumstances of the trial extraction and annual sales of the product (about 3,000 tons). Arrange coverage of the dispute in the Russian and UK media.

In Ukraine (Kiev), an operation has been conducted to obtain the collaboration of Energobank staff [...].

Within this period, disseminate news in the media about falsification of accounts and dubious transactions of Energobank. Requests by deputies addressed to National Bank, the State Property Committee and the Prosecutor General's Office for audits of the bank's activities for possible initiation of criminal proceedings. Acquire and exploit inside information from persons expressing a willingness to collaborate.

In Ukraine, a minority stake has been purchased in Energobank for use in appeals to the law enforcement agencies and to deputies.

Within this period, send enquiries to Verkhovna Rada deputies from the Party of Regions (Yanukovych) and send deputies' enquiries to the Prosecutor General's Office. Publish in the media expressions of concern by a group of shareholders regarding the state of affairs in Energobank.

In Ukraine (Kiev) the legal position is being explored in respect of the company jointly owned by the Presidential Administration and the Target which was formerly the proprietor of the Moscow Hotel (now Ukraine Hotel). An article has been published in the

Ukrainian issue of *Kommersant* indicating that the state is entitled to receive a portion of the funds contributed by the Target to the initial capital ($21.5 million) upon liquidation of the company. Final ruling by the Supreme Economic Court of Ukraine regarding liquidation of the company.

Within this period, expand discussion in the media of the damage caused by the Target to the state in terms of illegal privatisation of the hotel and the receipt of revenues from it, depositing of funds from the initial capital of the company owned jointly with the state in Energobank to enable it to function. Also, deputies' enquiries addressed to the State Property Committee and the Prosecutor General's Office. Work with the Prosecutor General's Office to initiate a criminal case relating to causing damage to the state.

From insider information from Ukraine, it has been established that the Target is involved with a public company which has been prepared in the United States for listing on the Nasdaq exchange for transferring and anonymising assets in excess of $100 million.

In the United States contact has been made with a security consultancy with close links to the FBI. It has discovered secret information about the Target dating to before 2009. The company is prepared to enter into a contractual relationship.

Within this period, prevent the use of this public company and find analogous companies with the same owners and directors and initiate an enquiry into them. Publish information in the foreign and Russian media about the creation of a tool for laundering illegally acquired funds.

Also from insider information from Ukraine it has been established that the Target has an involvement with the Pan-European Internet Communications Company, of which a Ukrainian Internet company (brand name RetNet) is part.

Within this period, establish where all divisions of the company are registered and the sources of its financing.

In Russia six people have been identified through the services of a recruitment agency who are current or dismissed employees of National Reserve Corporation, Prom Tech Leasing, the National

Housing Corporation, or Red Wings Airlines. These individuals have been interviewed regarding possible employment. Two of them [...] are potential sources of important corporate information.

Within this period, enter into relations with these individuals to obtain further corporate information and make use of it.

In Russia a statement has been prepared addressed to the Federal Agency for State Property Management (by prior agreement) from a company providing free servicing of minority stakes in banks, in order to raise the company's profile.

Within this period, obtain the right to represent the state's shareholdings in National Reserve Bank, Russian Capital and three miscellaneous other banks in order to acquire additional information and possibly file lawsuits on behalf of the shareholder.

Contact has been established with Natalia Arkhipova, the dispossessed founder of Kairos Bank, and an offer made to assist in restoring her violated rights and obtaining compensation. Her decision is awaited.

Within this period, publications in the media about the fraudulent acquisition of the shares of Kairos Bank.

The Ukrainian Independent Trade Union of Transport Workers has sent a request for information to the trade unions of workers in the German aviation industry seeking clarification of the situation surrounding the bankruptcy of the Blue Wings airline.

In the present period, conduct a journalistic investigation in Germany and transmit its results to Russia and the CIS.

In Russia the situation surrounding the Red Wings airline is being studied. It has become known that said company was acquired by the Target after the 'shutting down' of a criminal investigation into illegal operations with aircraft parts. It is surmised that this situation continues today.

Within this period, organise verification by Rostekhnadzor of the newness of the aircraft components used, and a tax inspection of schemes of withdrawal of resources. In Russia the Target has been contacted by a foreign businessman and preliminary agreement was reached for the transfer of a number of assets to his management. Contact has been interrupted owing to the Target's departure from Russia.

Within this period, resume contact for reaching a possible deal and gaining control of assets.

In the United Kingdom contact has been made with representatives of Rupert Murdoch's company (a media conglomerate in competition with the Target). A willingness has been expressed to publish materials about the Target as they become available.

Within this period, provide such materials.

Tasks planned for the period 31 January to 15 September 2013:

Exploit the evidence base and media background created during the initial period to inflict maximum damage on the Target in the West, making him the object of multiple investigations.

Expand the receipt and study of information needed for organising of civil, criminal and socio-political actions against the Target beyond the borders of Russia and the CIS.

Gain access to confidential information of the Target's key Cypriot agent, identify hidden connections and suspect transactions.

Within this period – gain access to the company documents of relevant individuals.

Identify players and associated individuals, accounts and transaction trails in the United Kingdom, Switzerland, Luxembourg, Germany, Cyprus and the United States.

Within this period, employ several detective agencies (with Interfor as base) to obtain confidential information about assets of the Target that have been discovered, as well as assets identified in the course of the investigation as being affiliated.

On the basis of results achieved in Russia and the CIS, disseminate information in the media of Western countries, urge their law enforcement agencies to scrutinise the Target's activities, and get this covered in media sources.

Use investigations initiated in Russia and the CIS to send enquiries in respect of the Target to law enforcement agencies in third countries. Provide materials and documents to the authorities and influential individuals in the United Kingdom, Switzerland and the United States giving evidence of illegal activity by the Target, draw their attention to the criminal nature of some of the funds used by the Target for transactions on their territory.

Within this period, elaborate information received in Russia and the CIS, and also incorporate information obtained from investigations.

Discredit the Target in the business and civil communities of countries where he owns property and operates, primarily in the United Kingdom where the Target has powerful official political support.

Within this period, disseminate to the media information generated in the initial period, recruit foreign professionals to become shareholders in National Reserve Bank, prepare features for them in the media and possible civil lawsuits.

Discredit the civil wife of the Target within her professional community.

Within this period, publish information in the Western media about the drug-dealing case and develop it.

Evaluation of Measures Taken in the Initial Period

Pros:

A fairly extensive amount of information on the Target has been assembled.

There have been four waves of social media campaigns and flooding of the blogosphere with negative information about the Target. Public events have been staged which have brought a response from the media and the public.

The Target has been negatively positioned in relation to the government authorities in Russia and (more actively) Ukraine.

The media and society are receptive to information about the Target: they find him interesting. The effectiveness of the activities undertaken is confirmed by the Target's reaction in his blogs, and later by an article on the front page of *Izvestiya*. The Target has been drawn personally into the flow of information, which indicates his sensitivity and vulnerablity to the situation which has developed.

There are fully prepared criminal lawsuits waiting.

Cons:

Insufficiently complete processing of information as a result of the limited selection of individuals who can be brought in to implement the project.

Insufficient representation of the campaign in the West.
Overall self-assessment: 7.5 on a 10-point scale.

The authors' self-assessment is clearly an overestimate, although they had certainly put in a lot of hard work. In addition to the media campaigns, complaints had been filed with the law enforcement agencies, criminal cases had been fabricated, enquiries from deputies had been stage-managed, there had been overt surveillance and covert monitoring of telephone calls, regulators had been appointed to inspect my companies and the bank, protest demonstrations by 'outraged members of the public' had been held and our email had been hacked. The budget was clearly in the millions of dollars. There was a ramified infrastructure and hundreds of underlings had violated a dozen Articles of the Criminal Code.

The roles in the organisation that was persecuting me were clearly apportioned, as in any criminal gang. The harassment was organised by an office called The Fourth Estate, whose boss is a certain Alexander Krestnikov. Black PR was subcontracted to Yury Patrin, former deputy editor of *Obshchaya Gazeta* under Yegor Yakovlev. He abandoned journalism to found the SiM-Media agency. The criminal *krysha* or overall patronage was provided by Colonel Dmitry Frolov of K Directorate of the FSB (who was subsequently sacked for 'no longer enjoying the confidence' of his superiors when they discovered a portfolio of real estate in Italy).

As the subsequent investigation revealed, the attack was financed by donations to a slush fund from people who had figured in my investigations into fraud in the banking system. I had given Pugachev a lot of grief with my publications in the Western press. After these, the British courts not only refused to grant him political asylum, but threw the book at him for trying to pervert the course of justice. Pugachev is currently lying low in France, where he mysteriously managed to acquire a passport of the Fifth Republic (despite the unassailable fact that there are no corrupt officials in France).

Here is an excerpt from the prospectus of The Fourth Estate that so enticed those who commissioned the campaign:

Fundamental to our work is the fact that, as a rule, all the articles we publish are prepared or signed by real journalists, experts or politicians. Among our constant authors are:
Mikhail Khazin, president of NeoCon, economist
Mikhail Tulsky, president of the Centre for Political Analysis,

political scientist

Pavel Danilin, expert consultant of the Business Russia society

Mikhail Vinogradov, president of the St Petersburg Politics Foundation

Konstantin Kalachev, compiler of the electability rating of provincial governors

Nikolai Petrakov, director of the Institute of Problems of the Market of the Russian Academy of Sciences, academician

Mikhail Delyagin, director of the Institute of Globalisation, economist

Alexander Nagorny, vice-president of the Aspek Association of Political Scientists

Kirill Kabanov, chairman of the National Anti-Corruption Committee, member of the Presidential Council

Sergey Sapronov, director of the Research Institute for Problems of Corruption

Yelena Panfilova, director of the Transparency International Centre for Anti-Corruption Investigations and Initiatives

Alexander Kynev, director of regional programmes of the Foundation for the Development of Information Policy.

We particularly specialise in journalistic and parliamentary investigations. Our contributors include the well-known television presenter and investigative journalist, Natalia Metlina (currently presenting 'The Metlina Defence' on Channel 5); Vladimir Prokhvatilov, president of the Real Politics Foundation; Oleg Matveychev, professor of the Higher School of Economics; such renowned bloggers as Oleg Luriye and Avtandil Tsuladze, and many others.

Here are some of their masterpieces that have come to light. They are correspondence between these 'information hitmen' and those who commissioned them (L is me. The spelling and punctuation are theirs.):

Hello, as you know, the President has nominated Nabiullina for the post of head of the Central Bank. This presents an opportunity not to be missed for preparing material. Specifically, about the fact that L very much dislikes Nabiullina and tried in every way to compromise her both in the media, and by spreading baseless rumours about her professionalism and personal qualities (this was during the time she was working in the government).

The said attitude towards Nabiullina is mainly linked to the fact that it was she who took a principled position over the sale of the shares in Aeroflot and Ilyushin Finance owned by L. Essentially, in his customary manner, L tried to backmail the government by using the fact that he had a liquid shareholding in Aeroflot and another absolutely nobody wanted in Ilyushin Finance. Therefore, through his friends, he lobbied for the sale of said shares to the state for a price that did not correspond to reality at all. As a result, the state would suffer a very serious loss, and L most likely would have bought something in the United Kingdom. If it had not been for Nabiullina, then everything would have happened that way.

Therefore the material should be devoted to illustrating the government position of Nabiullina, who was afraid of a big bust-up with L and pre-empted harm (in effect, theft), and also point out that our 'champion against corruption' was yet again trying to cut himself a slice of the gov. pie, which is what he is currently accusing everyone in the world of!

By the way, as one of the ways of having a showdown L wanted to initiate filing a collective lawsuit by the citizens of Russia against Nabiullina on a charge that as the head of the Ministry of Economic Development she ineffectively spent $500 million which were at the disposal of Financial Leasing Company. In other words, just another usual piece of nastiness on the part of this individual, which he was unable to bring about only on account of the absurdity of the whole idea.

It needs to be mentioned that Krestnikov's gang were not only at work on me. Among their other victims are well-known businessmen, officials and even judges. For example, in May 2013, the PR specialists conducted a campaign of 'information pressure on the judge and chairman of the court, deputy minister and opponents, making it possible to create the necessary conditions for changing a pre-determined court ruling.'

This was a propaganda campaign conducted at a time when the organisations controlled by Pugachev were suing the organisation controlled by businessman Alexander Sabadash (a former companion of Pugachev's, also an ex-senator, who was arrested in May 2014).

The dispute was about the land holdings of The Light of Lenin, an agricultural enterprise. In the 'Budget Plan for a PR Project' compiled by Krestnikov, were such items as:

> Placement of publications ... trolling of the deputy minister, supported by phone calls from journalists.
>
> Placement of a fake interview with Sabadash, in which he effectively admits his designs on the land and that the matter has been agreed with the courts. Presented so as to appear part of his own PR.
>
> A succession of phone calls from journalists to the court press service (Federal Arbitration Court of the Central Federal District, RF Supreme Arbitration Court) and to the clerk of the court asking for comment on news that the court decision has been 'bought', sending an official journalistic enquiry from the federal news agency to the court.

When Pugachev's lawyers appealed against a court ruling to arrest him in absentia, The Fourth Estate was set the task of influencing the Moscow City Court, which was considering the appeal. The estimate of costs names a dozen media outlets, with a price list for publications ranging from $2,600 to $14,400. There is a separate quote for the blogosphere, in a section titled 'Information support for bloggers', with a note:

> *Discussions on forums of publications, and in blogs of well-known people. Our team of bloggers will for the period of the campaign support and distribute in the blogosphere references and abstracts of publications we have issued, accompanied by various comments aiming to achieve maximum impact and maximise the number of readers. Some of the bloggers have access to (continuously post) on the personal blogs of Medvedev, Bastrykin and other well-known officials and public figures. They will present a daily report on work done (posts, comments, etc.) of up to 20–25 comments per 24-hour period. Budget: up to $5,500 per week.*

All this frenetic activity designed to wreck my business did unquestionably have an effect. In terms of depriving the 'Target' of his ability to carry on investigating it was, however, the opposite of what was apparently intended. It was simply not possible to create any serious, let alone 'critical', discomfort for me because, over time, you develop a kind of immunity to this kind of bullying. Although, who knows, perhaps my ordeal by depression was in fact linked to this 'stress testing' over many years.

They seem not to have succeeded in defaming me and trashing my reputation. The would-be hunters failed to take account of the fact that not only information technologies have progressed but so has society. Some fifteen to twenty years ago, it was possible to put out an anonymous false story and everyone would immediately start talking about it, transforming it into an event in the popular consciousness. Today, though, society has learned not to trust anonymous claims, and the status of sources is paramount. In order to implicate someone in dirt, you need to involve in your information war influential media and people who are authoritative figures in society.

I am grateful to Vladimir Sungorkin, the editor of the most popular newspaper in Russia, *Komsomolskaya Pravda*, for personally blocking defamatory material that the people who compiled that plan attempted to plant in his publication. They approached well-known people, politicians, commentators and experts both, be it noted, in the 'Kremlin camp' and in the opposition, but none would demean themselves. The upshot was that this entire campaign failed to catch the public's attention.

'Get 'im Out!'

As for the objective of 'depriving the Target of property and/or causing the maximum of harm to him', these characters assuredly did their level best. Frankly, this was the primary task they were set by the client. The outcome of their efforts in that direction was twofold. They certainly did harm, only not to me personally but to businesses that gave employment to thousands of people. If, before the attack, some 1,500 people were working at National Reserve Bank, by the end of 2014 there were only slightly over a hundred left. We closed down all our branch offices and cut our programme of mortgage lending. We returned all their money to our customers, ourselves lost tens of billions of rubles, but saved the bank. I believe that the only indicator of a bank's stability is its ability to pay off all its customers at any given moment.

Some odd things happened with our aviation assets. At New Year 2013, a Red Wings plane crashed at Vnukovo. Almost the entire crew were killed in this terrible disaster, with only a flight attendant and a stewardess surviving. They were flying home from the Czech Republic, all the passengers having disembarked in Pardubice. It was later established that the tragedy had occurred because of a highly improbable combination of circumstances.

The Tu-204, as on non-Russian aircraft of a similar class, has foolproof, fail-safe features. Reverse thrust of the engines can be engaged only when the landing gear detects pressure, that is, when the aircraft 'knows' it really has landed. At just that moment, however, a high wind was blowing and the plane was empty, so the landing gear had insufficient traction. The pilots believed they were already on the runway and continued to press reverse thrust, which was not functioning. Ideally, they should have raised the aircraft and made a second approach, but they were evidently disoriented and the aircraft came off the end of the runway at cruising speed.

An investigation began. The regulator, Rosaviatsiya in the person of Alexander Neradko, grounded all Red Wings flights. The official reason was not the disaster, but that the company was supposedly in an 'unsatisfactory financial state.' In fact, in respect of the ratio of debt to revenue, Red Wings was in a better state than Transaero. A few years afterwards the latter came to a predictable end and bankruptcy, while Red Wings is still flying. It recently announced it was breaking even and transports some two million passengers a year.

What are the implications for an airline of having its aircraft grounded? Every day of downtime represents costs without revenue, and loss of customers. We went through all that with Blue Wings. Rosaviatsiya showed no inclination to extend our operator's licence. I gave the company away for a symbolic one ruble. Next, the Government most generously made me a proposal in respect of Ilyushin Finance. Vneshekonom Bank finally valued the asset and bought a 48.4 per cent stake from United Aircraft Corporation for a stonking $300 million and a bit (to finance the 'Superjet', of course). That is, the entire company was valued at $700 million, and my modest contribution at $175 million.

I was informed, however, that I had to accept a cashless transaction and exchange my shareholding in Ilyushin Finance for two Ruslan (An-124) heavy cargo aircraft that belonged to Ilyushin Finance. To be frank, it was an unequal exchange: instead of almost 6 billion rubles worth of shares [about $200 million] I would become the owner of two aircraft worth at most 2.5 billion rubles [about $83 million]. I had no choice.

The aircraft were leased from a Voronezh aviation company called Polyot

(Flight), whose owner was a certain Anatoly Karpov, a namesake of the former world chess champion. This Karpov had worked as a radio operator in the agricultural aviation section of Voronezh airport, and had become the owner of several Ruslans during the wave of privatisation in the 'wild nineties'. There are not in the world all that many heavy-load-carrying planes capable of accommodating supersized cargoes, and the demand for such services is enormous.

Karpov soon recruited customers, and not only from Russia. Polyot became the overall transporter for Roskosmos space exploration. Its customers included companies like Volkswagen, Rolls-Royce, Siemens, Philip Morris, Ericsson, IBM, Lufthansa and many others. NATO too used Polyot to transport freight to its contingent in Afghanistan.

Anatoly Karpov had, however, structured his business very ingeniously. There were actually two companies called Polyot. There was the one that transported passengers, was registered with the tax inspectorate in Voronezh province, and made nothing but losses. The other one operated the cargo planes, signed contracts for millions, and was domiciled in Cyprus, where Karpov garnered his profits and squirrelled them away in the Bank of Cyprus.

The documents indicate that for twenty years the tax inspectorate paid not the slightest attention to these antics.

Karpov certainly was not short of money to provide his tax-free business with reliable patronage. His foreign customers also took no great interest in where they were asked to pay. The United Kingdom's Ministry of Defence, for example, in order not to be transferring money directly into an offshore company, insulated itself by using Chapman Freeborn Ltd, a wholesale consolidator. Between 1994 and 2014, Karpov's Cypriot company, Deltaline Overseas Ltd, brought in on average $40–50 million a year!

And everything would have been fine, but greed got the better of him. In order not to shovel any of his invisible money back to his homeland, he took out loans in Russia and then, because of debts, had to give up two of his Ruslans to Ilyushin Finance. Polyot promptly leased them back. The aim was to get money from Ilyushin Finance, but not pay it for leasing the aircraft. Karpov generally preferred not to pay anyone for anything, whether in taxes, for leasing, or even the salaries of his staff.

Something very curious is that Ilyushin Finance's CEO, Alexander Rubtsov, who began his career in the Russian branch of Ernst & Young, a British accounting company, and who later worked in our bank, took such a benign view of this situation. It was always a puzzle to me how Russia's biggest aircraft leasing company that, according to those same auditors, was receiving enormous revenues, in all those years never paid me, its founder and one of its main shareholders, or the state, a single ruble in dividends. One can only wonder whether perhaps Karpov was also incentivising the Ilyushin Finance management and bypassing the cashier.

In sum, all I received from a multi-billion-ruble investment was two old aircraft that, to add insult to injury, I had to prise away from a rogue partner. It reminds me of the joke about two peasant representatives who came to see Lenin. 'Vladimir Ilyich,' they complained, 'there's this really unpleasant fellow in reception. We ask him for a smoke, and he tells us to get stuffed.'

'Oh,' said Lenin. 'That's just Dzerzhinsky! Felix has a heart of gold. Anyone else would have punched you in the face.'

The upshot was that I was all but put out of business. To tell the truth, I took my farewell of it without regret. At this precise moment two reporters from the Russian version of *Forbes*, Alexander Levinsky and Yelena Berezanskaya, came to see me. They tried at great length to draw out how this had all come about, and at great length I told them.

The cover story about me, published in May 2013, was titled 'How Billionaire Alexander Lebedev Found Himself on His Uppers in Business and Politics'. The text was strikingly cynical, paid-for journalism:

It's no joking matter for Lebedev. In early October 2011, on the instructions of the Chairman of the Investigative Committee A. Bastrykin, a criminal case was initiated on a charge of hooliganism 'motivated by political, ideological, racial, ethnic or religious hatred'. It is the same Article – carrying a maximum sentence of five years – that the Pussy Riot dancers were tried under. One of the banker's former partners has not disagreed that he might secretly even be hoping to be sent to prison and become a martyr in order, if only for a short time, to stay in the limelight. But might it not be more sensible for Lebedev to emigrate to London, where he has for so long been at home, selling off such property as he still has left, and live a quiet, happy life?

Does that by any chance seem familiar? And the trial was only just beginning.

CHAPTER 13

A Courtroom Farce

The 'Polonsky Case': a U-turn

In October 2012, I was summoned once more to the Investigative Department of the Investigative Directorate of the Investigative Committee of Babushkin District of the Investigative Committee of the Russian Federation. I had been warned in advance that I was to be charged with a crime I had not committed. Before this visit to the investigators, I had a meeting with Henry Reznik. 'Are you sure you need this?' he asked. 'You can see where it is leading. From a legal viewpoint our position is unassailable, but I cannot guarantee you a favourable outcome. You know what our legal system is like ...'

The hint was more than transparent. I could just emigrate and avoid ending up in the dock. But that would mean giving up everything I valued and losing my self-respect. The next day Reznik and I presented ourselves at the Investigative Committee. Roman Sirotin read me the charge and put a document in front of me to sign: the notorious 'undertaking not to change the place of residence'.

At this I took the first of a series of actions that I hoped would enable me to create legal precedents. The Russian law-enforcement system has a noxious practice that, if a person is not arrested, he is required to sign a declaration. It is a reflex, automatic, way of exerting psychological pressure. It is openly said that, no matter how nonsensical the practice, the individual must be made to sign.

This is, nevertheless, a serious restriction of your freedom, and the investigator must have sound reasons to justify such a restriction. That is, he must have reasonable grounds to suspect that the accused might abscond, destroy evidence, or try to exert pressure on witnesses. For the past year I had been dutifully turning up to be questioned, and the investigator had no reason to suspect me of nefarious intentions.

In 1990, a UN Convention was adopted, which is known as the Tokyo

Rules. According to Clause 3.4 of this document, if a suspect or accused is not placed under arrest, then any restriction on his or her freedom (including a written undertaking not to change his or her address) can be applied only with the individual's written consent. And not otherwise. The Soviet Union ratified that convention and thus, according to the constitution, it passed into Russian law.

The Investigative Committee, needless to say, knew nothing of such subtleties, which is why I was being asked to sign the undertaking. I refused. What I did write was that I considered this proposed restriction to be unmotivated and had no intention of restricting my freedom of movement. In spite of that, by evening a message appeared on the website of the Investigative Committee that the document had been 'represented' (presented?) to me, and Investigator Tatiana Rusakova sent me a personal clarification in which she threatened to jail me if I tried to leave Moscow. At that I appealed to the Constitutional Court.

The ruling it issued on my complaint confirmed the right, enshrined in international agreements ratified by Russia, of suspects and defendants not to sign any undertaking not to change their address. The court's ruling reads: 'Of itself, the adoption of a directive on the choice of a preventive measure in the form of a signature not to change one's place of residence and behave in an appropriate manner does not, without the obtaining from the individual of the said written undertaking, allow the measure to be deemed to have been applied and to entail legal consequences.'

After the Constitutional Court's ruling, prominent lawyers debated the issue. Khodorkovsky's lawyer, Vadim Klyuvgant, for example, argued that this would only worsen the situation of those under investigation because, in case of refusal to sign, everybody in that situation would be imprisoned indiscriminately. Henry Reznik and I defended our view that only a court could order a citizen's arrest after the investigator had justified his or her position. Today lawyers everywhere, including in the remote provinces, make use of the Constitutional Court's ruling.

In late 2012, the charge against me of committing a villainous act on grounds of political hatred was forwarded from the Investigative Committee's Department for Investigation of Especially Important Cases of Crimes Against the State and the Economy to the Prosecutor's Office. The prosecutors mindlessly rubber-stamped the indictment and sent it to the courts. But at this point the life of the complainant took yet another dramatic twist: Sergey Polonsky was arrested at the New Year by the police of the Kingdom of Cambodia, where he been living since August 2012.

The developer and his retinue were carousing on his small island near the city of Sihanoukville. In a state of narcotic inebriation, he set off for more distant islands on a boat he had been given by his business partner, Nikolai Doroshenko, a local 'authoritative businessman'. During the party Polonsky, so to speak, went ape. He beat up the Khmer sailors and first locked them in the store room, then forced them to jump into the water and swim to the shore. They summoned a military patrol boat that, after gunfire, overtook the the developer's boat and arrested him. Polonsky and two of his IT specialists ended up in the local prison, where he broke a fan and caused a fire, which got him sent to the punishment cell.

When the case against me came to court, Judge Kostyuchenko refused to consider it before the Prosecutor's Office had notified Polonsky as required. But then the judge was changed to Bakhvalov, and in April the hearing began anyway.

Each hearing started with our demanding that the complainant should be brought to the court. Henry Reznik logically argued that the main element in the accusation of hooliganism was the alleged motive of 'political hatred'. That is, I was assumed to have had serious political differences with Polonsky, which had led to a scuffle. However, we knew nothing about the political views of that truculent gentleman, so my lawyer wanted to be able to question him in court.

On each occasion Dobrovinsky argued that was not possible, because his client was incarcerated in a jail in Cambodia. He even embarked on an expedition to that faraway tropical land and visited Polonsky in his dungeon there. Admittedly, the lawyer appeared in no hurry to extricate him. He came back to Moscow with a contract from Polonsky to sell his business to Dobrovinsky himself, and to another minority shareholder of the former Mirax, Roman Trotsenko, for $100 million. This was despite the fact that the company's public debt, against the collateral of numerous unfinished construction projects and Polonsky's personal guarantee, amounted to half a billion dollars.

At the end of April, a Cambodian judge released Polonsky on bail. He immediately fled the country, using his son's passport. He was first spotted in Europe, in Luxembourg and Switzerland, then turned up in Israel, where he attempted to obtain citizenship. All this time Dobrovinsky was reporting to the court that the offended party was in Sihanoukville under a restraining order not to leave the country.

The Israeli authorities wanted nothing to do with someone with such a scandalous reputation. Polonsky was taken in handcuffs to the airport and deported, with a prohibition against appearing again in the Holy Land. He found himself back in Cambodia.

There Polonsky had another unpleasant surprise when the Investigative Department of the Russian Interior Ministry filed a criminal case against him on charges of fraud. In 2007, he had collected over 6 billion rubles [$200 million] from investors in the Kutuzov Mile residential quarter, of which 3.5 billion evaporated in offshore accounts of the Mirax empire.

The investors were left with no money and no apartments. For five years they did the rounds of the law enforcement agencies, and finally – a result!

For me the certainty crystallised that we would not be seeing Polonsky in court. If he returned to Russia it could only be in handcuffs, which clearly was not part of his plans. The Article of the Criminal Code covering assault and battery was a matter of a personal accusation and required the presence of the complainant in court. Since Polonsky was plainly going to be a no show, it only remained to close the case.

It had anyway been falling apart before our eyes. How could it be otherwise when, as Reznik said, Themis was here not encountering even a trumped-up charge, but a case which had been dreamed up completely out of thin air. The main document on which the charge of 'political hatred' was based, a 'Culturological Determination by Professor Komkov', had to be withdrawn from the evidence for the trial because, in a gross violation of the Code of Criminal Procedure, it had been concocted even before criminal proceedings were instituted.

At the request of the prosecution, a viewing of the recording of that ill-starred television programme was arranged. It was played from a computer disk in the courtroom. It was curious to watch the expression on the faces of the judge and prosecutor. It seemed to me from their reaction that they were seeing the talk show for the first time in their lives.

At the end of the viewing, all that remained was for Reznik to theatrically spread his arms wide. He asked the prosecutor to indicate at which moment exactly I manifested political disagreements with Polonsky. She looked at the floor and said nothing. It was clear from the recording that I had not said anything to the complainant at all. The investigators themselves, when they officially reviewed the recording in autumn 2011, noted in their report that 'up until the forty-ninth minute' (until Polonsky's remark about airmen and chicken farmers) they 'found nothing of relevance to the criminal case'.

Then it was time for a circus turn from the witnesses. Anton Krasovsky, one of the presenters of *The NTV Show*, declared he was baffled as to why he had been summoned to attend the hearing at all. 'Everything is recorded on many cameras and from different angles. What am I doing here?' the TV professional exclaimed. He explained that, in the three days between the recording and the broadcast, the footage with the incident was deliberately promoted on the instructions of NTV's CEO, Vladimir Kulistikov. It would contribute to the station's viewing figures, and higher ratings meant higher rates from advertisers. Nothing personal, just business.

Olga Romanova testified in court that Polonsky had been insulting me in the dressing room. The judge spent a lot of time trying to extract from her the precise obscenity beginning with a 'd' he had used and ultimately obliged Olga to pronounce it. Others who had been involved in the recording, Herman Sterligov and Sergey Lisovsky, clearly stated that Polonsky had been behaving abnormally, aggressively provoking the other guests, and had attempted to bully me. 'I left early,' Sterligov said. 'Otherwise I would now be where Alexander is sitting.'

At this something distinctly odd happened: prosecution witnesses were brought into the courtroom who had not even been in the NTV studio, but only watched the programme on television. And all of them were from Ruza district in Moscow province and their testimony had been added to the case file only in summer 2012, nine months after the 'crime'. How they came to figure in the case is a story in its own right.

One woman said an FSB officer had approached her at the trolleybus stop and asked if she had watched *The NTV Show* last September. When she said she had, the young gentleman invited her to accompany him to the Investigative Committee and give evidence. Another girl, who had just turned eighteen, was invited to the Investigative Committee because her mobile phone had been stolen. This, by the way, was on a Saturday evening, so the investigators were being exceptionally conscientious. The investigator told her the phone had been found, but if she wanted it back, she would need to provide testimony. The third 'television viewer' actually declared he remembered nothing, because it was such a long time ago.

In the end, the judge's nerves snapped, and he reprimanded the prosecution. 'There were three hundred people in the audience. Why are you dragging people in here from a bus stop?'

'Disrespecting society'

I was accused of 'gross violation of public order, having expressed clear disrespect for society' (which is the definition of hooliganism in the Criminal Code). I had to demonstrate to the court that I do in fact have respect for society, which is often reciprocated.

I invite you to judge for yourselves.

The Charitable Reserve Fund implemented programmes in the medical field. It built one of Russia's largest cancer clinics for children, the Raisa Gorbacheva Institute for Paediatric Haematology and Organ Transplants in St Petersburg. It paid for children to be treated at the N.N. Blokhin Russian Cancer Research Centre. For many years, annual charity events have been held in the United Kingdom attended by cultural figures and show business celebrities, to raise money to help children.

The fund financed reconstruction of the Spaso-Yakovlevsky and Assumption cathedrals in the town of Rostov the Great and a memorial to the eighteenth-century Generalissimo Alexander Suvorov was restored in Switzerland. Other statues were erected: in London, 'Sorrowing Woman' in memory of the citizens of the USSR who died during the Second World War; in Voronezh, to the poet Osip Mandelstam. In Krasnaya Polyana, Sochi and in Smolensk province, memorials honoured the fallen heroes of the Second World War.

In Italy, the twelfth-century fortifications of Friedrich Barbarossa were restored; as was, in Switzerland, the historic nineteenth-century Château Gütsch, where Sergey Rachmaninov, Richard Wagner, Queen Victoria and many other historical figures were guests. I was a patron of the Chekhov Moscow Art Theatre's Pyotr Fomenko Theatre Workshop, and of the Galina Vishnevskaya Centre for Opera Singing. For ten years, a Yury Kazakov Literary Prize was awarded annually.

A considerable part of my life has been devoted to journalism and publishing, and from 2006 I was the publisher of *Novaya Gazeta*. Mikhail Gorbachev and I 'bought' 49 per cent of the newspaper's shares, while 51 per cent remained in the hands of the newspaper's staff, under the direction of its outstanding editor, Dmitry Muratov. I put the word 'bought' in quotation marks because, although I paid several million dollars for the asset, the shares were actually worthless.

The newspaper did not make a profit and, in order for it to continue to appear, I made charitable donations each month from my own account to that of the newspaper. Because *Novaya Gazeta*'s journalists always reported what they considered important in the manner they considered appropriate, I periodically got into hot water with some of those who featured in their articles, despite the fact that I exercised no influence on editorial policy and the most I allowed myself was to publish a column in its pages.

In late 2007, I began publishing a daily newspaper called the *Moscow Correspondent*. By this time, Mayor Yury Luzhkov's office had a complete monopoly of all the city's media, and the basic idea was to provide Muscovites with alternative news and tell the truth about what was happening in their city. Alas, we overlooked the fact that it is not enough to publish a newspaper: it then needs to be distributed to its readers. The mayor's office systematically deprived us of the opportunity to advertise, stopped the paper from being sold in newsagents' kiosks, and drove us out of the Metro. We then began to distribute the newspaper free of charge, but the police arrested the students selling it and took them off to the police station.

The result was that in April 2008 the *Moscow Correspondent* died, strangled by the city authorities. There was no point in continuing to publish it. In the newspaper's office the mood was one of despondency and people engaged in irresponsible drinking. Evidently the editor decided to go out with a bang and published some tittle-tattle about the president and Olympic sports medallist Alina Kabaeva, which created a considerable stir. Anyway, the newspaper was shut down not because of censorship, but as the result of harassment by Luzhkov's Administration.

In 2009, Lord Rothermere, the owner of the Daily Mail and General Trust, which published the *Daily Mail*, the most popular tabloid in Britain, sold me his evening newspaper, the *Evening Standard*, for a symbolic £1. This was no gift: the newspaper, published since 1827 and part of the history of the capital of the United Kingdom, was burdened with debt, making a loss and facing closure. The team my son Evgeny assembled took the bold decision to transform the *Evening Standard* into a free newspaper. We lost revenue, but the circulation increased dramatically and advertisers were attracted. The newspaper even began to make a profit, which was unprecedented for the modern British press.

In 2010, we analogously acquired the *Independent* newspaper, founded in 1986 by three former journalists of the *Daily Telegraph* – Andreas Whittam Smith, Stephen Glover and Matthew Symonds. This independent, liberal publication, respected for its analytical reporting, was also in a parlous financial situation. In order to keep it afloat, we launched a 'sister' to the *Independent*, the newspaper '*i*', a lighter version of the main edition, aimed at young people and costing only 20 pence. The '*i*' rapidly won a following. A few years later we were able to sell it, gaining extra funds with which to develop the overall holding.

At about that time we launched the London Live television channel from scratch, and moved the *Independent* online, terminating the newsprint version. Today the *Independent* is a global brand, a publication with an impeccable reputation. The *Evening Standard* is the most popular daily newspaper in London. Together with the television channel and *ES Magazine*, the readership of our media is around 180 million unique users per month.

These successes by 'the Russians' in Foggy Albion's media market (in fact, by the English themselves, because it is they who are the managers of our newspapers and television channel) have been ruffling feathers for a few years now among the traditional players.

In March 2012, in London, an attempt was made on the life of fraudster Herman Gorbuntsov, a fugitive from Russia who gutted Russian banks with the same abandon as Jack the Ripper disembowelled his victims in Whitechapel. The media tycoon Rupert Murdoch, who owns *The Times* and *Sun* newspapers in Britain, the *Wall Street Journal* and Fox News television channel in the United States, as well as, until recently, the 20th Century Fox film company, wrote waspishly on Twitter, 'Another Russian shot down in London. Wonder what ex-KGB boss could tell his paper *Independent*.'

Unlike Murdoch, I have never meddled in the editorial affairs of publications I happened to own, either in Russia or in Britain. This is common knowledge. To me, European and American journalism has always, ever since I worked in London in the 1980s, seemed an amazing cultural phenomenon, one of the treasures of civilisation.

It is the 'fourth estate' that has made the Western system of democracy what it is, competitive and remarkably transparent. The journalists have stood sentinel over this system: investigative journalism did not just appear by magic, and journalists themselves have come to be called the 'watchdogs of democracy'. I include myself among those who practise this profession, because watchdog journalism is precisely the genre of the dozens of articles I have published over the past ten years in a great variety of publications, from the *Guardian* and *Financial Times* in Britain to the *New York Times* and *Wall Street Journal* in the United States, to *Novaya Gazeta* and *Moskovsky Komsomolets* in Russia.

In a word, by the time I was to be tried as a 'hooligan' I believed I had accumulated a respectable stash of merit in the eyes of society. But how was I to get that all down on paper and presented to a court of law? At that moment my case file contained precisely one compliment, from the Sloboda District Duma. I decided to appeal to everyone with whom I had engaged in work for charity to send me a favourable character reference. Within a couple of weeks, I had secured over a hundred letters, addressed to the court, in which people lavished praise on me in every conceivable way.

They came from the Tatar actress Chulpan Khamatova and supermodel Natalia Vodianova, from venerable Liya Akhedzhakova and theatre director Sergey Yursky, from Foreign Intelligence Agency General Yury Kobaladze and the president of the Chess Federation, Kirsan Ilyumzhinov, from academician Alexander Nekipelov and Corresponding Member of the Russian Academy of Sciences Ruslan Grinberg, from Deputy Finance Minister Sergey Storchak and economist Sergey Guriev, from Director of the State Hermitage Museum Mikhail Piotrovsky and film and theatre director Kirill Serebrennikov, from *Novaya Gazeta* and the company of the Chekhov Theatre in Yalta, from high-up members of the Orthodox Church hierarchy and the Association of Relatives of the Kursk Submariners.

Brilliant Dmitry Bykov wrote his character reference in verse:

> *I Lebedev have known for many a year.*
> *He talent has, and knowledge, and charisma.*
> *I'm not a business partner, have no fear.*
> *My reference stems from nothing so abysmal.*
> *Our* Novaya Gazeta *had support from him,*
> *and still I think he may support it.*
> *I have betimes collected there a fee, but*
> *frankly not enough to keep me sorted.*
> *So it is not his silver bright I seek, and*
> *not from fear the boss may fill my face in,*
> *I here confirm that Lebedev's all right.*
> *Indeed for Russia now he's just amazing.*
> *He once was tempted by the lure of cash,*
> *set up a bank, succeeded with potatoes,*
> *and owned some media – but does he bash*
> *his fellow man? His is a loftier status.*

In Moscow and Crimea we've hung out.
I breakfasted with him on one occasion.
He did not seem to me at all a lout,
or someone who was prone to ostentation.
Instead a hint of irony perhaps,
plain food and everything in moderation.
(Myself I think he ought to let it lapse
sometimes, but understand his reservations.)
In London doubtless he feels quite at home.
His first job there, the world now knows, was spying.
A KGB man through the City roamed.
I mostly spend my time that lot decrying. [...]

In short I wish that more would cock a snook
like Lebedev at boorishness unbounded:
as was his right, assail with a right hook
the loutishness by which he is surrounded.
If my voice counts for aught as now I roam
the intellectual wreckage of these times,
I would propose that he should be sent home
and carry on along those selfsame lines.

My friends abroad also responded. 'Character references' were sent by such internationally renowned stars as Elton John and Sting, the actors Kevin Spacey, John Malkovich, Hugh Grant, Ian McKellen, Keira Knightley, director Tom Stoppard, sculptor Anthony Gormley and many others.

Here, for example, is what sage Stephen Fry wrote:

I have had the pleasure of knowing Mr Alexander Lebedev for some years now, through an introduction by my friend, his son Evgeny.

Alexander Lebedev has always struck me as a man who combines authority, integrity, decency and intelligence with the greatest charm and self-deprecation. That he, like all human beings, is capable of losing his temper is beyond question. But then, which of us is not? What I believe is utterly inconsistent with Alexander Lebedev's character is hooliganism or the idea of him inciting anyone to hatred.

He is a man who, more than most, can listen to arguments with which he disagrees. I have met many people of great wealth and achievement in the financial and corporate field, but none with so small a sense of self-importance and so great an intellectual curiosity and openness to new ideas.

The kind of outburst the world saw from Mr Lebedev happens thousands of times an hour around the world in bars, salons, boardrooms and bedrooms, and is generally followed by an apology, a slap on the back, a drink and a handshake. It would be a sad, strange and unjust day if this one ill-judged moment should be singled out for special and unusual punishment.

We have all seen the incident on YouTube and we have all seen much, much worse. I hope the good offices of the court and its instincts for natural justice will come to the view that this molehill does not have to be seen as a mountain.

With very many thanks,

Stephen Fry

Ring down the curtain

At the end of June, after several months of court hearings, it became obvious that the charge of hooliganism motivated by 'political hatred' was laughably absurd. Predictably, the case fell apart. The Prosecutor General's Office itself abruptly 'withdrew' the charge, declining to continue to prosecute me under Article 213. That left Article 116, Part 2 'Battery motivated by hooliganism'. The prosecutor demanded that I should be found guilty and subjected to a restraining order for one year and nine months. This was effectively house arrest.

Reznik was fully determined to prove that not only was there not 'motivation by hooliganism', but neither had there been 'battery'. I had merely tried to thump a boor who launched himself backwards and fell off the stage together with his seat.

Here is Henry's virtuoso speech, delivered in the debate prior to sentencing. It deserves to be included in handbooks for lawyers:

Your Honour!

I confess I simply cannot recall another similar case where, whichever aspect of the criminal charge you inspect, whichever circumstances are cited as evidence proving it, the charge immediately begins to crumble. The prosecutor has withdrawn the charge of hooliganism and initially I considered asking the court to clarify the procedural form of that withdrawal. The case was, after all, at the outset initiated on a charge of hooliganism and only subsequently did a further Article relating to battery appear. It would have seemed that under Part 7 of Article 246 of the Code of Criminal Procedure relating to charges of hooliganism the case should be terminated.

Upon further reflection, however, I came to the conclusion that the prosecutor was right insofar as the formulations in the indictment of 'hooliganism' and 'battery' are absolutely identical, they are presented as a single criminal act corresponding to more than one definition. We can consider this a minor matter, but neverthess it is a legal masterstroke: hooliganism and battery cannot be identical crimes in any ideal sense, only in practical terms. This explains the prosecutor's withdrawal of the charge of hooliganism as superfluous. She considers the charge of battery to be proven, but we shall return to that.

The prosecutor has given the absence of any motivation by political hatred on the part of Lebedev as her reason for withdrawing the charge of hooliganism. That was wholly unsurprising. The charge of political hatred was plucked from nowhere, in a word, it was a pure fabrication. No political differences of any kind were to be observed between Polonsky and Lebedev during the broadcast. That too is unsurprising: politics and ideology had no place in a discussion of how ordinary citizens and businessmen should survive the financial crisis. I had intended to dwell in some detail on the absence of any motive for political hatred. I will not do so in detail, because the prosecutor's withdrawal of the charge is binding on the court.

I shall, however, consider it a little, because the complainant's representative is continuing to insist that political hatred was present. The representative of the complainant feels compelled to continue to insist on this non-existent motive, because of the appearance at this hearing of an individual by the name of Komkov, whom he has invited as an expert witness. From considerations of professional decency, I shall not mention the name of this charlatan again.

All the participants in this trial have had an opportunity to judge for themselves the value of his specialised knowledge, which is zero. His qualification as a culturologist – I leave to one side the manifest irrelevance to this case of culturology – this pathetic individual has been unable to demonstrate by reference to any degree from a Russian institution. It was, however, precisely his culturological report, created to order of representatives of Polonsky, that was the sole foundation of the prosecution's charge of criminal hooliganism. The fact of the matter is that in Polonsky's initial statement not a word was said about any political differences with Lebedev.

Polonsky asked that a criminal case should be instituted in respect of a crime he had found in another paragraph of Article 213 of the Criminal Code, namely the use of weapons or items adapted for use as weapons, considering Lebedev's fists to fall within that definition. Next, of course, lawyers came on the scene. They will undoubtedly have explained to him that this was totally nonsensical, and the phrase now appears in Polonsky's testimony: 'But it all came about because of our differences.' Polonsky finds it difficult, however, to define their nature, calling them in one place political and in another ideological. What the nature of these disagreements was is something Polonsky's representative also failed to clarify during the court debate.

I fully appreciate the complexity of the position of lawyers in a number of trials whether in the role of defence counsel or as representatives of the complainant. Our activity is one-sided. It can happen that we are obliged to defend the unsustainable, or indeed simply foolish, position of a client. Nevertheless, when interpreting the facts of a case in a register favourable to the client, putting forward value judgements which do not follow from the circumstances of the case, a lawyer should not make statements he or she knows to be factually untrue.

In this broadcast, Lebedev said not one word about the Federation Tower. Neither did he say anything about Polonsky only building luxury accommodation and never doing anything to help the abandoned, the poor and those living in penury. That simply did not happen.

In the prosecution's winding-up speech, a remark was

represented as betokening political differences which Lebedev made in response to Polonsky's assertion that, before the crisis, Mirax occupied first place in terms of charity. Lebedev is perplexed: 'Hang on a moment! What's this you're trying to say? Where did this first place came from? Did you award it to yourself?'

This was the response of a man, perhaps the most consistent and generous philanthropist in the Russian Federation, who has been engaging in charitable activity for a very long time. He is naturally surprised by what Polonsky has said, who has come to business considerably later, and he is fully aware that no competitions are held among philanthropists to determine their ranking, who occupies first place, who is second, who third. It would be, to put it mildly, odd if the situation were any other. Just as it is odd to try to portray this episode as political!

With the exception of that one question addressed by Lebedev to Polonsky, in the course of the entire transmission there was no communication between them, no dispute of any description. For this reason, we have heard nothing from the complainant's representative specifically about political disagreements during the broadcast.

And so we see that the Prosecutor's Office, which rubber-stamped the indictment with its fabricated assertion of political hatred, did eventually consider it impossible to publicly disseminate outright lies in these court hearings. The withdrawal of the assertion of motivation by political hatred is sufficient in itself to nullify the charge of criminal hooliganism. But I would very much like to hear another ground for this in the verdict, one which seems to me very important.

That is that there has been no hooliganism at all in Lebedev's actions. Neither from an objective, nor from a subjective point of view. And not only because of the absence of a particular motivation which would categorise his actions as criminal. The present case, about an entirely run-of-the-mill episode, has attracted wide publicity because of the social prominence of the accused and the complainant. The court's verdict will accordingly be discussed in the legal community.

I have in my hands the *Course in Criminal Law* of our leading academic criminologist, Anatoly Naumov, now head of the

Criminal Procedure Department at the Academy of the Prosecutor General's faculty of criminal law. In it the author, considering the crime of hooliganism on page 395 of Volume 2, relates an aphorism which took root among legal practitioners after adoption of the Criminal Code of 1960, which was in force until adoption of the present one in 1996.

This aphorism reflected judicial practice, which held the definition of hooliganism as a kind of 'reserve': 'There is no analogy in criminal law, but there is the Article covering hooliganism.' For many years, 'hooliganism' was used as a catch-all, a gutter to which instances of bad behaviour could be consigned.

In the course of the past twenty years, our judicial practice has made great strides in the definition of criminal liability for hooliganism, and that is reflected in a 2007 Directive of the Plenum of the Supreme Court. Russia's supreme judicial body finally removed the category of 'indirect intent' from the definition of criminal hooliganism. 'Hooliganism,' the Plenum explained, 'can only be committed if there is direct intent.'

That is, it has to be shown that the perpetrator not only caused a certain amount of inconvenience to those around him or her, but intentionally caused a gross breach of the peace, wishing to express manifest disrespect for society. The Plenum further stated that being in a public place did not automatically qualify such actions as hooliganism. The manner, intensity, duration and other circumstances of the acts committed had to be taken into account.

The prosecutor's position is entirely at odds with the directive of the Plenum. In place of direct intention, 'wished', we find indirect intention 'cannot have been unaware', analysis of the circumstances of the incident is replaced by mere indication of its occurring in a public place. If this court were to concede these points, it would set judicial practice back two decades.

I remind the court that the defence asked the prosecutor to specifically define in the formulation of the alleged offence the concept of hooligan motivation. That was because this motive can take many forms. It can manifest itself in drunken bravado, gross impudence, mischief, a desire to show off, to deride other people, and to draw attention to oneself through objectionable behaviour. A hooligan deliberately sets out to cause outrage, upset or affray.

The state prosecutor made no attempt to analyse how Lebedev's two-second act could be construed as motivated by hooliganism. He did not, because it is impossible to do so. Neither did we hear anything about hooligan motivation from the prosecutor during his speech.

I turn to the charge of battery. If I approached the analysis of hooliganism from the subjective aspect of the crime, I shall approach analysis of the charge of assault from an objective aspect. Here there was evident a difference in the positions of the public prosecutor and the complainant's representative. The state prosecutor proceeds from the claim that there were two blows, and that these are sufficient to comprise the offence of assault.

The complainant's representative disagreed: 'No. There were more than two blows and accordingly they were not counted, but there were markedly more than two.' The fact that there were two blows was plain to see, but this obvious fact did not suit the complainant's representative, an experienced lawyer. He needed more blows. And with good reason.

Well then, let us turn to authoritative academic and practical commentaries to the Criminal Code. I could adduce a dozen such commentaries, but will confine myself to three, namely such as are addressed directly to those charged with administering the law: judges, investigators and prosecutors.

Here is the first. It dates from 1996 and was published under the general editorship of the then Prosecutor General of the Russian Federation, Yury Skuratov, and the Chairman of the Supreme Court of the Russian Federation, Vyacheslav Lebedev. Here is what is written in the commentary to Article 116 'Battery'. 'Battery is the inflicting of multiple blows to the victim's body, his being battered. The blows are, moreover, inflicted repeatedly using a hard, blunt instrument (three times or more).'

The second commentary dates from 2001. It was published by the Prosecutor General's Office of the Russian Federation, Institute for Advanced Training of Senior Staff. The authors of the commentary include, arguably, all our foremost authorities in criminal law. I quote: 'Battery is the inflicting of multiple blows to the victim's body, his being beaten up. The blows are, moreover, inflicted repeatedly using a hard, blunt instrument (three times or more).'

And one final commentary, fresh from 2011. It states that it has been published for the use of staff of the Prosecutor General's Office. Its general editor is the Deputy Prosecutor General, State Councillor of Justice (1st class), Distinguished Lawyer of Russia, Vladimir Malinovsky. On page 347 of the commentary, staff of the Prosecutor General's Office have it explained to them that, 'By battery is understood the inflicting of multiple (not fewer than three) blows to any part of the victim's body.'

So, for fifteen years in legal theory and judicial practice, there has been no doubt that the objective aspect of battery consists of multiple blows, and 'multiple' means three blows or more. Even the preliminary investigation into this case accepts that, yes, obviously, three blows are needed. So in the indictment it pulls out all the stops. It embarks on outright forgery, distorting the content of the available evidence.

The defence raised the issue of the number of blows already at the stage of the preliminary hearings. The complainant's representative agreed with us and started trying to stretch two blows to make them three. But now the prosecutor is saying two will be enough. At this rate we'll live to see the 'good' times roll, when a couple of slaps or kicks up the backside will count as battery. Then, in practice, they'll dispense with the so-called 'physical offence' and before you know it everything will be battery!

To summarise. As for the first issue, there is no ambiguity. There is no objective basis for considering a crime to have taken place. Let us consider the second issue. Let us suppose there really were three blows: did they land on Polonsky's head? The prosecutor claims they did, referring to the testimony of Polonsky and witnesses, and the conclusion of a forensic expert report. At this point some specialist knowledge is essential if we are to answer this question, only not from the sphere of forensic medicine, but from that of sporting and other martial arts.

The defence has sought the opinion of such specialists and is in possession of their conclusion. The crux of the matter is that the human eye can be deceived. In our instance it was clear to everyone that there were two percussive movements. But whether Lebedev's fist actually made contact with Polonsky's body is not visible. That can only be established by a detailed frame-by-frame examination, which the investigation did not undertake.

In bringing the conclusion of experts in the martial arts to your attention, I will note that it fully conforms with all the requirements of the Criminal Procedural Code. There is in it no clouding of the brain by enumeration of complicated scientific methodology. What is involved is the viewing of a video recording of a television broadcast with the aid of specialist knowledge. When experts base their conclusions on a frame-by-frame examination, it is clearly seen that the blows never reached Polonsky's head.

Zaichikov, an expert in the field of martial arts, explained everything clearly and intelligibly. And the value of the conclusion and testimony of the specialists is that all their comments can be verified by those involved in the trial and by the court by viewing the frame-by-frame breakdown. It is only by viewing this that it can be seen that Lebedev's left arm, with which he originally blocked Polonsky's hand, moves on and is seen to be beyond the vicinity of Polonsky's head.

This confirms Lebedev's testimony that he put out his left hand to ensure that any blows would fall on it, not in order to strike Polonsky's head. Experts who have worked in their field for decades are fully conversant with biomechanics. They say, 'Look there. If the blow had reached a target, the position of the head would have been different, because it would have been forced back by the blow.' In this case, however, it is clear that Polonsky's head is actually tilted forward.

Blows to the head, if they had landed, would have caused the fall to be different. The fall was what would be expected if effort was applied to the lower, not the upper, part of the body. Accordingly, with a high degree of probability, it was caused by Polonsky pushing against the floor. The conclusions of these experts corroborates the testimony of the only person in a position to see the contact of Lebedev's arms and Polonsky's head, namely Lisovsky. This eyewitness was standing literally alongside, and he tells us that no blows reached Polonsky's head and that he just pushed himself back with his feet.

And, finally, I refer to the testimony of Polonsky himself. Polonsky in his statement and in his testimony categorically claims, 'The blows were targeted at my temple. They could have led to all manner of consequences, including serious injuries, but thanks to my physical fitness and army training in the parachute troops, I was able to avoid them.' It is possible to avoid such damage only by avoiding the blows, so the conclusion of the experts is, contrary to the opinion of the prosecutor, confirmed by other evidence and not refuted by it.

Finally, to the question of injuries. I would suggest that the fact of approaching a forensic medic only three to five days later in itself raises questions as to where these injuries actually came from. Furthermore, at the initial reference to Botkin hospital, no abrasion on Polonsky's cheek was registered at all. The conclusion of Medic Ltd is that it appeared five days after the incident.

Given these circumstances, it cannot be asserted that any blows actually landed on Polonsky. The other injuries described in the forensic medical report were registered on his thigh. Plainly they could not have been caused by blows by Lebedev to Polonsky's head.

I put to you the following question. Even if there had been three punches and they had landed on Polonsky's head – would that suffice to establish criminal responsibility on Lebedev's part for battery? Well, no, because one further component of this kind of action would need to be examined: motivation. It is motivation alone which can give us an answer to the question of the reason for these punches.

Here too the preliminary investigation gave birth to another of its masterpieces. The first, as I have said, was the 'ideal identity' of battery and hooliganism. According to the charge sheet Lebedev, in striking Polonsky, had simultaneously two motivations: that of hooliganism and that of political hatred. This, however, is not logically possible, ever. Motivations by hooliganism and by hatred are in competition with each other.

Hatred is an extremely strong emotion, which takes possession of a person. It takes over consciousness. It gnaws at a person to such an extent that they are unable to control themselves. In Russian dictionaries, hatred is defined as extremely strong hostility and dislike. Extremely strong! Hatred causes people to shake, it stifles them. It stifles them to such an extent that, as the hero of a famous film says, 'I feel such dislike for him that I can't eat.'

Now we have a rather interesting situation. 'Political hatred' has been withdrawn. It remains unclear what the motivation of hooliganism might be. The formulation in the accusation is: 'Lebedev inflicted blows on Polonsky not at all because of feelings of personal dislike, but made use of insignificant pretexts to express his disrespect for society.' This is a reference to the wish Polonsky expressed to punch him in the face and the arm extended in the direction of Lebedev.

The preliminary investigation was naturally aware that this was less than coherent, and therefore, in the indictment, the phrase uttered by Polonsky is distorted and moved to a different context. Polonsky did not express the wish, quoted in inverted commas in the indictment, to 'give someone a punch in the face'. He very definitely expressed that desire in respect of Lebedev and Lisovsky who were sitting next to him, calling them 'the airman' and 'a chicken farmer', respectively.

The complainant's representative is clearly being disingenuous when he insists he cannot imagine how Lebedev could have perceived Polonsky's desire to punch someone in the face as referring specifically to him. I have an imaginary scene going round in my mind. Those present are the complainant's representatives: Dobrovinsky who left us before the debate, my colleague Samsonov, and me. But we are playing different roles. Dobrovinsky is still a lawyer, my colleague Samsonov is the prosecutor, and I, may the heavens forfend, am the representative of the Investigative Committee.

We are on a talk show discussing some question, simplification of the procedure for the preliminary investigation, for example. At some point I say, 'Listen, everybody seems to think they are the top dog: some people are prosecutors, other people are lawyers. I'm just tired of it all. I'd like to punch them in the face.' I somehow doubt strongly that my colleagues would take kindly to that. If they did just swallow it, that would place them in the category of people who meekly swallow insults and only rub their face after getting a punch.

I can, for example, foresee the reaction of Dobrovinsky, whose physical condition, it can fairly be said, is less impressive than my own. He would probably screw his finger at the side of his head and lodge a complaint with the Investigative Committee. But as for big, burly Samsonov, I imagine he would most likely say, as Lebedev did to Polonsky, 'You talking about me?' If I then answered this enquiry with a clearly aggressive counter-question in the idiom of Odessa, 'Do you want to try?', I suspect the incident would not be resolved to my advantage. That is a straightforward insult!

I will continue the analysis which the counsel for the prosecution chose to evade. Lebedev, after Polonsky's remark about wanting to punch someone in the face, asks, 'You talking about me?' and gets a response from Polonsky: 'Want to find out?' If, in response, Lebedev resorted to physical force, Polonsky would have grounds to file an application in the civil court to institute criminal proceedings for battery. This would be a private prosecution in respect of a purely personal conflict. The next step would be to understand how many punches there had been and whether they reached their target. The proceedings would be, of course, in respect of a personal conflict with the immediately obvious motive of personal dislike.

If, I repeat, the percussive movements were in response to an insulting statement. But that is not what happened. Contrary to what is claimed in the indictment, Lebedev did not just react to Polonsky's insulting statement by punching him. The dialogue between Lebedev and Polonsky concludes with a conciliatory phrase from Lebedev.

When Polonsky repeats to him, 'You want to find out?' Lebedev replies, 'Just control yourself, pal!' From any dictionary we can establish that the word 'pal' is used either in a friendly or in a familiar manner. Synonyms for the word are 'friend', 'buddy', 'old man', 'old chap', 'old boy'. Lebedev exercises self-control, he quashes the conflict with an amicable form of words addressed to Polonsky. The End.

But now I would like to ask those involved in this trial to press rewind, go back to their schooldays and recall the basics of causality, which we learned at some point in eighth grade in our lessons on logic and physics. There is a given set of circumstances, but despite their existence, an expected event does not occur. Then a new circumstance is added to that set of circumstances and the event occurs. This new circumstance is the cause of the event.

And so, the verbal skirmish has ended with Lebedev's conciliatory phrase. But then a new circumstance arises, namely Polonsky's arm in front of Lebedev's face. The prosecutor and the complainant's representative emphasise that Polonsky, when he made his gesture towards Lebedev, was not looking at him. What actually matters, however, is not that Polonsky was not looking at Lebedev, but that Lebedev was not looking at Polonsky, because he was sitting sideways on to him, or rather, he was in the process of sitting down, still heated over Polonsky's loutish utterance.

The audience and viewers who watched this show head on could see there really was no attack on Lebedev on the part of Polonsky, but Lebedev was sitting sideways to Polonsky. Lebedev has faulty eyesight. It is -6.5. When someone as shortsighted as this has an object immediately before his eyes, he cannot see it properly, everything is blurred. In order to see something nearby, he must take his glasses off.

Lebedev, who had just been informed of Polonsky's wish to punch him in the face, reacted to the sudden appearance of Polonsky's arm in front of his face, interpreting it as a transition on Polonsky's part from verbal to physical aggression. How? He blocks Polonsky's arm by gripping it and instantly, literally in the course of two seconds, makes two percussive movements, beginning them while seated and completing them while standing.

The fact is that this situation is a classic example of what is known as 'mistaken defence', where one person reacts to a mistakenly perceived attack. In the criminal law, there have for centuries been principles qualifying this situation, and they have been confirmed by the recent directive of the Plenum of the Supreme Court. It needs to be established whether a person had grounds to believe they actually were being attacked. I believe, Your Honour, that Lebedev did have such grounds.

Look where all this began: with insults in the dressing room. You will recall Olga Romanova's testimony. She was extremely reluctant to repeat the insulting term Polonsky used, so she related it as 'What is this thickhead doing here, beginning with the letter "d".' There was only one man in the room at that moment – Lebedev. He, naturally, took these words as referring to him.

Next. The explicit desire to punch someone in the face. Was it expressed by some decrepit 75-year old professor? No. It was expressed by a 100-kilogram bruiser, who fought in the war in Nagorno-Karabakh and served in the parachute regiment.

The next factor: Polonsky's personality. Polonsky is well known for his turbulent behaviour, for constantly insulting and humiliating people, for impulsiveness, for dishing out aggression. In particular, there had been widely known incidents when he flung his employees' telephones at the wall, when he chased a journalist into the toilet. He is a person who, as many witnesses have testified, behaved during the programme in a generally insulting and provocative manner towards Lebedev.

Lebedev's body language. Lebedev had not even had time to resume his seat after saying, 'Just control yourself, pal!' He was in the process of sitting down again, as is clearly visible in the frame-by-frame replay. At just this moment there appears in front of his face the arm of a man who just said he would like to give him a punch in the face. Let us not forget Lebedev's deficient eyesight. Is the aggregate of these circumstances not sufficient to confirm that Lebedev believed he was being attacked and defended himself?

How else can Lebedev's actions be explained? Mentally healthy people do not act without motivation. What was Lebedev wanting to achieve? Given the complete unsustainability of the attempt to attribute the motivation of hooliganism to him, it could only have been a wish to take revenge on Polonsky for his insults. But we already know that Lebedev did not make use of that readily available pretext and addressed Polonsky as 'pal'.

The prosecution are doing their best to ignore the words Lebedev addressed to Polonsky after the scuffle: 'Are you completely crazy? You keep your fists to yourself!' These words finally make everything fall into place. It would have been impossibe to devise them in the ten seconds which elapsed between Polonsky's fall and his getting back up as a flimsy excuse for a wilful crime. These words are irrefutable evidence that Lebedev had perceived Polonsky's gesture as a real attack.

When individuals have every reason to believe they are being subjected to a real attack and, moreover, do not exceed the limits of force necessary to defend themselves, their actions must be judged under the rules of necessary self-defence. They are not subject to criminal liability.

The harsh criticism I have directed at the prosecution naturally leads to the question of how it happened that this case ever came to court. How did it happen that a charge was brought, the main part of which the state prosecutor has subsequently repudiated?

I will not dwell on the rumours that this act of injustice was instigated by powerful forces of some description, who wished to take revenge on Lebedev for his civic position, for his free-thinking; for the fact that he finances *Novaya Gazeta*, whose critical articles affect the interests of corrupt officials who are still influential; for the fact that in his business practice he does not countenance questionable deals, he does not pay kick-backs to high-ranking officials.

Although it may be that these rumours are not without foundation. I will speak about what I know. We have a bad tradition that, if in the course of a criminal investigation a suspect emerges, every effort is made to ensure the case is brought to court. Terminating an investigation is regarded as a fault, as failure. The case gets sent to court, because our prosecution and investigative authority has no respect for the court. A large part of the blame for this lies with our judicial practices, which reject grounds for acquittal. Accordingly, our Pinkertons are confident that all their confections will result in a verdict of 'guilty'. The courts will put up with anything, they will digest anything in such a manner as to ensure that something criminal can be discovered. They will not dare to acquit.

I am comforted, despite a reality which is so regrettable for the defence, by the conduct in this case of those investigators who sabotaged the unlawful orders of their superiors, who did not agree to support a charge of hooliganism, and refused to tailor the evidence to fit the ridiculous accusation of political hatred.

I would like to believe that you will compel greater respect to be shown to the court, not only by acquitting Alexander Yevgenievich Lebedev, but also by adding a rider condemning the preliminary investigation for its artistic creativity and the outright fabrication which has been revealed in the preparation of the indictment.

CHAPTER 14

From Popovka to Monaco
An Epilogue

Bye-bye, *Forbes*!

I hope Henry Reznik was not too upset. He defended me brilliantly during the trial, and it should be mandatory for students and experienced lawyers to attend his speeches in court. The judge listened to him attentively, although the young girl from the Prosecutor's Office probably had no idea what he was talking about. Someone had evidently just asked her superiors what was happening and recommended a particular course of action.

I had no difficulty understanding the subtext of the verdict: this guy is not about to run off abroad, and what's the point of sending him to rot in prison? The investigation and the trial itself had already been sufficient punishment. He's got three children, two of them minors, and Polonsky's criminal patron is already in retirement.

For 'battery' I was, nevertheless, sentenced to perform 150 hours of community service. I could easily have avoided even that penalty. We did, needless to say, appeal the sentence in the Moscow Municipal Court and there was a second trial. The last session was scheduled for Friday 12 September 2013. If on that day I had simply not turned up in court, the statute of limitation would have terminated the case automatically, because the 'crime' (according to the official version in the verdict) had been committed two years previously. To do that, though, I would have had to pretend to be ill and obtain a false medical certificate, or arrange some reason why the lawyers were unable to attend.

I decided to force a definite verdict, a course of action that from the point of view of pragmatic logic was verging on imbecility. However, it was clear that I would not be receiving a more severe sentence, the most threatening outcome had been left in the past. It is not pleasant when you have a family, children, plans for the future, to be constantly recalling that you are shortly to be imprisoned for several years for a crime that you quite obviously did not commit.

At the height of the trial, when I really did face the prospect of seeing the world from behind bars, I wrote entirely seriously to Prime Minister Dmitry Medvedev asking him, within the framework of the anti-smoking campaign, to ban the imprisonment of smokers in the same cell as non-smokers. I was readying myself. The letter had no useful impact. Perhaps our sport-loving president should start a campaign against the smoking of the 750 billion cigarettes annually manufactured by America's tobacco monsters.

The idea of working for the benefit of the village of Popovka, where my National Land Company has its headquarters, occurred to me as soon as it was clear I had managed to avoid jail. My home address was registered as being in the Basmanny district of Moscow, and in theory that was where I should serve my punishment. One more manual labourer was, however, hardly going to make much difference to the Muscovites. The capital's housing and communal service already have plenty of guest workers prepared to clear the streets of mud and snow, and in the process hand over part of their salary to whoever expects them to do so. All they would get from me would be a lot of aggravation.

I therefore rented a house in Popovka and officially changed my place of residence: today that is a simple matter of notification. This obliged the Federal Penitentiary Service to transfer the case to their department in Chern district of Tula province. Our company had been maintaining the local children's day care centres for the past eight years as the state could not afford to. I correctly calculated that the local branch of the FPS would never have had to deal with someone with such an untypical sentence. In 99.99 per cent of cases, those before the courts are imprisoned, and any others get acquitted. Accordingly, they were unable to find anything else for me to do than toil on our own 'collective farm'.

And so in December 2013 I set to work renovating the children's day care centre, which in any case we needed to put right. On the first day of my community service, the media turned up in force. The national television channels sent cameras and did live broadcasts. It was practically the top news story of the day. Given that previously I had never been featured on state-run television to my advantage, the coverage was fairly positive. Here was a rich oligarch redeeming his guilt through manual labour in his native land.

The greater number of journalists declined, but some still visited. *Komsomolskaya Pravda*'s correspondent in Tula, Alexey Tumanov, actually moved to Popovka, wrote daily reports, and helped me with the work. We set out a new playground for the kids and finished renovating the inside of the building. We made a mini-football stadium. The village authorities have no money for such 'luxuries'.

The entire budget revenue for Popovka was 6 million rubles [$200,000]. They had debts for electricity and problems with water pumping stations, and renovating a day care centre for the children was going to cost in the region of 10 million rubles [$333,000]. This was where A. Lebedev, felon, came in useful.

There are a lot of children in Popovka now. They flock to the day care centre in new, smart clothes. Thanks to our farm, the villagers have started earning money and Popovka is no longer moribund. You can tell that from the houses. They are newly painted, sheathed in cladding, and almost all have satellite dishes.

Elvira Goryukhina is one of my favourite journalists and has been observing the evolution of Popovka for many years. Here is what she wrote:

> When you reflect on the phenomenon of Maxim Gorky Ltd, the main thing that strikes you is the wisdom of not destroying what is already there, not destroying village life, which is where large conglomerates often start. In Popovka they did not padlock the old farm office. Without doing away with the existing system (not even the former director, whom many suspect of conniving at bankruptcy), the 'newcomers' have put money in the production process and advanced technology.

Elvira Nikolaevna is right. In the countryside you can see your investments yielding a new harvest of homes, of smiles on people's faces. That is what money is really for.

Victor Pelevin has a story, 'Friedman's Space', in which the intelligence agencies' special services send money-laden 'buckonauts' (by analogy with cosmonauts) beyond the 'Shvartsman horizon', where there is a corridor that alters human psychology. Alas, money remains for the majority the main criterion of both human ability and character, and also of the talent of scoundrels and swindlers.

I was reminded of this in the office of Akin Gump Strauss Hauer & Feld, when I learned from the lawyers that the latest issue of *Forbes* magazine had my name on its rich list with a valuation of $1.6 billion. I was not a little surprised, and considerably more annoyed. That day the American lawyers themselves surprised me a lot. They suddenly became much more attentive, not to say obsequious, and also more eager to give the appearance of being very active. And it was only appearance. They were 'conducting' a lawsuit against the Administration of President Yanukovych over the expropriation of my fifty-per-cent stake in the Hotel Ukraine, while also having a contract on behalf of Yanukovych against Yulia Tymoshenko.

Forbes magazine was first published in 1917, a momentous year in world history. It very superficially believes that having a fortune is a great boon, and has no inclination towards moral judgement. Its journalists are not interested in where money comes from, and even less in what people spend it on. I still cannot understand how they arrive at their totals. One year my fortune had grown to $3.6 billion, and then suddenly disappeared. I wrote a letter to Steve Forbes, who is the chairman and editor-in-chief, asking him to explain their methodology and not to include me in this strange rating in future.

How, for example, are you to measure the fortune of an oligarch, whose indebtedness to state-owned banks of the Russian Federation might be double the valuation of the capital of his companies? By what means was *Forbes* magazine able to include Joaquín 'Shorty' Guzmán in its list of billionaires, a Mexican drug lord who has spent his entire life outside the law? This rating is another small cog in the mechanism for transferring that trillion dollars a year out of the pockets of the poor and into the pockets of rich crooks.

I took my leave of the notorious list in 2013–15, when I said goodbye to my business interests. Everything was relatively straightforward: National Reserve Bank had deposits of about a billion dollars of its clients' money. The bank was attacked by ill-wishers, who had no scruples about their methods. Their techniques have been described in detail above. We needed to return that money to our clients in a hurry. They were not interested in discussing postponements, and you cannot instantly sell shares in Gazprom and Aeroflot, a mortgage portfolio and real estate other than at major discounts.

I had to sell assets worth $1.5 billion for $1 billion. They included a cultural centre near Paris, A-321 planes, a Global VIP jet, an apartment in

London, and buildings in Moscow and St Petersburg. However, having repaid our clients their money to the last penny, I retained my reputation. I proved that, if you do business honestly, you can repay all your depositors even in the most acute run on your bank.

Today National Reserve Bank is not a business, it is a showcase. It owes nothing to clients, does not accept prepaid liabilities, does not make loans or buy securities, and it does not take risks. It survives by placing its capital in Savings Bank of Russia on the interbank market. A more solid bank is inconceivable: it can be destroyed only by nuclear war. It stands as a mute reproach to the individuals who have filched $100 billion from the 900 Russian banks they deliberately bankrupted since 2006, and who believe that in our country reputation counts for nothing.

I will not deny that this very thought did often cross my mind at those times when, since I was young, I was jealously guarding my honour. My banking colleagues screwed a finger at the side of their head: no one had behaved like this before. For them the main priority was to steal their clients' money, siphoning it off under the guise of technical loans to their shell companies, bankrupting their bank, and handing their depositors on to the Deposit Insurance Agency. This institution until recently covered up that artless mechanism, taking the view, evidently, that if a bank went bankrupt, that was that and there was no reason to pursue the matter further.

Some of the techniques used by these people I have described above, and how they live is described in a touching report in a London newspaper about the lifestyle of a 'Russian oligarch'. It tells us that, for €400 million, the shipwrights at German Naval Yards in Kiel built a superyacht, actually his second, for a certain gentleman in the fertiliser trade in Russia. They satisfied all their client's whims. The yacht, with the original name of *A*, is the biggest yacht in the world. It has a panoramic underwater bay, four lifeboats and a mini-submarine.

The only problem was that, to get out of the Baltic Sea, it needed to pass through the Drogden Strait between Sweden and Denmark, which proved, unfortunately, impossible. Because of its dimensions (it has fixed masts) and the draught, it could not squeeze through. There are no opening bridges along the route. The problem was ultimately solved in some way, but the story was all over the Western press. The whims of the Russian yachting enthusiast cost the ordinary farmer in Russia a 25-percent increase in fertiliser prices in the course of a year, even though the guy had already made an extra 1.5 billion from devaluation of the ruble. Why would I, having spent the same amount not on a yacht but on the world's biggest potato farm, join in the jubilation of the German shipwrights?

I do not like yachts, villas, private jets and similar luxury goods, whose purpose is merely to demonstrate an ostentatious superiority over the 'suckers'. I protected the most trusting and simple people from the one-armed bandit gambling mafia by dragging a law through the State Duma. I sank €200 million in Crimea rather than in the Maldives or the Côte d'Azur, and returned to my bank customers the full $1 billion they had entrusted to me. I want to invest in a network of Petrushka cafes, where my compatriots will be able to eat healthy food at an affordable price. This book aims to explain some aspects of my motivation. Do I have allies? Time will tell.

My Manifesto

Oligarchs, semi-oligarchs, would-be oligarchs, corrupt officials and their numerous retinues of staff come out to graze in the south of France in the summer and disport themselves in Courchevel in the winter. Is it possible that the wily French authorities have arranged this deliberately – this whole vanity fair which is yours to command? Beneath the palm trees and the gentle sun, this fauna bears a striking resemblance to the Papuans of the Wamena tribe, among whom I lived during my trip to New Guinea.

Men of this tribe wear a holim to cover their manhood, a hard cover from the shell of a tropical fruit. European tourists gaze in amazement at the diversity, configuration and, most importantly, dimensions of these holims, the size of this phallic simulacrum proclaiming the social status of the male. In fact, the women of the tribe say, it's all just for show, like the yachts in the Monaco marina.

The indigenous French population views the Russian parvenues with a degree of bafflement and ill-concealed contempt. No wonder that many of these Russian crooks have been robbed in their villas, and not only once. The whole Dolce Vita scene is an ostentatious sham. Behind it is cynicism and envy, loathing and servility, and always straightforward human fear.

In the subcortex of every monstrously superior movie-set alien squandering hundreds of millions in Monaco, there lurks an awareness that his status symbols have been bought with someone else's money, money embezzled from the state, from a bank's customers, or skimmed off some loan. On their home planet they could at any time be seized by the holim and carted off to lie on a gruesome bed of nails. Alternatively, some local French wizard may tire of the sight of them and turn these casino-crazy extra-terrestrials into cacti.

In 2003, during President Vladimir Putin's visit to France, a major event was held at our cultural centre near Paris. Pyotr Fomenko's company presented his take on *War and Peace* for the visitors. I was keen for the cultural centre to be talked about on the national channels of Russian television but, to my regret, I was not seeing eye-to-eye with Ambassador Avdeyev and things turned sour.

Instead, a different building was featured on Russian TV, an exact replica of the Washington White House, which a Russian oligarch had bought in the south of France. I asked the oligarch afterwards, 'Don't you see this does nothing for the reputation of our business class? The yacht, the new villa ... Is it really not possible to come up with something a bit different: restore a historical monument, create an art and culture centre, instead of buying your twenty-fifth property for $100 million? That's downright sad! And that's the reputation it will get you.'

His response was, 'You know, I don't sleep well anywhere. With every new purchase, I hope my sleep will improve.' No doubt he was joking, but the new Rybolovlevs continue their pointless extravagance.

How did the pseudo-state of Monaco appear on the map of Europe? On 8 January 1297, Francesco Grimaldi, a scion of one of the ruling families of Genoa, seized a castle on a cliff on the Ligurian Riviera. It was all rather sordid. Francesco and his comrades, disguised as Franciscan monks, knocked at the gates in bad weather, and when the guards took pity and let the 'poor pilgrims' in, they whipped their swords out from beneath their habits and murdered their guileless benefactors. This incident is cynically depicted on the coat of arms of the ruling dynasty.

Since then, Monaco can be considered a true offshore tax haven, which owes its existence to the commercial and fiscal privileges it provides to 'non-domiciled residents'. Its rulers have manoeuvred between the great powers of Europe, becoming at one time a protectorate of France, then of Spain, then of Sardinia. On 15 February 1793, the French

Convention decided to annex Monaco, and the principality, renamed Fort-Hercule, became a canton within the French Republic. All the riches of the Grimaldis were confiscated, their paintings and works of art sold off. The palace became a barracks, then a hospital and shelter for beggars. After the collapse of Napoleon's empire, Monaco's sovereignty was restored.

The French authorities might do well to take a closer look at the practices of the First Republic in this respect. And Russia might perhaps ask Citizens Pugachev and Motylyov, who now sip Crystal Rosé on board their yachts in the Monaco Roads, what happened to the money from Mezhprombank, Globex Bank, Russian Credit, a dozen other banks and pension funds, fleeced of something north of $5 billion.

Or enquire how exactly Georgiy Bedzhamov, fugitive swindler and friend of the prince, was able to avoid extradition to his homeland after he had stolen $4 billion from Vneshprombank with which, among other things, he opened the Wine Palace bar in Monte Carlo, acquired a thirty-per-cent share in Badrutt's Palace Hotel in St Moritz, and a dozen aircraft, yachts and villas.

Many Russians have, because of these Yeghiazaryan-Bukato-Pugachev-Borodin-Voronin-Motylyov-Alyakin-Romanov-Antonov-Ivashchenko-Bedzhamov-Yurov-Bulochnikov-Malchevsky-Zakharchenko-Plyakins, 'almost lost faith in the human race', as Ostap Bender put it. According to my calculations, in the past ten years over $100 billion has been stolen from wilfully bankrupted Russian banks. And if that is the case, then the banking system described by Adam Smith and David Ricardo has completely ceased to perform its useful functions.

All these hundreds of private banks swallowed up by the waters of Lethe have not contributed anything like a benefit to the real sector of the economy that would outweigh the damage inflicted by the fraudsters. Russia does not need so many small banks. And there is no question but that we should be fighting for the return of those 100 billion stolen dollars. They add up to more than Russia's National Wealth Fund!

The main question is – how? By hiring foreign lawyers and going through foreign courts? Well, certainly we could follow the example of the Kazakh authorities in the Ablyazov case or, as in our Russian case with Pugachev, spend years and pay astronomical fees to lawyers. I calculate that, for every stolen $1 billion, Russia would have to find $100–150 million from the Russian budget and, after ten or so years of litigation, would most probably lose. The other side would lay out $200–300 million and get better lawyers working for it.

Even if it proved possible to freeze the embezzlers' assets, which, as well as being expensive, is no simple matter, it is unlikely that it will prove possible to realise them for anything like their real value. The game is not worth the candle. The money will be left in the Western banks and investment funds which, in reality, created this reservoir of tainted money in the first place, welcoming into it a new trillion dirty dollars every year. They will continue to exploit this capital and make new money from it. We need a different approach.

I propose that getting the stolen money back should be made a priority of a purposeful national policy, and that all the resources at the disposal of the state should be mobilised to that end. The entire export of arms and agricultural products from Russia in 2015 amounted to $31 billion, and the profit was no more than a few billion. Getting this stolen capital back is net revenue for the treasury.

We are talking here about establishing a sector whose activities will bring the state budget a sum comparable with the income from the export of hydrocarbon natural resources. Faced with Western sanctions, which primarily limit access to the capital markets, these funds could be a key factor in ensuring financial stability, investment and growth of the Russian economy. Repatriating illegally exported capital should become one of the state's top priorities.

The measures currently being undertaken by the Prosecutor General's Office are insufficient. Thus, in 2015 only 6 billion rubles (less than $100 million) were repatriated out of an officially recorded outflow of 28 billion. This relates only to recovery of funds stolen as a result of corruption-related crimes. The colossal amounts taken out of the banking and financial system under fraudulent schemes, whose victims are business entities and the citizens of Russia, do not in general even come within the purview of the law enforcement agencies.

The example of Police Colonel Dmitry Zakharchenko is very illuminating, but there are other Zakharchenkos, generals at that, still around. The main problem is that prosecutors act formally, within the framework of existing international legal agreements. International experience shows that considerably better results can be achieved in this area.

Take the example of the United States. Over the past ten years, the US Attorney's Office, making use of information from their intelligence agencies and the threat of criminal prosecution, has succeeded in persuading some of the world's leading banks (UBS, Goldman Sachs, BNP Paribas and others) to transfer more than $350 billion to the state budget in out-of-court settlements for protecting tax evaders, involvement in fraud, violations of sanctions, and so on.

So why can't we? Why not produce similar incriminating evidence and get results? There are, separately, questions to be asked of the international auditing companies that have facilitated embezzlement: Ernst & Young, KPMG, PricewaterhouseCoopers and Deloitte Touche Tohmatsu. Either they return that money, or they are declared persona non grata. They all have major business interests in Russia, so I am confident they will find it more expedient to return, if not all, then at least part of the money.

What does this mean in specific cases, for example, that of Bedzhamov? In the first place, it is time to throw the book at this 'principality', which belongs in an operetta. The current ruler of Monaco, Albert II, loves to dress up as the best friend of the Russian people when welcoming the owners of superyachts bought with money stolen from that people. The nouveaux riche organise a vanity fair on the sea every year right in front of his residence.

For a start, we need to summon to the Russian Ministry of Foreign Affairs the French Ambassador, who represents Monaco's diplomatic interests in Russia, and hand him a note of protest. Secondly, break off all relations with Monaco and forbid Russian individuals and legal entities to conduct transactions with the principality's financial institutions, or invest in real estate in the principality. Thirdly, we need to address specific complaints to the financial institutions that hold the billions stolen by Bedzhamov.

As a rule, these are the foremost Western banks and investment funds. (Fraudsters will not try to hide the money they have stolen in dodgy banks: they know from their own experience in this area how easily they could become the victims of other fraudsters.)

These techniques can be employed in all similar cases. We need a systemic struggle against the international offshore financial oligarchy. The reservoir of tainted money needs to be drained, and the money thus obtained needs to be used for the development of human potential. This should be one of the leitmotifs of Russian foreign policy, the work of the competent ministries and departments and of the media.

Russia has a unique opportunity to turn the tables and shape a new global agenda by instituting its own campaign of international investigations and diplomatic efforts. If we shut down the offshore tax havens and make the financial world transparent and fair, then life for those living in Popovka will be no worse than it is in the villages of Provence.

I believe that is no more than our people deserve.